Taking Confucian Ethics Seriously

SUNY series in Chinese Philosophy and Culture
———————
Roger T. Ames, editor

Taking Confucian Ethics Seriously

Contemporary Theories and Applications

Edited by

Kam-por Yu
Julia Tao
and
Philip J. Ivanhoe

Published by State University of New York Press, Albany

© 2010 State University of New York

All rights reserved

Printed in the United States of America

No part of this book may be used or reproduced in any manner whatsoever without written permission. No part of this book may be stored in a retrieval system or transmitted in any form or by any means including electronic, electrostatic, magnetic tape, mechanical, photocopying, recording, or otherwise without the prior permission in writing of the publisher.

For information, contact State University of New York Press, Albany, NY
www.sunypress.edu

Production by Cathleen Collins
Marketing by Michael Campochiaro

Library of Congress Cataloging-in-Publication Data

Taking Confucian ethics seriously : contemporary theories and applications / edited by Kam-por Yu, Julia Tao, and Philip J. Ivanhoe.
   p. cm. — (SUNY series in chinese philosophy and culture)
Includes bibliographical references and index.
ISBN 978-1-4384-3315-8 (hardcover: alk. paper)
ISBN 978-1-4384-3314-1 (pbk. : alk. paper)
   1. Confucian ethics.   I. Yu, Kam-por, 1957–   II. Tao, Julia Lai Po-Wah, 1946–   III. Ivanhoe, P. J.

BJ1289.3.T35 2010
170.951—dc22
                                                  2010004937

10 9 8 7 6 5 4 3 2 1

Contents

Acknowledgments — vii

Introduction: Why Take Confucian Ethics Seriously? — 1
Kam-por Yu, Julia Tao, and Philip J. Ivanhoe

Chapter 1. What It Means to Take Chinese Ethics Seriously — 13
Heiner Roetz

Chapter 2. The Handling of Multiple Values in Confucian Ethics — 27
Kam-por Yu

Chapter 3. Humanity or Benevolence? The Interpretation of Confucian *Ren* and Its Modern Implications — 53
Qianfan Zhang

Chapter 4. East Asian Conceptions of the Public and Private Realms — 73
Chun-chieh Huang

Chapter 5. Trust Within Democracy: A Reconstructed Confucian Perspective — 99
Julia Tao

Chapter 6. A Defense of *Ren*-Based Interpretation of Early Confucian Ethics — 123
Shirong Luo

Chapter 7. Is Sympathy Naive?: Dai Zhen on the Use of *Shu* to Track Well-Being — 145
Justin Tiwald

Chapter 8. The Nature of the Virtues in Light of the
Early Confucian Tradition 163
 Eirik Lang Harris

Chapter 9. The Values of Spontaneity 183
 Philip J. Ivanhoe

List of Contributors 209

Index 213

Acknowledgments

The editors would like to express our sincere gratitude to several organizations and individuals who contributed to the success of this volume. The Governance in Asia Research Centre (GARC) of City University of Hong Kong and the Hong Kong Polytechnic University sponsored the initial conference that served as the source of several of the papers in this volume. GARC generously supported the preparation of the manuscript, which was done in a most precise and thorough manner by Katherine E. Lawn and Bruce Tindall. We also would like to extend our appreciation to all the contributors for their creativity, care, diligence, and patience.

Introduction

Why Take Confucian Ethics Seriously?

Kam-por Yu
Julia Tao
Philip J. Ivanhoe

Many—though surely not all—people who have lived in Confucian societies have taken Confucian ethics seriously for hundreds of generations, but why should one study Confucian ethics today? One could do so in order to learn more about an ancient and unfamiliar school of thought or to understand or deepen one's understanding of some aspects of East Asian cultures. To be sure, these are legitimate and respectable objectives. But to approach the study of Confucian ethics in such ways is to take it only as something we can *learn about*, not something we can *learn from*. For the purposes of this volume, to take Confucian ethics *seriously* means that one does not see it simply as something East Asian or Confucian; to take Confucian ethics seriously is to be concerned with the contemporary philosophical relevance of the Confucian tradition.

An ethics can be understood simply as a description of the moral outlook of people remote to us in time, space, or point of view. But an ethics can also be taken in terms of what it purports to be: a collection of answers to ethical questions that are thought to describe, in part or whole, not how some people do live but how all should live. To take an ethics in this way allows one to engage it with an eye toward discerning its contemporary relevance: to defend and uphold its strengths, to criticize and oppose its weaknesses, to further pursue its arguments and lines of thought, to develop it with the aim of making it more robust, and to consider what we can learn from it that we cannot readily learn from other systems of ethics.

This volume takes Confucian ethics as a living ethical tradition, one that offers a range of principles, ideals, and arguments of contemporary relevance and philosophical interest. While we, the editors, have endeavored to maintain the highest standards of historical scholarship and textual evidence, we have sought contributions that focus on and explore issues that have more than historical or cultural interest. Our volume is addressed to fellow philosophers and those interested in ethics in general, though we hope that fellow scholars and students of Confucianism will appreciate it as well. The issues discussed in this volume, such as the nature of virtue, the distinction between the public and the private, the value of spontaneity, the place of sympathy in moral judgment, the meaning of what it is to be humane to people, the way to handle multiple values, the relation between trust and democracy, are all living issues in play in contemporary philosophical discourse and debate. Our contributors take Confucian ethics seriously by showing that they are not satisfied with merely stating or explicating Confucian views; they consider how far such views remain philosophically significant and perhaps even compelling in contemporary times.

The task of taking Confucian ethics seriously in the sense that we have described above can involve one or more general approaches. For example, one can approach the study of the Confucian tradition primarily as a task of philosophical retrieval. One's goal might be to show, through interpretation and analysis, that the Confucian tradition advocates principles, ideals, or arguments that support, augment, or extend our understanding of contemporary ethics. The aim of such an approach always is to find what is philosophically significant and relevant about Confucian ethics; what one finds can be more or less familiar and in some cases may be distinctive if not unique. An alternative is to approach Confucian ethics primarily as a task of philosophical reconstruction. Such an approach relies more on the spirit or implications than the exact words or teachings of traditional Confucian philosophers. The goal is not to present some Confucian way of thought as it is or has been, but rather to make it more tenable, sophisticated, and compelling for contemporary consideration. Confucian ethics is taken not as something completed and ready for incorporation or adoption, but rather as something still developing and very much a work in progress. As we see in the course of our brief descriptions of the contributions to this volume, the chapters in it employ one or more of the approaches discussed above.

In "What It Means to Take Chinese Ethics Seriously," Heiner Roetz criticizes a major and influential approach to the contemporary study of ancient Chinese thought—what he describes as the "contrastive approach." The contrastive approach differs from an equally influential yet earlier Sinological approach, which he deems the "comparative approach." The latter tries to understand Chinese ways of thinking by comparing them with Western models and looks for similarities; the former avoids using Western categories to analyze what it regards as a remote and alien culture and tends to look for differences rather than similarities. The comparative and contrastive approaches, however, share some common ground. Both of them "objectify" what they study; they take Chinese authors as objects of study rather than people who made claims that they regarded as true. But, when traditional Chinese authors said or wrote what they did, they were asserting the validity of what they said or wrote. Roetz insists that in order to take them *seriously* we must interpret their claims as validity claims and not just as descriptions of the views of various authors. In his contribution, Roetz refers to the "eye-level principle" and "communicative hermeneutics," which describe an interpretive posture that takes the authors as our equals and understands them as making validity claims that we should assess and respond to, rather than just as providing texts to be analyzed and exposited. If Confucian ethics is valuable as a resource for contemporary ethics, then certainly it must contain claims that are true and valuable and not simply descriptions of what ancient Chinese people thought or believed.

In chapter 2, "The Handling of Multiple Values in Confucian Ethics," Kam-por Yu employs an interpretation of the Confucian concept of *zhongyong* 中庸—often understood as denoting something like a sense of a "harmonious mean"—not only to shed light on the meaning and coherence of certain seminal Confucian texts, but also as a contribution to the philosophical understanding of ethical pluralism. Yu rejects two popular interpretations of the concept of *zhongyong*, the first of which understands it as recommending a moderate position between two extremes and the second, which interprets it as being able to hit upon the right response by cultivating an unbiased inner state. Instead, he argues that *zhongyong* is a way to handle multiple values. Yu argues for his preferred interpretation by setting up two tests that any adequate understanding of *zhongyong* must meet and then shows how his meets these criteria better than the most popular and influential alternatives.

Yu's interpretation of *zhongyong* is relevant not only for understanding the Confucian texts in which this concept appears, but also for our understanding of the nature of morality. According to Yu's understanding of *zhongyong*, ethical thinking contains more than the distinction between good and bad or the choice between right and wrong. Often we are faced not just with a single good but many, and these many goods may compete, conflict, and resist reduction—either one to the other or to some independent third standard. In such cases, the right thing to do is not to pick one value over another but to strike the best balance among these competing claims to our moral attention. Moreover, in order to fully or adequately appreciate the entire range of values we are facing, we need to consider different perspectives on the moral issue before us, not because all perspectives are equally valuable, but because the values that can be seen from one perspective may not be seen or adequately appreciated by another. The view here is not that human values are relative or subjective but that they are complicated, and so it is unrealistic and harmful to think that we can fully appreciate them by adopting just one perspective. In ethical debate, often it is not that one side is completely right and the other completely wrong; rather, different perspectives often have distinctive and important insights into the complex issues involved. In order to work out an ethically adequate solution, we must discover and fully appreciate what each perspective has to offer and give due recognition to the legitimate values upheld by each. This is not to say that different perspectives are equally right, but that each may offer us a way to see important values that cannot be seen or fully appreciated from other points of view.

In chapter 3, "Humanity or Benevolence? The Interpretation of Confucian *Ren* and Its Modern Implications," Qianfan Zhang analyzes and evaluates different conceptions of the traditional Confucian concept of *ren* 仁 by exploring the implications these hold for a range of practical issues in contemporary politics and social justice. He illustrates and motivates his analysis by discussing the particularly tragic case of Sun Zhigang, a young college graduate who was unjustly detained by the Guangzhou city police and later died from injuries suffered in a beating by fellow inmates in the detention center.

Zhang's chapter looks at an important theoretical question in Confucian ethics that has direct and serious practical implications for contemporary political and social theory and policy. His first and primary aim is to provide an account and analysis of the Confucian concept *ren*. Zhang identifies two main lines of thinking on this issue within the Confucian tradition. The first is associated with the concept of "humanity"—the principle of respecting people as individual persons with dignity. The second is associated with "benevolence"—the view that we should treat people with care because they are centers of well-being and suffering. Zhang argues that these two lines of thinking about *ren* do not enjoy equal status in contemporary ethical and political philosophy, and they have dramatically different implications regarding the obligations a government has toward its people. According to Zhang, the first conception of *ren* is not sufficiently developed in traditional Confucian sources, while the second is well developed but proves to be ethically inadequate in a number of respects. Zhang takes Confucian ethics seriously by criticizing certain weaknesses in Confucian views about "benevolent government" and by pointing toward a way to reconstruct Confucian political philosophy based on the Confucian concept of *ren* that regards human beings not simply as receivers of benefits but also as individuals with moral worth and dignity.

In "East Asian Conceptions of the Public and Private Realms," Chun-chieh Huang explores a problem that has attracted a great deal of attention from a wide variety of Confucian thinkers. At the same time, his central concern—the distinction between the "public" and "private" realms—continues to have great contemporary relevance—in the West as well as throughout East Asia—and remains the focus of lively philosophical debate. One of the many virtues of Huang's contribution is that it provides a vivid illustration of the richness and complexity of the Confucian tradition. It shows that Confucian ethics is not a single static set of principles, ideals, and arguments but is an ongoing discussion and debate revolving around a constellation of common themes. The tradition has continued to develop throughout its long and impressive history, and this process remains active and ongoing.

Huang shows in a careful and convincing manner the ways in which the concepts of "public" and "private" changed—in some respects quite dramatically—from the Western Zhou (1045?–771 BCE) down to the Warring States period (403–222 BCE). He explains how a range of classical Confucian philosophers conceived and handled this perennial problem, and how debate about this issue continued throughout the tradition's history and across a number of different East Asian cultural contexts. Huang argues that to a significant extent, the central problems that motivated and defined this debate remain to be solved. For example, he shows why appeals to higher standards such as *tianli* 天理 (Heavenly principle) or *tianxia* 天下 (the world) displace rather than resolve the problem of justification. Such proposals offer no clear criteria and only serve to open opportunities for hijacking and manipulating these purported "higher standards." Though many people might agree that "Heavenly principle" should prevail, no one can provide any clear and persuasive explanation for ascertaining what Heavenly principle directs us to do. As Huang points out, this tends to leave such decisions in the hands of reigning elites. If Huang's analysis is correct, then East Asian Confucians—like their Western counterparts—still have not resolved "the conflict between the public and private realms," and further effort is required.

In "Trust within Democracy: A Reconstructed Confucian Perspective," Julia Tao explores the nature of trust and its relationship to democracy. Through a critical evaluation of some of the prominent contemporary literature on trust and political theory, Tao analyzes different kinds of trust: strategic trust and moral trust, general trust and particular trust, and their implications for governance in a world of diversity. She asks whether trust is in any sense necessary for democratic governance and where one might look for the source of such trust in a contemporary society.

Tao explores the cultural roots of trust and in particular resources for the cultivation of trust. She points out that even the best account of trust in regard to governance, "offers no philosophical analysis of the importance of moralistic trust for the purpose of government or for the ideal of democratic governance." She suggests we turn to Kongzi (Confucius) and the Confucian tradition as a philosophical resource able to supply these critical, missing features of our understanding of trust.

Tao shows that Confucian trust is an expression of moral trust and that it begins—as scholars such as Uslaner suggest—in the family and in particular from our relationship with parents. But Confucians insist that this is just the first blossoming of a more general and robust virtue that must be enlarged and extended to inform the common enterprises we share with nonfamily members. This effort of extension can give rise to civic trust and a kind of civic friendship that finds its final expression in benevolent government.

Confucians regard trust as a fundamental virtue for family, civil society, and government, which provides the basic environment for human thriving. As Tao points out, the Confucian conception of trust can serve to remind us of "our shared fate and mutual responsibility at all levels of our human connectedness, at both the local level and the global level." Tao suggests that this view of the self and its potential flourishing puts trust back into democratic governance to underpin equal respect and mutual concern for humankind in order to achieve not only a stable democracy, but also and more importantly a stable world order.

In "A Defense of *Ren*-Based Interpretation of Early Confucian Ethics," Shirong Luo argues that early Confucian ethics offers an example of what Michael Slote calls an "agent-based" virtue ethics. Agent-based ethical theories are distinctive for holding that "ethical assessment be based entirely on the admirableness or reprehensibility of the inner qualities of the agent." Luo argues that Kongzi offers a special form of agent-basing, one centered on the virtue of *ren* (benevolence). He refers to this distinctive early Confucian view as a *ren*-based theory.

Luo begins chapter 6 by arguing against a range of other interpretations of Kongzi's ethics. He discusses and rejects the possibility that Kongzi ultimately bases his ethics on a prior conception of the way (*dao*) or ritual (*li* 禮). The former would offer an example of *dao*-basing, while the latter would be a case of a *li*-based ethical theory. He proceeds to argue against the influential interpretation of D. C. Lau, who argues that Kongzi's ethics is *yi*-based; that is to say, it depends on a prior conception of what is *yi* 義 (right).

Luo then makes his case that Confucian ethics is best understood as *ren*-based. Such an interpretation entails that Confucian ethics is a form of virtue ethics but one quite distinct from the kind of virtue ethics system that one finds in thinkers such as Aristotle, which Slote has argued are agent-prior as opposed to agent-based. Kongzi's ethics shares much in common with other agent-prior ethical theories, such as Nel Noddings's ethics of care, though Luo has argued in his "Relation, Virtue, and Relational Virtue: Three Concepts of Caring" (*Hypatia,* 22.3, 2007) that Kongzi's ethics avoids a number of philosophical problems that remain challenges for Noddings's view.

Luo's chapter offers an excellent example of both philosophical retrieval and reconstruction. He aims not only to present Confucian ethics as it has been, but also as it could be. He seeks to strengthen Kongzi's original view by extending some of its implications in light of recent insights in ethical theory. As Luo says, "A recasting of Kongzi's moral teachings in agent-based virtue ethics terms will enable us to make cogent arguments for its relevance to many issues within as well as beyond the purview of ethics." He also intends his account of early Confucian ethics to contribute significantly to contemporary debates about the nature of ethics in general and virtue ethics in particular, arguing that it holds exceptional value for our understanding of moral education. Unlike many contemporary versions of virtue ethics, Confucian ethics is not just a theory about the meaning of being virtuous, but also a theory about "how we should acquire virtue, i.e. the issue of moral self-cultivation."

Justin Tiwald's contribution to our volume relies on an exposition of central features of the philosophy of Dai Zhen, an important Qing dynasty Confucian, to set and explore a range of issues in contemporary moral psychology. Specifically, Tiwald presents Dai Zhen's teachings as offering a more plausible and powerful account of the role that sympathy should and must play in moral understanding. In "Is Sympathy Naive?: Dai Zhen on the Use of *Shu* to Track Well-Being," Tiwald begins by discussing the widely held view that sympathy offers us a way to discover and appreciate what is good and bad for creatures such as ourselves. He argues that the common conception of sympathy is incapable of guiding us to such knowledge in a reliable or adequate way. If we think of sympathy simply in terms of perspective taking—imaginatively taking up another person's point of view—it will lead us to confer value on too broad and undisciplined a set of desires. Sympathy in this naive sense condones desires uncritically and is not a good guide for understanding what truly is in another person's best interests. Dai Zhen's account of *shu* 恕 (sympathetic understanding)—a term of art that appears in the earliest Confucian texts and has commanded attention and commentary throughout the tradition—is more complex and plausible than the simple perspective-taking account of sympathy.

Dai Zhen's interpretation of *shu* does not entail making the common mistake of simply projecting one's own desires onto another, nor does it lead one to take all the actual desires of a person equally seriously. For a variety of reasons, one's own desires often are not a good way to determine what is really in the best interests of another person, especially if we are aiming at the good of the other *for her own sake*. However, some desires that a person may happen to have are of no moral value, while other desires that she does not have might be very much in her best interests. Dai is concerned only with certain kinds of desires; he refers specifically to the "ordinary feelings of human beings" (*ren zhi changqing* 人之常情). Such desires are rooted in human nature and are universal, at least under the right counterfactual conditions.

The ordinary feelings of human beings are not as whimsical or insatiable as our unevaluated, individual desires. Unlike the latter, "ordinary" desires are required for "life fulfillment" (*sui sheng* 遂生). This important concept sets the nature, purpose, and scope of a particular set of desires that have special ethical status, for these desires describe in outline a common human conception of personal well-being. Dai Zhen's account of *shu* provides a standard for distinguishing between desires that should be counted ethically and desires that can be taken less seriously or altogether ignored from the ethical point of view. It does not have many of the problems that plague the common conception of sympathy described above and offers a significant contribution to our understanding of human moral psychology.

In "The Nature of the Virtues in Light of the Early Confucian Tradition," Eirik Lang Harris uses an analysis of certain aspects of early Confucian ethics to challenge and amend an important and influential contemporary philosophical account of the nature of the virtues. Philippa Foot, in her justly famous essay "Virtues and Vices," argues that virtues are related to the will and serve as correctives, in the sense that in order for something to be a virtue, it must counteract some temptation or augment some deficiency in human behavior that stands in the way of our leading good lives. Moreover, such temptations and deficiencies are things that we as human beings are inclined to suffer. It is only by choosing to cultivate virtue that we can shape ourselves to act for the good in a reliable fashion.

Harris begins by showing that being a corrective is only a contingent feature of at least certain virtues. If the world or human nature were different, such traits of character would still be needed to live well—and hence would still qualify as virtues on a widely accepted conception of what virtues are—but they would not stand as correctives to temptations or deficiencies. Harris goes on to argue that self-love is plausibly understood as a virtue, and one that bears many similarities to other so-called corrective virtues. And yet, when properly understood, self-love clearly is not corrective, even in a contingent way.

Harris draws on resources in the early Confucian tradition and especially the *Mengzi* to demonstrate that there is an entire class of virtues, which he calls "inclinational virtues," that cannot plausibly be understood as correctives. He describes such traits of character by saying that "inclinational virtues are virtues due to their being good inclinations, traits that incline one toward the direction of what is good." For example, in *Mengzi* 2A6, Mengzi argues that all normal human beings possess "sprouts of virtue" that incline them toward good actions of various kinds. These sprouts do not arise as counterbalances to temptations or motivational deficiencies; rather, they are natural *inclinations* rooted in human nature. Although it is true that something like the will is needed to focus on and develop such virtuous inclinations, in such cases, volition is not acting in opposition to natural desires and tendencies. If this account of human nature contains any grain of truth, then Harris's arguments appear quite compelling, and we must enlarge and enrich our conception of the virtues.

In the final chapter, "The Values of Spontaneity," Philip J. Ivanhoe seeks to realize several related goals. His primary aim is to present an account of two general conceptions of spontaneity as a normative ideal that are found in early Chinese philosophy. The first, "untutored spontaneity," is more characteristic of early Daoist thinkers, while the second, "cultivated spontaneity," is most often found in thinkers from the Confucian school. The former describes a type of action that arises with little or no prior training or reflection and is thought to flow out of natural dispositions to perceive, feel, evaluate, and act in certain ways. The latter describes a related kind of action, but one that can only be realized after a concerted and sustained course of training. Untutored spontaneity reflects unadulterated nature, while cultivated spontaneity manifests an acquired and internalized "second nature." Both types of action though are thought and felt to connect one with patterns, processes, and forces greater than one's individual self and thereby provide one with a highly valued sense of belonging in and to the world. In the case of untutored spontaneity, the deeper, grander scheme is Nature, while in the case of cultivated spontaneity, culture or tradition serves as a kind of Second Nature.

Ivanhoe presents his two forms of spontaneity as ideal types and notes that one rarely finds pure forms of either. Nevertheless, these types are helpful guides for understanding two general visions about the fundamental grounds for ethics in early China. While the advocates of untutored and cultivated spontaneity often hold different views about the value and reliability of such things as our uncultivated inclinations or traditional moral standards, they both insist on the importance of spontaneity when describing their ideal ethical agents and the lives they lead. A proper grasp of their respective conceptions of spontaneity is an excellent way into their ethical philosophy and arguably represents an essential, though often underappreciated, aspect of their views.

Ivanhoe concludes the chapter by suggesting that his study of spontaneity in early Chinese philosophy holds significant promise for ethics more generally. First, if we understand ethics to have among its concerns an account of what human beings value, then the widespread intuitions about the value of spontaneity—shared by contemporary people in both the East and West—offer at least *prima facie* evidence that early Chinese discussions of spontaneity may help us to understand not only the early Chinese but ourselves as well. Second, Ivanhoe shows that certain prominent Western thinkers invoke their own distinctive conceptions of spontaneity in the course of presenting their ethical philosophies. These references to spontaneity are overlooked by contemporary expositors because spontaneity is not thought of as an ethical term of art or even as a central normative concept. Ivanhoe suggests that an understanding of early Chinese views of spontaneity can help us understand not only our own intuitions, but also prominent members of the Western philosophical tradition more accurately and deeply. Once we return to these familiar texts with spontaneity in mind—we find it almost everywhere.

The nine chapters forming this volume focus on a broad range of topics, employ a spectrum of philosophical styles, and pursue a variety of different aims in the field of practical and theoretical ethics. Our contributors represent a selection of approaches and interests but are united in their attempt to take Confucian ethics seriously as an equal participant in a larger global conversation about human value and well-being. Taking Confucian ethics seriously, in the sense we intend, requires one to employ a certain critical conception of charity. We assume that the East Asian thinkers whose work we present here were sincerely expressing views not only that they took seriously, but also that they thought others should as well. One of their aims in writing the texts that we read was to convince other people of the correctness of their views and to move others to adopt those views. To take the thinkers seriously is to honor this original intent. Because we are separated from these philosophical conversation partners both culturally and temporally, in order to give their views a fair hearing we must, at least initially, endeavor to understand them as best we can within their particular historical and cultural context. However, with such an understanding in hand, we must then move on to question and evaluate the views they advocate. Taking them seriously entails an obligation to disagree, when appropriate, as well as to interpret, but it opens up the possibility of learning from as well as about other points of view.

Hong Kong
2009

Chapter 1

What It Means to Take Chinese Ethics Seriously

Heiner Roetz

When in 238 BCE his "guests" (*ke* 客) had compiled the *Lüshi chunqiu* 呂氏春秋 (Master Lü's Spring and autumn annals), a work "completely covering all topics of heaven and earth, of the myriad things, and of ancient and present times," Lü Buwei, the chancellor of Qin, displayed the work at the market gate of Xianyang, hung one thousand pieces of gold over it, and promised the money to any one of the wandering scholars from the other states or any one of the "guests" who was able to add or subtract a single word.[1]

If we take this episode from the third century BCE not as a singular event, but as representative of the intellectual situation of the time, it contains two important aspects of relevance for the topic of my paper. First, the Chinese authors creating the body of texts that we deal with today when we speak about "Chinese philosophy" or philosophy in China and philosophical ethics in particular laid claim to the validity of what they said or wrote. Second, the authors addressed this claim to an audience that we may call a public audience. Even if their writings, as in the case of the *Lüshi chunqiu*, were meant to influence the rulers of their time, they presented the writings to a general public that at least comprised the literate intellectuals of the then known world. Many late Zhanguo (5th century–221 BCE) texts were distributed extensively, and they prove the existence of widespread intellectual discussion. Rather than being isolated events, in Legalist judgments these developments "brought into disorder the common people" and became a serious threat to political stability (cf. Li Si's famous speech at the palace banquet in Xianyang in 214 BCE).[2]

Why are these aspects of relevance for "taking seriously" Chinese thinkers? My simple answer to this question would be: Because these aspects show that these thinkers themselves expected to be taken seriously, and that they addressed this expectation to all of their possible listeners or readers. By "taking seriously" I mean above all respecting their claims to the rightness and truth of their positions and statements and treating these claims as we would treat any other claims of this kind in normal conversation.

The texts in question are not "dead" bodies as are their physical media (silk, paper, wood, etc.) but, in general, they are expressions of meaning (*Sinneinheiten*) authored by human beings and directed to other human beings. The basic hermeneutical relation is a relation between subjects on equal terms, not between a subject (the researcher) and an object (the text as a "source"). It is only within the framework of this basic relation that an objectifying attitude (speaking *about* a text or the human being behind it rather than speaking *with* him or her), too, has its legitimate place. The objectifying attitude is appropriate inasmuch as we do not only have to *understand* the *reasons* of an author, but we also have to *explain* possible *causes* behind his or her work. Nevertheless, in the final analysis, when dealing with a text, we are never merely dealing with some "material" but also with a human subject that is addressing us and whom we ourselves can address.

If it is true that behind the "sources" we have to deal with human co-subjects, we cannot assume rules for engaging with these subjects other than those rules that we observe in everyday communication with human co-subjects in general. This would mean that a text imparts sense to the reader and that the reader can comment on this sense with "yes" or "no" answers. In doing so, he or she will do justice to the *dialogical*, and not monological, situation of understanding, which philology shares with normal conversation. Thus, in understanding (*verstehen*) a text, one should take into account that understanding is embedded in the context of coming to an understanding about something (*sich verstaendigen über etwas*). As Hans-Georg Gadamer has put it, "Understanding means, first of all, understanding each other. Understanding is first of all agreement (*Einverständnis*). To understand is always to come to an understanding about something."[3]

In order to illustrate my point, it is helpful to observe how we ourselves approach philological work (I again speak from the perspective of a Westerner dealing with Chinese texts, reading, for example, the *Lunyu* (Analects) or the *Mozi*, although this perspective is not Western-specific). The fact that what appears to be an interesting or good argument in these texts appeals to us, or what appears to be a poor argument might cause us to shake our head, bears witness to an imagined simultaneousness, a conversation between reader and author. Thus, we not only try to understand the meaning that the author intended, but to come to an understanding with him or her on a certain topic—in the given case, his or her ethics. In taking Kongzi and Mo Di (Mozi) as an example, I would like to suggest that this is true even when our authors have long been dead, as is the case in all classical philologies. These authors, too, are never mere objects of research, but partners in a conversation, albeit a *virtual* one. And the conjectures, hypotheses, and interpretations by which we try to make sense of their writings are only substitutes for our questions to the authors and for the answers they can no longer give.[4] The philological standards of objectivity, correctness, conscientiousness, and so forth, are rooted in the ethical "eye-level principle" (*Prinzip Augenhoehe*) rather than in a separate scientific ethos—they directly follow from the respect and sincerity that is due in communicating with human beings regardless of epoch or culture. This frame of mind is crucial in dealing not only with one's own tradition, but also with foreign thought. There is a restriction in Gadamer's hermeneutics in this respect that has to be overcome in order to make his approach fruitful for intercultural understanding (see below).

If the communication model for philology is sound, we cannot remain indifferent to the intentions and normative goals that have flowed into the text, just as in actual conversation; the texts are not only a "source," they, or their authors, also speak to us. Except for texts written for purely private reasons—and even these texts are in a public language that is not the sole possession of the author—they address a world of recipients that is open in time and place. Sociologically, this does not necessarily correspond to a full-fledged "civil society" in late Zhou China, but to the existence of an enlightened intellectual layer of society with open membership, and self-conscious in the sense of recognizing the binding force of intellectual ties vis-à-vis all other specific social relationships—as in the Greek idea of *cosmopolis*, the humanistic "conversation of high minds," or Mengzi's "friendship with the scholars (*shi* 士) of the world."[5] Strictly speaking, however, the argument is not sociological. It is rather assumed that together with the intellectual activity as such a universal horizon of meaning and validity claims is opened that encompasses all recipients wherever and whenever. Thus, the philologist who tries to understand a text shares a world and starts a shared history with it.

When philology begins, an intellectual community comes into being that comprises the interpreter, the (scientific) community to which the person addresses the work, and the authors of the texts in question—the relationship is a triadic rather than a dyadic (researcher and audience) one. In philological work, we not only anticipate the expectations of our future readers toward us (i.e., to deliver a competent work), but also the expectations of the ancients both toward their contemporaries and their future audience. It is only the positions that change: We have to take "our" authors just as seriously as we ourselves would like to be taken by those who follow us.

Taking the foreign authors seriously concerns already the accurate translation and interpretation of a text—foreign authors have a right to be represented as objectively as possible in other languages, and we have a corresponding obligation to them, not only to our readers. Foreign authors likewise have the right to have their validity claims respected by those to whom they speak or write, and this is any possible reader at any time and in any place. This does not imply that we should embrace antique ideas and forms of life. But it does imply that we should endeavor to separate what is anachronistic from what is not. In other words, it implies that we should examine the truth and rightness of the respective positions that may hold even today and be ready not only to criticize, but also, as the case may be, to learn something—not only *about* the authors, but also *from* them. As Max Scheler, who has declared himself a follower of a "cosmopolitan world-philosophy," has written, what matters is "not only to register historically Chinese and Japanese 'wisdoms,' but also at the same time to scrutinize them objectively (*sachlich prüfen*) and make them a *living* element in one's own thought (emphasis added)."[6]

However, the hermeneutical approach I am suggesting here is far from uncontroversial. It contradicts assumptions about understanding otherness (*Fremdverstehen*) in general, a widespread self-image of the hermeneutical sciences dealing with other cultures including Chinese studies, and a certain view of Chinese thought.

As to "understanding otherness" in general, in the corresponding literature the possible outcome of the process of intercultural understanding is often anticipated by—as I see it, premature—misgivings of all kinds. The classic representative of this position is Victor Segalen, who argued that with regard to foreign thought we have to "begin with the admittance of noncomprehensibility."[7] The main motive for this cautiousness is a fear of ethnocentrism, of reading one's own categories into foreign thought. According to Peter Weber-Schaefer, to take an example from German East Asian studies, *Fremdverstehen* is "occidental self-interpretation resulting in inevitable distortion." If we can understand East Asia, then it is only as "a European construct," not as an "external reality."[8] An important source for such a radical perspectivism is Gadamer's *Wahrheit und Methode*. As quoted above, Gadamer stresses on the one hand that understanding cannot be reduced to a mere "understanding of sense" (*Sinnverstehen*) but implies "coming to an understanding about something." On the other hand, he assumes that the interpreter is part of what he or she is trying to understand

(*Zugehoerigkeit des Interpreten zu seinem Gegenstande*), inasmuch as he or she is subject to the "concrete bonds of custom and tradition" (*konkrete Bindungen von Sitte und Ueberlieferung*).[9] Paradoxically, this has made Gadamer an inspiration for East Asian cultural traditionalism, although the reduction of the "matter" (*Sache*), of the "something," which is the topic of "coming to an understanding" (*Einverstaendnis*), to an element of a shared heritage limits the relevance of his approach for a theory of *intercultural* understanding.

As to the self-image of Western cultural sciences (*Kulturwissenschaften*), it is more or less comparatistic, although in practice research can be "dialogical" in the sense that I am defending here on a theoretical level (this might be the case particularly in the United States, given the large number of Chinese scholars in the American scientific community). The preferred hermeneutical point of view is that of the neutral researcher who collects facts and, perhaps, discusses similarities and distinctions in comparison to his or her own historical or contemporary home discourse. Most Sinologists would regard leaving the distanced perspective on the "sources" for getting involved in the "message" of the text as unscientific. As Hans-Georg Moeller has put it with regard to the topic of human rights in a critique of my own approach, "the question as to whether or not traditional Confucianism is compatible with the modern conception of human rights can be put either as a scientific question or as a political or juridical one, but not for all these fields at the same time." As Moeller says, what one expects in a "scientific publication" has to be "descriptive and analytical."[10]

Weber-Schaefer has called East Asian studies (*Ostasienwissenschaften*) "comparative cultural sciences" that try "to explain East Asia to themselves rather than to the East Asians."[11] Undoubtedly, comparison is a necessary and legitimate element of cultural sciences. The problem is the programmatic priority attributed to it in its self-definition, which means to substitute conversation *with* others for conversation *about* them. I fully agree, therefore, with Hermann-Josef Roellicke's polemic against the "priority of comparative methods" in Sinology, because it undermines the real primacy of being addressed or even "being hit" (*getroffen werden*).[12] If comparison in the final analysis is not embedded in the endeavor to come to an understanding about something (*Verstaendigung ueber etwas*), it remains instrumental and haphazard, and it can just be replaced by the search for mere contrast.

This is indeed suggested by a number of Sinologists, including Rolf Trauzettel ("In conscious one-sidedness, I would like to take only the first step of the comparative method and that is to confront in a contrastive way the phenomena which at first sight seem to have similarities"[13]), Mathias Oberth (Sinology should "think in the direction of difference, not in the direction of unity"[14]), and Hans-Georg Moeller ("The task of comparative studies is precisely to make the texts more comprehensible by contrastively 'dispelling' them of seemingly similar 'ideas' "[15]). Perhaps the most prominent advocate of this view in Chinese studies is Chad Hansen, who suggested as early as 1972, "In such cases where parallel comparisons are invalid, a new approach is required. Contrastive analysis must replace comparative analysis in comparative philosophy.... We ought to abandon the frenzied search for forced parallels between Chinese and Western thought."[16]

Against these approaches, I would like to defend an alternative conception of understanding alien thought (*Fremdverstehen*) that does not necessarily discard the spectator's perspective altogether but embeds it in the wider perspective of a participant in a dialogue.

However, there are arguments in favor of the position of the quoted authors. I have already mentioned the well-founded suspicion that an accommodationist heuristic might lead to the projection of our own ideas and values into foreign thought (a historical example of this is the "figuristic" approach to China by seventeenth-century Christian authors eager to discover traces of the biblical tradition in China). This suspicion, however, does not take us far from a principled point of view, since it makes us sensitive to *empirical* problems of interpretation that, once known, do not remain the same but can be avoided or at least lessened.

Another type of argument suggests that an accommodationist heuristic fails not only because of ethnocentric prejudice on the part of the interpreter, but also because it is not corroborated by the other side of the process of understanding, the Chinese "material." Many Sinologists or Western philosophers would find the idea of "taking Chinese philosophical ethics seriously" meaningless, because they question to the present day that "philosophy" and "ethics" ever existed in China in the first place. They argue that due to linguistic, mental, or developmental reasons philosophy could not emerge in China, that it is an exclusively Western tradition invented by the Greeks, and that it was only much later imported into other cultures. Accordingly, "Chinese philosophy" is an invention of the twentieth century in the course of modern Chinese identity management.[17] And given the absence of philosophy in premodern China, "ethics" as a theory of moral action would become a misnomer, too. Doubt has also been cast on whether the term "truth," certainly a cornerstone of a hermeneutics that takes validity claims seriously, can be meaningfully applied to the texts in question.[18]

One type of argument poses a special challenge to my hermeneutics of communication or serious conversation. It is, in short, the argument that such a hermeneutics must fail because the *language* of the texts in question has no communicative function, at least not in the sense that I have suggested. Rather, it serves other purposes.

The weaker variant of this view is that the normative Chinese texts in question are not addressed to a general audience but only to the powerful, above all to the ruler. According to the German Sinologist Hans-Otto Stange, this marks the decisive difference between Greek and Chinese thought.[19] A similar view has been put forward by Nathan Sivin and G. E. R. Lloyd in recent publications.[20] Accordingly, Chinese authors would reject conversation with discussants outside the hierarchy, and even more so with foreigners.

The harder variant is that Chinese texts in general do not aim at being "understood" in the sense of an intellectual, rational apprehension of ideas or argumentative agreement (*argumentative Verstaendigung*). The texts rather aim to achieve the *practical effect* of a direct influence on the members of the language community. Marcel Granet, the initiator of this view, has even attributed this feature to the Chinese language itself. In his *La pensée chinoise*, perhaps the most influential Western Sinological work of the last century, Granet writes that Chinese language has a "latent imperative value," that it aims at "effectivity" and "action effects" rather than "following strictly intellectual requirements."[21] Chinese words function like models (Granet's expression is *emblemes*), which through an "affective and practical force" evoke a certain behavior.[22] Language is not meant to make propositions on facts; it is not descriptive, theoretical, or argumentative; but, in the terminology of modern speech act theory, it is one-sidedly perlocutionary.

It is generally overlooked that this influential theory is not just one theory among other Sinological theories about China and that it not only concerns a specific Sinological topic. Rather, the theory is *paradigmatic* in the sense that it affects the whole attitude of Sinology to its subject matter. It concerns language per se as our common medium and therefore has grave hermeneutical implications.

Chad Hansen has reformulated Granet's theory independently of the French Sinologist on a much more elaborate Sinological and linguistic basis. According to Hansen, the grammatical features of the Chinese language, above all what he calls the "action structure" of verbs denoting mental activities, foster a function of knowing in terms of the practical "knowing how" referring to habitual, correct behavior rather than a propositional, theoretical "knowing that."[23] Correspondingly, the Chinese texts would not aim at truth—a word that should accordingly be eliminated from our vocabulary for analyzing Chinese "philosophical" texts—but at effecting social results. Following Hansen, Roger

Ames and David Hall have ascribed a "nonpropositional character" to the Chinese language.[24] Whatever this might mean, such a language would hardly communicate *reasons* that could be the topic of an evaluating discourse and of "yes" or "no" comments, but it would operate as a nonreflected *cause* to shape conventional behavior.

It appears unfeasible to enter into a virtual "discourse" with the authors of the ancient Chinese texts on this basis. It would also have a bearing on the translation and interpretation of these texts: the claim to a good translation and interpretation would be based only on the expectations of our own readers, but not on those of the Chinese authors. This is because the—allegedly—syntactically rooted uniquely suggestive power of Chinese would necessarily be lost when translated into differently structured languages.

Views of the Chinese language in the tradition of Granet can also be found in the writings of the German Sinologists that I have quoted already as advocates of a contrastive heuristic. Here, too, the key to understanding—or, better, *explaining* Chinese culture—is the relationship of the Chinese thinkers to language. According to Moeller, language for these thinkers is "not yet medial, not communicative, and not an expression of thought"; it is not for "expressing individual consciousness," but for the "suggestive control of behavior." In short, it has "no hermeneutical function."[25] Trauzettel has ascribed to ancient China "a usage of language in an early stage of civilization that was retained much longer than in the Occident." The characteristic of this language lies in its "prescriptive" rather than "descriptive" function. In the "monism of the old Chinese systems of thought," which does not make a difference between language and the world in the first place, language is not seen as a "medium" but as "a thing among other things."[26]

If these statements are sound, they would rule out a communicative hermeneutics and would, by confounding content and method, not only justify but necessitate a contrastive approach. The respective theories can only be presented as objectifying and external, and their representatives cannot see themselves as "spoken to" by the corresponding texts and in a shared situation of "coming to an understanding." The respective writings are clear about this implication. To take Moeller as an example, the behaviorism he ascribes to the Chinese mind repeats itself in the scientific practice of the Sinologist—he pursues "perception in the sense of *observation*" (*Erkennen im Sinne von Beobachten*).[27] The language of the Chinese texts does not allow for coming to an understanding on a common topic—"one cannot have a conversation in this language."[28] Thus, what is missing on the Chinese side is not only *subjects* with a sovereign command of language, but also *co-subjects* of a communication. In the final analysis, this conception leads directly into behavioral science.

However, can we be sure that these heuristic approaches, which replace the "principle of eye-level" by a "principle of difference" or a "principle of divide," are appropriate to the Chinese "sources" in question? Is it perhaps true that the Chinese "authors" do not want to "be taken seriously" in the sense described above, let alone by a foreign interpreter? To my mind, the reverse is the case: the mentioned theories project their own pattern into their research objects. It is interesting to notice that Max Weber, one of the most influential multipliers of the contrastive approach to China, admitted this when he explicitly omitted all commonalities between China and the Occident in favor of a counter picture experiment.[29]

Still, we have to look at the Chinese texts and see which one of the conflicting approaches is suggested by them.

Let me start with the thesis that normative Chinese texts, and thus the group of documents that, more than other documents, bring up the question of coming to an understanding about a common concern, are not directed to a public audience, but to the rulers. As I see it, this thesis fails to take into account the intellectual atmosphere of "axial age" China, where the belief in all authorities is severely shaken in the political, social, and mental crisis of the epoch. In this crisis, which induced the new normative thinking and Chinese philosophical ethics in the first place, the normative discourse takes on much broader dimensions and much more critical directions than merely being a vehicle of consultation for the powerful. There is plenty of positive and even more negative evidence of this fact. Nearly every late Zhou text bears witness to the wide influence of all kinds of theories and opinions even among the "stupid masses."[30] It was exactly this *public* reasoning, not only some private opinions of critical intellectuals, that motivated the Qin to launch their attack on the "scholars" in 214 and 213 BCE.[31]

As to the linguistic arguments, they deprive classical Chinese of its propositional dimension in favor of its performative and perlocutionary dimension. That language is not regarded as "medial," that is, as a means for conversation about something, but as a direct cause, contradicts the view of the *Zhuangzi* that "words are there for getting hold of meaning" 言者所以在意.[32] Xunzi's conventionalistic theory of language,[33] again, is hardly compatible with a view of language in terms of "things" (cf. Trauzettel's statement above). I have argued elsewhere that normative Chinese texts are not marked by a one-dimensional regulative structure, but by a constative-regulative double structure.[34] It is true that the authors in question also aim at the "effect" of their ethical teaching. However, effect is not achieved by causal conditioning and immediate triggering of a certain behavior but—exceptions notwithstanding—by giving arguments, and these arguments can in turn be evaluated as convincing or not convincing. In order to give force to these arguments, it is a frequent rhetorical device to present ethical statements, in other words, rightness claims, by analogy with logical statements or statements about facts (*Tatsachenbehauptungen*), that is, truth claims, routinely combined by conjunctive elements like 猶, "it is like...," 譬之猶 or 譬之若, "it can be compared with...," and others. Examples are Mengzi's statements, "Human nature is good as water flows downward" 人之性善猶水之就下, or "Humaneness wins over inhumaneness just like water wins over fire" 仁之勝不仁也猶水勝火,[35] or Han Fei's statement, "A starving man will not survive if he does not eat anything for a hundred days in order to wait for millet and meat. If one waited for Yao and Shun in order to govern the people of today, this would be like the talk of waiting for millet and meat in order to rescue a starving man" 且夫百日不食以待粱肉, 餓者不活; 今待堯舜之賢乃治當世之民, 是猶待粱肉而救餓之說也.[36] Here, both authors obviously furnish their different normative programs rhetorically with one and the same claim to objective truth, a truth that is evident for anyone who lives in the same world of facts, rather than in the same world of culture-specific convictions. In these and similar cases, there is a special preference for "hard" facts like water flows downward, water wins over fire, a blind man cannot see colors, a deaf man cannot distinguish sounds, and so forth, which is surely due to the conviction that these facts are so unshakable that they cannot be called into question. If we make explicit the validity claims in those arguments in direct speech, it would, to take Mengzi as an example, go as follows: "Everyone who accepts the sentence 'Water flows downward' as true, and that is every human being, has also to accept my sentence 'Human nature is good' as true, together with all consequences for the right moral practice. And since it cannot be doubted that water flows downward, it can also not be doubted that human nature is good." Mengzi's aim to influence the behavior of his contemporaries and Han Fei's aim to destroy the belief in past models are communicated by way of demonstratively fostering the ethical and political claims with the force of an objective truth that can rationally be accepted by every human being who is a member of the same objective world.

I therefore draw the conclusion that Chinese texts do not undermine, but rather corroborate the appropriateness of, even the indispensability of, the culture-transcending communicative hermeneutics that I have suggested, with the implication of taking validity claims seriously, irrespective of time and place. This would rule out the systematic priority of comparative, contrastive, and objectifying approaches without denying their scientific value altogether and would give a systematic priority to those heuristic approaches that from the beginning assume a common horizon of meaning and make it possible to understand the foreign world and foreign history as part of our own world and our own history—like Karl Jaspers's theory of the "axial age," Lawrence Kohlberg's "cognitive developmental theory," or Karl-Otto Apel's discoursive ethics, which I have used in my own Sinological research.[37]

To take validity claims "seriously" is not to endorse them without examination. It means the decision for a hermeneutical paradigm based on the principle of eye-level communication that includes judgment—it does not rule out "yes" or "no" comments, but rather facilitates and enforces them. One will not necessarily become a Confucian by taking Confucian ethics seriously, the more so since, by the same logic, one would also have to become a Daoist or Mohist by taking Daoist and Mohist arguments seriously. There is only one preference for specific ethical positions that is justified by the hermeneutics of communication: a preference for those positions that on thorough examination help to promote or anticipate the principle of communication itself, as against tutelage, force, and exclusion.

Notes

1. *Shiji, Zhonghua shuju bianjibu* (ed.), (Beijing: *Zhonghua Shuju*, 1959), 85:2510.

2. Ibid., 6:254 f.

3. Hans-Georg Gadamer, *Wahrheit und Methode* (Truth and Method) third edition, (Tuebingen: Mohr, 1972), 168 ("Verstehen heißt zunaechst, sich miteinander zu verstehen. Verstaendnis ist zunaechst Einverstaendnis. . . . Verstaendigung ist also immer: Verstaendigung über etwas").

4. Cf. for this topic Karl-Otto Apel, "Die hermeneutische Dimension von Sozialwissenschaft und ihre normative Grundlage" [The hermeneutical dimension of social science and its normative foundation], in *Mythos Wertfreiheit? Neue Beitraege zur Objektivitaet der Human und Kulturwissenschaften*, eds. Karl-Otto Apel and Matthias Kettner (Frankfurt and New York: Campus), 17–47.

5. *Mengzi* 5B8, in *A Concordance to Meng Tzu*, Harvard-Yenching Institute Sinological Index Series (reprint, Taipei: Chengwen, 1966).

6. Max Scheler, "Der Mensch im Weltalter des Ausgleichs" [The human being in the world age of equalization], in *Philosophische Weltanschauung* by Max Scheler (1927; Munich: Lehnen, 1954), 106.

7. Victor Segalen, *Die Aesthetik des Diversen: Versuch über den Exotismus* [Essay on exoticism: An aesthetics of diversity] (Frankfurt: Qumran, 1983), 44.

8. Peter Weber-Schaefer, "Spiegelbilder Oder: Was geschieht, wenn Ostasienwissenschaftler versuchen, Ostasien zu verstehen?" [Mirror images: What happens when East Asianists try to understand East Asia?], in *Politisches Denken Chinas in alter und neuer Zeit*, eds. Oskar Fahr, Wolfgang Ommerborn, and Konrad Wegmann (Muenster: LIT, 2000), 13, 15.

9. Gadamer, *Wahrheit und Methode*, 249.

10. Hans-Georg Moeller, "Menschenrechte, Missionare, Menzius: Überlegungen angesichts der Frage nach der Kompatibilitaet von Konfuzianismus und Menschenrechten" [Human rights, missionaries, and Mengzi: On the question of the compatibility of Confucianism and human rights], in *Menschenrechte in Ostasien: Zum Streit um die Universalitaet einer Idee*, ed. Gunter Schubert (Tuebingen: Mohr Siebeck, 1999), 121 for the first quotation and 112 for the second.

11. Peter Weber-Schaefer, "Ostasien verstehen: Moeglichkeiten und Grenzen" [Understanding East Asia: Possibilities and limits], *Bochumer Jahrbuch zur Ostasienforschung* 19 (1996): 11.

12. Hermann-Josef Roellicke, "Die Ausgelegtheit der Welt: Zur Kritik komparatistischer Methoden" [The "interpretedness" of the world: A critique of comparativist methods], *Orientierungen* 1 (1996): 5; "Plaedoyer für eine 'Phaenomenologie der eigenen Zunge': Noch einmal über 'die Ausgelegtheit der Welt'" [A plea for a 'phenomenology of one's own tongue.' The 'Interpretedness of the world' revistied], *Orientierungen* 2 (1998), 16.

13. Rolf Trauzettel, "Denken die Chinesen anders? Komparatistische Thesen zur chinesischen Philosophiegeschichte" [Do the Chinese think differently? Comparativist theses on the history of Chinese philosophy], *Saeculum* 41, no. 2 (1990): 81.

14. Mathias Obert, "Sinologie als Geisteswissenschaft heute, mit besonderer Berücksichtigung der Philosophie" [Sinology as one of the humanities today, with special reference to philosophy], *Orientierungen* 2 (2001): 3.

15. Hans-Georg Moeller, "Sino-Nietzscheanismus: Eine geistesgeschichtliche Analyse und ein Plaedoyer für eine negative Dialektik in der philosophischen Komparatistik" [Sino-Nietzscheanism: A historical analysis and a plea for negative dialectics in philosophical comparisons], *Minima Sinica* 2 (2000): 51.

16. Chad Hansen, "Freedom and Moral Responsibility in Confucian Ethics," *Philosophy East and West* 22, no. 2 (1972): 169–186.

17. Cf. for this topic Heiner Roetz, "Philosophy in China? Notes on a Debate," *Extreme-Orient, Extreme-Occident* 27 (2005): 49–65.

18. Chad Hansen, "Chinese Language, Chinese Philosophy, and 'Truth,'" *Journal of Asian Studies* 44, no. 3 (1985): 491–519.

19. Hans Otto Stange, "Chinesische und abendlaendische Philosophie: Ihr Unterschied und seine geschichtlichen Ursachen" [Chinese and Occidental philosophy: Their difference and its historical causes] *Saeculum* 1 (1950): 380–396.

20. G. E. R. Lloyd, *Adversaries and Authorities: Investigations into Ancient Greek and Chinese Science* (Cambridge: Cambridge University Press, 1996); G. E. R. Lloyd and Nathan Sivin, "Why Wasn't Chinese Science about Nature? With a Discussion of Concepts of Nature in Ancient Chinese and Comparisons," in *Concepts of Nature in Traditional China: Comparative Approaches*, eds. Guenter Dux and Hans-Ulrich Vogel (Leiden: Brill, 2010).

21. Marcel Granet, *La pensée chinoise* (Paris: La Renaissance du Livre, 1934); quotations on pages 40, 43, 59, 43, respectively.

22. Granet, *La pensée chinoise*, 43, 27 ff.

23. Cf., for example, Chad Hansen, *Language and Logic in Ancient China* (Ann Arbor: University of Michigan Press, 1983); "Chinese Language, Chinese Philosophy, and 'Truth.' " I have discussed Hansen's theory in Heiner Roetz, "Validity in Zhou Thought: On Chad Hansen and the Pragmatic Turn in Sinology," in *Epistemological Issues in Classical Chinese Philosophy*, eds. Hans Lenk and Gregor Paul (Albany: State University of New York Press), 69–112.

24. David L. Hall and Roger T. Ames, *Thinking through Confucius* (Albany: State University of New York Press, 1987), 301.

25. Hans Georg Moeller, "Die chinesische Lehre von Formen und Namen (*xing-ming zhi xue*) aus der Sicht einer Philosophie des Zeichens" [The Chinese teaching of forms and names (*xingming zhi xue*) seen from the perspective of a philosophy of the sign], in *Zeichen lesen, Lese-Zeichen: Kultursemiotische Vergleiche von Leseweisen in Deutschland und China*, ed. Juergen Wertheimer (Tuebingen: Stauffenburg, 1999), 494 ff; *Die Bedeutung der Sprache in der fruehen chinesischen Philosophie* [The meaning of language in early Chinese philosophy] (Aachen: Shaker, 1994), 136, 145.

26. Rolf Trauzettel, "Mystik im chinesischen philosophischen Denken" [Mysticism in Chinese philosophical thought], *Minima Sinica* 2 (1997): 11.

27. Moeller, *Die Bedeutung der Sprache*, 115.

28. Moeller, "Die chinesische Lehre von Formen und Namen (*xingming zhi xue*)," 28.

29. Cf. Max Weber, *Die Wirtschaftsethik der Weltreligionen: Konfuzianismus und Taoismus, Schriften 1915–1920*, Studienausgabe der Max Weber-Gesamtausgabe Band, vol. 1, no. 19, eds. Helwig Schmidt-Glintzer and Petra Kolonko (Tuebingen: Mohr, 1991), 19. Weber gives a "typological" account that presents what is "of typical importance with regard to the great distinctions of the spirit of economic activity" and "neglects other aspects." It does not claim to give a "well-rounded" picture, but stresses opposites. A portrayal without this accent "would have to express more emphatically than is possible here that all qualitative differences in reality can somehow be interpreted as quantitative differences of mixtures of single factors" (ibid.).

30. *Xunzi*, chap. 6, p. 57, in Wang Xianqian, *Xunzi jijie*, vol. 2 of *Zhuzi jicheng* (Hong Kong: Zhonghua, 1978).

31. *Shiji*, 6:254 f.

32. *Zhuangzi*, chap. 26, p. 407, in Guo Qingfan, *Zhuangzi jishi*, vol. 3 of *Zhuzi jicheng* (Hong Kong: Zhonghua, 1978).

33. *Xunzi*, chap. 22, p. 274; Heiner Roetz, *Confucian Ethics of the Axial Age: A Reconstruction under the Aspect of the Breakthrough towards Postconventional Thinking* (Albany: State University of New York Press, 1993), 295, n. 23.

34. Roetz, "Validity in Zhou Thought."

35. *Mengzi* 6A2 and 6A18, in *A Concordance to Meng Tzu*; cf. also *Mengzi* 2A4, 2A6, 4A3, 4A7, 4B7, 5B7.

36. *Hanfeizi*, chap. 40, p. 300, in Wang Xianshen, *Hanfeizi jijie*, vol. 5 of *Zhuzi jicheng*, (Hong Kong: Zhonghua, 1978).

37. Cf. Roetz, *Confucian Ethics of the Axial Age*, chap. 3.

Chapter 2

The Handling of Multiple Values in Confucian Ethics

Kam-por Yu

Central Question

In this chapter, I present a line of thinking in Confucian ethics that recognizes the existence of multiple values, sees the value of preserving and promoting competing values, and proposes a way to accommodate multiple values.[1] According to this line of thinking, there is more to ethical thinking than the distinction between good and bad or right and wrong. There is not just one good (*shan* 善) but many goods, and one good may not be reduced to another.[2] Due recognition has to be given to all the competing values, and effort has to be made to preserve and promote the competing values as far as possible. The challenging task in ethics is not so much to identify *the best solution*, as there may not be one, but to recognize the values contained in different solutions and to take this recognition into account in making moral judgments.[3]

Three Lines of Interpretation

The core concept of this line of thought is *zhong* 中, and related concepts include *zhongdao* 中道, *zhongxing* 中行, and *zhongyong* 中庸. There have been two main lines of interpretation for this set of concepts. One can conveniently be called moderatism, which regards the right course of action to be somewhere between excess and inadequacy. The other can conveniently be called internalism, which holds that if we get our internal mental state right we will also get our external behavior right. The view that I shall present differs from these two lines of interpretation in that it sees ethical thinking not only as a choice between good and evil, but also a choice among various goods. This view may be conveniently called pluralism.

My analysis is based on a wide range of Confucian classics and other works within the Confucian tradition, but the *Zhongyong* 中庸 (commonly called the *Doctrine of the Mean*) is my primary source. Just as the word *zhong* 中 has two meanings,[4] there are also two uses of the word *zhong* in the *Zhongyong*. This has long been recognized by Confucian scholars such as Cheng Yi 程頤 (1033–1107) and Zhu Xi 朱熹 (1130–1200). The first sense refers to the unbiased state one is in before one acts; Cheng Yi calls this *zaizhong* 在中. The second refers to the appropriate way one acts; Cheng Yi calls this *zhong zhi dao* 中之道.[5] Chapters 2 to 20 of the *Zhongyong* are related directly to the expression *zhongyong*, and they are on the theme of personal and political morality. Chapters 21 to 32 present a moral metaphysics based on the concept of sincerity (*cheng* 誠). It has been said that these two parts may come from different sources. I will not comment on that issue here. This chapter is focused on that part of the *Zhongyong* where the focus is on *zhong* 中 as an appropriate way of acting rather than a proper inner state associated with sincerity.

Two Tests for an Acceptable Interpretation

Many things have been said about the notion of *zhongyong* in the Confucian classics. Two very strong claims, in particular, have been made: first, that it is impossible to fully realize *zhongyong*; second, that *zhongyong* is the supreme virtue. It is a challenge to any interpretation of *zhongyong* to explain the reasons underlying these claims.

In several passages in the *Analects* (*Lunyu*) and *Zhongyong*, Kongzi (Confucius) is quoted as saying that it is impossible to put *zhongyong* into practice.[6] But if *zhongyong* is the middle state between two extremes, why is it impossible to put it into practice? We may not always be able to locate the middle, but this does not mean that it is impossible to do so. In any event, it does not seem more impossible to do the moderate action than the extreme ones. If, as many have claimed, *zhongyong* is about the value of the common or the familiar, then it is even more puzzling why Kongzi said it is so difficult or impossible to put *zhongyong* into practice.

A second puzzle is why *zhongyong* is regarded as the supreme virtue.[7] What has *zhongyong* to do with virtue? Why is it regarded as a virtue that has higher status than other virtues? Is there a reason for giving *zhongyong* a prestigious position in the hierarchy of virtues or for regarding it as a higher order virtue?

Any acceptable interpretation of *zhongyong* should be able to answer these two questions. We can regard the explanation of the two claims as two tests that an acceptable interpretation has to pass.

Similar and Dissimilar Concepts

Before I begin my account of multiple-value ethical thinking, I would like to compare the concept of *zhongyong* with a few other concepts that have been associated with it.

In a number of writings in the Confucian tradition before the Song-Ming period (960–1644), *zhongyong* is contrasted with the concept of *pianzhi* 偏至 (excelling in one single aspect, or overemphasizing one important aspect) and is regarded as synonymous with the concept of *zhouquan* 周全 (holistic, or all-round).

In the *Houhanshu* (*History of the Later Han Dynasty*, by Fan Ye 范曄, 445), the concept of *zhongyong* is regarded as meaning all-round or general excellence, as contrasted with one-sided excellence.

> Kongzi said, "If *zhongyong* is not available, we have to opt for the undisciplined or the overcautious." Kongzi also said, "The undisciplined is eager to act while the overcautious will refrain from doing certain kinds of actions." This describes cases when all-round excellence cannot be found, and one-sided excellence is approved.[8]

Chapter 81 of the *Houhanshu* is a collection of stories about a number of remarkable individuals who have displayed at least one aspect of virtue in an impressive and memorable manner. Their behavior offers examples of *pianzhi*. They are regarded as exemplary because they are serious in their pursuit of virtue, but they are not regarded as the highest model, because they may overlook other important aspects in their pursuit of one specific virtue. By contrast, a person who follows *zhongyong* is able to take multiple values into consideration. If only one value or part of the values is emphasized, then even if the value or values are realized to the full, it is still a case of *pianzhi*. The mode of *zhongyong* may not take some of the values as far as the mode of *pianzhi*, but all the values are given due recognition, and there is a better balance among them all.

In the *Gazette of Human Nature* (*Renwu zhi* 人物志), which was written by Liu Shao 劉劭 (b. 168–172, d. 240–249) of the Wei dynasty and provides a taxonomy and evaluative system of personality, *zhongyong* is also defined by its all-roundedness. In the chapter on "nine features" (*jiu zheng* 九徵), it is said that there are five virtues: "To possess all the virtues, and to the highest possible extent, is called *zhongyong*. *Zhongyong* is the name for the sage. To possess all the virtues to some extent is called a good moral character. To excel in just one aspect is called specialized excellence."[9] Here *zhongyong* is characterized not by its moderate nature, but by its inclusive nature. *Zhongyong* is not concerned with having a good quality to a moderate degree, but having as many good qualities as possible to the highest possible degree relative to the possibilities afforded by the particular situation.

The use of the difference between a whole picture and a partial picture as a metaphor (*quanpian zhi yu* 全偏之喻) for the difference between a superior ethical view and an inferior ethical view is quite familiar in the Confucian tradition. An inferior view is regarded as inferior not because it is completely wrong, but because it reveals only part of the truth (but pretends that it is the whole truth or the most important part of the truth). The contrast here is not between right and wrong, but between complete (*quan* 全) and partial (*pian* 偏). An inferior view (*yipian zhi jian* 一偏之見) is a partial truth, but it is not wholly incorrect. A superior man is able to see the value of all the partial truths, without overemphasizing any one of them.

The above view prevails in the *Xunzi*. The following two quotations, from the "Jiebi" 解蔽 chapter and the "Bugou" 不苟 chapter, respectively, are obvious examples.[10]

> It is a common flaw of people to be blinded by one aspect of truth and fail to see the overall pattern.

> The problem people usually have is one-sidedness. When they perceive the desirable qualities, they ignore the undesirable qualities. When they see the benefits that might be brought, they overlook the harms that might be incurred.

The concept *zhouquan* (holistic, all-round approach) is used to explain the concept *zhongyong*, but another concept, *zhizhong* 執中, is regarded as different from *zhongyong* and should not be confused with it. A distinction between these two concepts is useful for a better understanding of the concept of *zhongyong*.

Mengzi points out that the problem with *zhizhong* (holding on to the middle ground) is like the problem with *zhiyi* 執一 (holding on to one aspect but ignoring other aspects) in that it is one-sided and not well-balanced:

> Mengzi said, "Yangzi advocates self-love. Even if he could benefit the whole world by pulling out one hair, he would not do it. Mozi advocates equal love. Even if he has to make his head bald and walk on bare feet, he would do it if it could benefit the world. Zimo holds on to the middle ground. Holding on to the middle ground is closer to being right. But to hold on to the middle ground without proper weighting is no different from holding to one side. The reason that I hate holding to one side is that it is harmful to the *Dao* [Way]. It emphasizes one aspect at the expense of one hundred other aspects." (*Mengzi* 7A26)

Here Mengzi is considering two values: love of oneself and love of other people. According to Mengzi, both of these values should be recognized. Zimo's position is said to be closer to being right, because his position involves recognition of these two values to some degree, instead of affirming just one of them and turning a blind eye to the other one. Mengzi thinks that we should affirm both values and strike the right balance between them. But striking the right balance between the two requires more than adopting the middle ground. It is interesting to note that the *Dao* is known, not by excluding the two competing views, but by including them and giving them some kind of affirmation or recognition at the same time.[11]

For the time being, it is enough for us to notice that *zhongyong* is different from holding on to the middle ground. It is to be contrasted with a one-sided view and is holistic. The holistic view is formed not by excluding the one-sided views, but by including them while recognizing the limited value that each has.

Two other expressions, *zhongdao* 中道 and *zhongxing* 中行 should be regarded as synonymous with the term *zhongyong*. *Zhongyong* is usually compared with two other ways: the undisciplined and the overcautious. On such occasions, the expressions *zhongdao* and *zhongxing* have been used in place of *zhongyong*. In *Analects* 13.21, the term *zhongxing* is used: "Kongzi said, 'If *zhongxing* is not available, we have to opt for the undisciplined and the overcautious. The undisciplined are eager to act. The overcautious refrain from doing certain kinds of action.'" In *Mengzi* 7B37, the term *zhongdao* is used:

> Mengzi said, "Kongzi could not find the company of those who follow *zhongdao*; he could only fall back on the undisciplined and the overcautious. The undisciplined are eager to act. The overcautious refrain from doing certain kinds of actions. It is not because Kongzi did not want those who follow *zhongdao*. He could not be sure that he could find them. So, he thought of the second best."

From the above passages, we can conclude that *zhongdao* and *zhongxing* are other names for *zhongyong*. The term *zhongyong* has been used in a number of ways. If we are aware that it is synonymous with *zhongdao* and *zhongxing*, then we may want to avoid interpreting *zhongyong* in some of these ways.

The term *zhongdao* also appears in certain Buddhist texts. However, the Buddhist use of the term is different from the Confucian. The Buddhist *zhongdao* is obtained by avoiding or excluding both of the sides (*buluo liangbian* 不落兩邊).[12] The Confucian *zhongdao* is obtained by incorporating both sides into a comprehensive point of view.

The commentary of Wang Fuzhi 王夫之 (1619–1692) on *zhongdao* is particularly enlightening. He points out that the *zhongxing*, the undisciplined, and the overcautious are not three separate paths. The *zhongxing* incorporates the merits of the other two, and that is why it is superior to the other two. The undisciplined are eager to do the right thing, but they violate some moral constraints in trying to do the right thing. The overcautious are careful not to violate any moral constraints, but they may not try hard enough to do the right thing. The *zhongxing* sees the value of both of these two alternatives. The right thing should be done, and the moral constraints should be respected. To uphold these two points means trying to do the right thing within the moral constraints.[13]

Three Illustrations

Kongzi has offered three memorable illustrations of the meaning of *zhongyong*. The first is a story about the sage-king Shun 舜. The second concerns Kongzi's best and favorite disciple, Yan Hui 顏回. The third concerns Kongzi's disciple Zilu 子路, a student who is best known for his courage.

In *Zhongyong*, chapter 6, the sage-king Shun is referred to as an exemplary person who is skillful in putting *zhongyong* into practice.

> Kongzi said, "Great indeed is the wisdom of Shun! Shun likes to ask [the views of all kinds of people] and to investigate the words

of those who are close to him. He omits the bad and propagates the good. He holds fast the two ends (*duan* 端) and uses the *zhong* for the people. This is what makes him Shun!"

In what sense is Shun a man of great wisdom? He is regarded as wise because he knows a good way to find out what is right. Note how different his process of thinking is from the "internalism" of the Song-Ming philosophers. Shun first inquires widely about the views of different people. Other people may have valuable opinions that Shun may not be able to think of by himself alone. He invites views from different parties so that he has the greatest chance not to miss any worthwhile views. He is able to distinguish between those views that are valuable and those that are not.[14] He is not unduly affected by views that are not valuable and appreciates those that are valuable. In regard to those who are close to him, he remains alert not to accept their words too easily or lightly. Words of advice are not to be accepted but investigated. After investigation, we can separate the valuable parts from those that lack merit. We can then forget about those views that are without value and give due recognition to those that possess value. A proper *zhong* resolution can only be determined by holding fast to all the values that we have discovered.[15] This story about Shun illustrates the *zhongyong* way of ethical thinking.

Often when people have different opinions, especially in ethical matters, it is not that some views are completely right and some views are completely wrong. Even though a view is basically wrong, it may still contain *some* reasonable elements. People who hold such views would not be convinced regarding what is truly right if the reasonable elements of their views were not recognized. Shun is regarded as wise because he can make use of the wisdom of other people. He is able to extract valuable opinions from different parties and hold them consistently at the same time. As pointed out by R. M. Hare, the difficult thing in doing philosophy is not so much to grasp the truth but the *whole* truth:

> If you take a bunch of supposedly divergent theories on almost any philosophical question, you will find in each of them some points which are right, and some which are wrong. Those who criticize these theories often rightly attack the points that are wrong, but do not see that not everything in a theory is wrong; it also, usually, has hold of important truths. So, in putting forward their own opposing theories, these philosophers discard the good with the bad, denying truths that their victims had grasped. So they too land themselves in a mixture of truth and error.

The difficult thing, as I said, is to grasp the whole truth. This entails carefully disentangling the truths from errors in *all* the theories one studies. It is the mark of the good philosophers to be able to do this. All philosophers can profit from the advice that I regularly give to my students: pinch your opponents' clothes. That is, find out what is right about what they are saying, and say it yourself.[16]

In the case of Shun, the *liangduan* 兩端 ("two ends," or "two different or opposing aspects") are not something that we should get rid of. On the contrary, they should be grasped tightly. The resulting *zhong* is determined as a result of grasping the two ends. If the two ends are the wrong paths of excess and inadequacy, then it is unreasonable to say that they should be grasped tightly. If they should be grasped tightly, then the two ends must be something valuable.

Now look at the second story, which is about Kongzi's best student, Yan Hui. Kongzi very clearly states that Yan Hui is able to make his choice according to *zhongyong*. And what is it like to make one's choice according to *zhongyong*? "Kongzi said, 'Yan Hui made his choices according to *zhongyong*. Whenever he got hold of one good, he grasped it firmly, cherished it dearly, and never let go.'" (*Zhongyong*, chapter 8) If what Yan Hui grasped was *just one* good, how can he be said to be choosing according to *zhongyong*? What is so special about Yan Hui is that he is able to do this not just for one good, but whenever he encounters a good. This means that Yan Hui is able to grasp all the goods he encounters, and this is why he is regarded as making a choice according to *zhongyong*. The goods may compete or conflict with one another. It is common for people to accept one value and reject or ignore other values that are in conflict with the value they have already accepted. But Yan Hui is able to recognize each good when he sees it, grasp hold of each of them, and make his judgment taking into account all of them.

Some writers are puzzled by expressions in the *Zhongyong*, such as "seizing the two *duan* 執其兩端" (chapter 6), "clasping to the breast 拳拳服膺" (chapter 8), and "holding steadfastly 固執之 (chapter 20)." It is said that in regard to the last phrase "the insertion of the adverb *ku* 固 (firmly) . . . reinforces the sense of holding fast to just one end of the moral spectrum."[17] It is indeed puzzling if *zhong* is regarded as opposing the two ends, rather than including them.

In a number of Confucian writings, we find that the different *duan* are to be examined, included, and given their proper place, instead of being denied, excluded, or attacked.

> Organize different *duan*, such that they do not contradict one another.[18]
>
> Kongzi said, "To attack a *duan* different from yours can do nothing but harm." (*Analects* 2.16)[19]
>
> Kongzi said, "Do I know anything? No, I don't.... I just examine the two *duan* and exhaust what is contained in them." (*Analects* 9.8)

The important point that the different *duan* are to be grasped and assimilated is noted by the Japanese scholar Kanaya Osamu:

> A lead for a fresh examination of the Mean is provided by a passage in *The Mean* that describes the government of the sage-king Shun: "Shun loved to question others, and he carefully considered what was said within his hearing. He praised what he thought to be good and concealed what he thought to be bad and grasping these two extremes employed the middle in his government of the people." Special note should be taken of the final words: "grasping (*zhi* 執) these two extremes" means that instead of rejecting them he took firm hold of them. Although it is the middle that is actually adopted in government, it may be assumed that the two extremes are assimilated by and put to good use in this middle. In other words, the middle between two extremes, inclining neither to the left nor to the right, is in fact endowed with the capacity to encompass both the left and the right.[20]

The nature of *zhongyong* is also illustrated by our third story, which concerns a judgment between two values. It contrasts the value of contending and self-asserting on the one hand with the value of tolerance and forgiveness on the other hand.

> Zilu asked about strength. Kongzi said, "Are you asking about what the southerners call strength, or what the northerners call strength, or the kind of strength that you should have? To have tolerance and gentleness in teaching others and to take no revenge on those who have acted against the proper way is what the southerners

call strength. This is what the gentlemen today regard as strength. To sleep on one's shield and armor and meet one's death without remorse is what the northerners call strength. This is what the strong regard as strength. Thus, the gentleman cultivates harmony without submitting to pressure. Great indeed is his strength! He takes up the position of *zhong* and does not incline to either side. Great indeed is his strength! When the way prevails in the country, he does not change the principles he sticks to in difficult times. Great indeed is his strength! When the way does not prevail in the country, he does not change his principles even though his life is at stake. Great indeed is his strength!" (*Zhongyong*, chapter 10)

It is interesting to note that Kongzi, in his reply, affirms both of the two competing conceptions of strength. Instead of criticizing the two conceptions, he points out the merits of both and puts forward his own conception that incorporates the merits of both. He presents a picture of someone who insists on his own principles and is ready to make a sacrifice but who also respects differences and works at not being oppressive. The recommended resolution is not a rejection of either of the two competing answers but a synthesis of them, giving their insights due recognition by incorporating them.

From the above three illustrations, it is clear that *zhongyong* has a holistic and inclusive nature. Unlike other perspectives, which affirm one aspect while denying others, the approach of *zhongyong* is able to see the value of different points of view at the same time. The recommended resolution of *zhongdao* or *zhongxing* is determined by taking all the relevant aspects into consideration and giving due recognition to all the values involved.

The *zhongdao* or *zhongxing* approach can be applied when we are considering just one value, when we are considering two values, as well as when we are considering multiple values. In the following section, I examine the three models one by one.

One-Value Model

In the *Analects*, we can find a number of expressions in the form *X but not Y*:[21]

> Have self-confidence but do not engage in contestation. Get along well with others but do not form cliques. (*Analects* 15.22)

The Handling of Multiple Values in Confucian Ethics

> Give benefit to the people but do not spend much. Demand that the people contribute but [do] not [burden them] to the extent that they would complain. Have desires but do not be greedy. Take things easy but do not be arrogant. Be dignified but do not be fierce. (*Analects* 22.2)

Many of the above statements have been taken as expressing the Aristotelian mean. For example, we should have the right amount of dignity; if we go too far, we will become fierce. Similarly, if we have too much desire, we will become greedy. If we take too many things too easily, we will become arrogant. If we demand too much from the people, then we will reach the extent of burdening them. If we give too much benefit to the people, we will be spending too much of the state's resources.

The following quotation from the *Xunzi* has been translated along this line of interpretation:

> The gentleman is magnanimous, but not to the point of being remiss. He is scrupulous, but not to the point of inflicting suffering. He engages in argumentation, but not to the point of causing a quarrel. He is critical, but not to the point of provoking others. When he upholds an upright position, he is not merely interested in victory. When hard and strong, he is not haughty. When flexible and tractable, he does not merely drift with the demands of the occasion. He is respectful, reverent, attentive, and cautious, but still remains inwardly at ease.[22]

In each of the above expressions in the form *X but not Y*, we find one quality being affirmed (e.g., *jin* 矜, *qun* 群, *hui* 惠, *lao* 勞, *yu* 欲, *tai* 泰, *wei* 威) while the other is being denied (e.g., *zheng* 爭, *dang* 黨, *fei* 費, *yuan* 怨, *tan* 貪, *jiao* 驕, *meng* 猛). We can understand the above expressions in a single-value model. In each expression, only one thing is considered a value. The important point is to be neither excessive nor fall short in the pursuit of the value.

But how do we determine whether we are going too far or falling short? When we say that we are going too far, there must be a second value to which we are referring. The pursuit is regarded as problematic because while upholding one important value, it threatens another important value. For example, consider the expression "Be dignified but do not be fierce." What is the problem with being fierce? The problem is not that we are too dignified, but because while we dignify ourselves we may hurt the feelings of other people. We can either put this point in the form of *X but not Y* (where *X* is something desirable or good and *Y* is something undesirable or bad) or we can put this point positively in the form *X and X'* (where both *X* and *X'* are desirable or good). We can put this point as "Be dignified and respect the feelings of other people." In this expression, there are two values that we want to promote. I call this a two-value model. What I want to show is that the one-value model described above is actually a disguised form of what I call a two-value model. The *zhongyong* approach is always associated with the handling of multiple values.

Two-Value Model

The *Zhongyong* begins with a contraposition of two values: "Following our nature is the way. Improving the way is education." The first statement affirms the value and importance of following one's nature. We cannot totally alienate our nature in our moral pursuit. Our nature should not be the end of our moral pursuit, but it has to be the beginning, and there is no other place from which we can begin. The second statement, however, affirms the value and importance of improving on what we have as our nature. So, the two statements side by side affirm two values: (1) following our nature; (2) improving our nature. Moral pursuit is at the same time affirming and transcending our nature. The *Zhongyong* does not regard these two aims as incompatible. What we should do is not to take one and reject the other, but to strike the right balance between the two.

In the *Zhongyong*, the following pairs of values are contraposed: simplicity (*jian* 簡) and refinement (*wen* 文), and being cordial (*wen* 溫) and principled (*li* 理) (chapter 33).

In the *Analects*, we can find a number of expressions in the form *X and X'*, where both *X* and *X'* are desirable values. Kongzi's view is that both values should be pursued at the same time. It is problematic if one value is pursued at the expense of another. Such competing qualities include the following: refined (*wen* 文) and substantial (*zhi* 質) (*Analects* 6.18); cordial (*wen* 溫) and stern (*li* 厲) (*Analects* 7.38); respectful (*gong* 恭) and easy (*an* 安) (*Analects* 7.38); and simple (*jian* 簡) and reverential (*jing* 敬) (*Analects* 6.2).

If only one of the two competing values is upheld, the deficiency of one value cannot be compensated for by additional quantities of another value.

> The Master said, "When there is a preponderance of native substance over acquired refinement, the result will be churlishness. When there

is a preponderance of acquired refinement over native substance, the result will be pedantry. Only a well-balanced admixture of these two will result in gentlemanliness." (*Analects* 6.18)[23]

> In ruling over the common people, is it not acceptable to hold oneself in reverence and merely to be simple in the measures one takes? On the other hand, is it not carrying simplicity too far to be simple in the way one holds oneself as well as in the measures one takes? (*Analects* 6.2)[24]

If there is more than one value that should be upheld, then concentrating on just one value while ignoring other values is a moral deficiency. As pointed out in the *Huainanzi* 淮南子, the son who gave evidence against his father who had stolen a sheep and the young man who kept his promise and refused to leave when the river rose are examples of people who know only one value.

> Honoring one's word and keeping one's promise are regarded as exemplary behavior by the whole world. The "Upright Boy" bore witness against his father for stealing a sheep. Mr. Wei made an appointment with a woman and chose to die rather than miss the appointment. This is uprightness that bears witness against one's own father. This is honoring [one's word] that drowns one to death. Though [these are cases of] uprightness and honoring [one's word], who would treasure them?[25]

It is never denied that these two cases are examples of uprightness and honoring one's word. It is also never denied that uprightness and honoring one's word are good. The problem is that the people in these stories knew only one value and failed to appreciate other values besides the value they held so dearly.

The recognition of two competing values, however, does not necessarily lead to the conclusion that there must be a golden mean—that it is ideal to maintain a perfect proportion between the two competing values.

In the *Book of Rites* (*Liji*), Kongzi speaks of the importance of two opposing aspects: tense (*zhang* 張) and relaxed (*chi* 弛). Both of these aspects are valuable. But the best option is not the middle ground between these two ends, nor a perfect proportion of these two attributes. The suggested solution is an appropriate alternation of the two states. This solution implies that when we are relaxed we can be very relaxed, and when we are tense we can be very tense.

> Zigong had gone to see the agricultural ceremony at the end of the year. Kongzi said to him, "Did you enjoy it?" Zigong replied, "The whole country seemed to have gone mad. I didn't enjoy it." Kongzi said, "After a hundred days of labor, people have one day of fun. That's not something you understand. To be tense all the time and never relax, that is too much even for King Wen and King Wu. To be relaxed all the time and never get tense, that's not what King Wen and King Wu would prefer. To alternate being relaxed and tense—that is the way of King Wen and King Wu." (*The Book of Rites*, "Miscellaneous Records," part 2)

Multiple-Value Model

Chapter 20 of the *Zhongyong* talks about the three virtues, the five relations, and the nine guiding principles (*jiujing* 九經). What have they to do with *zhongyong*, and why should they be mentioned at all?

James Legge is not unreasonable in making the following complaint:

> The twentieth chapter, which concludes the third portion of the Work [*Zhongyong*], contains a full exposition of Kongzi's views on government, though professedly descriptive only of that of kings Wen and Wu. Along with lessons proper for a ruler there are many also of universal application, but the mingling of them perplexes the mind. It tells us of "the five duties of universal application,"—those between sovereign and minister, husband and wife, father and son, elder and younger brother and friends; of "the three virtues by which those duties are carried into effect," namely, knowledge, benevolence, and energy; and of "the one thing, by which those virtues are practiced," which is singleness or sincerity. It sets forth in detail the "nine standard rules for the administration of government," which are "the cultivation by the ruler of his own character; the honoring men of virtue and talents; affection to his relatives; respect towards the great ministers; kind and considerate treatment of the whole body of officers; cherishing the mass of the people as children; encouraging all classes of artisans; indulgent treatment of men from a distance; and the kindly cherishing of the princes of the States." There are these and other equally interesting topics in

this chapter, but, as they are in the Work, they distract the mind, instead of making the author's object more clear to it.²⁶

That the *Zhongyong* appears to talk about a number of unrelated things has not gone unnoticed. Cheng Yi in his preface to the *Zhongyong* says, "The Book first speaks of one principle; it next spreads this out, and embraces all things; finally, it returns and gathers them all up under one principle. Unroll it, and it fills the universe; roll it up, and it retires and lies hid in mysteriousness."²⁷ But the problem with this explanation is that it can explain everything. Any digression in the middle of the text can be explained in this way. If it can explain everything, then it cannot explain anything at all. The question is: What have the things said here to do with the theme of *zhongyong*? Why talk about these things rather than something else? In what sense are they more relevant to the topic?

But if I am right in saying that the *Zhongyong* is a treatise on how to handle multiple values, then it is quite straightforward to see what the nine guiding principles have to do with *zhongyong*. The nine guiding principles are the nine aspects of good governance. Good governance is achieved if we can take care of all the nine aspects and strike the right balance among them. The nine guiding principles define the components of good governance and are as follows: cultivate one's person (*xiu shen* 脩身), honor the good and capable (*zunxian* 尊賢), be devoted to one's kin (*qinqin* 親親), respect the senior ministers (*jing dachen* 敬大臣), understand the difficulties of the various officials (*ti qunchen* 體群臣), love the common people (*zi shumin* 子庶民), attract the various artisans (*lai baigong* 來百工), give preferential treatment to people from afar (*rou yuanren* 柔遠人), and pacify the feudal states (*huai zhuhou* 懷諸侯). These nine aspects compete for our attention and resources, and as a result there is tension among them. The important thing is not to focus on just some of them but to ensure that none of them has been neglected.

The idea that there are multiple values and that effort should be made to promote all of them and strike the right balance predates Kongzi. In an important treatise (*Yin Zhou zhidu lun* 殷周制度論)²⁸ on the institutional reforms and cultural changes during the Yin-Zhou period (c. 1111 BCE), historian Wang Guowei 王國維 explained and illustrated with numerous examples that the institutional reform initiated by the Duke of Zhou was designed to strike the right balance among three important values: (1) respecting those who have high status (*zunzun* 尊尊); (2) caring for those who are related to us (*qinqin* 親親); and (3) recognizing the worth of those who are good and capable (*xianxian* 賢

賢). These three emphases have different functions: Respecting people who have high status is necessary for stability. Caring for those who are related to oneself is necessary for social cohesiveness. Finally, recognizing the worth of those who are good and capable (instead of selecting people for office on the basis of status or relation) is necessary for building a reasonable and good society. According to Wang Guowei, the institutions were designed by the Duke of Zhou as a result of taking these three important aims into consideration.[29]

The Moral Methodology

The story of how Shun finds out what is the right thing to do implicitly contains the methodology of an important form of moral thinking. There are six steps: (1) being fond of asking questions (*haowen* 好問); (2) being fond of [careful] investigation (*haocha* 好察); (3) omitting what is unworthy (*yine* 隱惡); (4) propagating what is worthy (*yangshan* 揚善); (5) holding firmly to all that is worthwhile (*zhiliang* 執兩); and (6) locating the right balance and applying it (*yongzhong* 用中).

We cannot assume that we have all moral knowledge inside us, such that we can bring it out simply by reflection. To find out what is the right thing to do, we need to have an open mind, the willingness to listen to different opinions, and be sensitive to new information. "Being fond of asking questions" means taking the initiative in seeking out new information. However, we cannot accept new information uncritically. We have to make judgments about its worth. "Being fond of [careful] investigation" means we need to screen the new information and check its validity. "Omitting what is unworthy" means that after critically examining the new information, we omit whatever is without merit. We then need to fully understand and appreciate the value of what is worthwhile. As Kongzi said, "investigate the two *duan* and exhaust what is contained in them" (*Analects* 9.8). The people who express a certain view may not have fully grasped the worth of their own views. So, further investigation is needed to carry out the phase of the process called "propagating what is worthy." The next step, "holding firmly to all that is worthwhile," means we should affirm simultaneously all the competing values that have been identified. As it is said in chapter 20, "Select what is good and hold it firmly." After making sure that we have not left out any significant aspect that should have been taken into consideration, we can consider which is the best way to give due recognition to the importance of all the relevant aspects. That is the last step: "locating the right balance and applying it."

These steps roughly correspond to the explicit five-step guide provided in the *Zhongyong*: "the extensive study of what is good, accurate inquiry about it, careful reflection on it, the clear discrimination of it, and the earnest practice of it."[30]

Although we know that there are multiple values and we should consider all of them, the question remains: In what way can we handle multiple values? If there is a common currency, we know how to compare two options. But if there are two values, and one option is better in one dimension while the other is better in another dimension, how can we determine which one is the better option?

Part of the implication of accepting a pluralistic approach to value is that there may not always be an answer to the question "What is the better option?" An option may be better in one way but worse in another. Of course, this does not mean that an answer is never available or that we should not try hard to determine what the better option is. What I would like to do here is to point out some direction that may shed light on moral deliberation in the context of multiple values. From the resources that we can find in the Confucian ethical tradition, there are several distinctions that we can make, and these distinctions are helpful for ethical thinking involving multiple values. I mention three distinctions here: (1) the distinction of domains—different values should prevail in different domains; (2) the distinction of agents—different standards can be used when we are referring to different people; and (3) the distinction of levels—the moral task may be broken down into different levels and there is a difference of priority.

The three values *zunzun* (respect those who have high status), *qinqin* (care for those who are related to us), and *xianxian* (recognize the worth of those who are good and capable) have different weightings in different domains. *Qinqin* should be the major value within the family, but *xianxian* should be a more important value in the government.

The *Book of Rites* says: "Inside the gate [family door], affection overrides rightness. Outside the gate, rightness overrides affection" (*The Book of Rites*, "Sangfu xizhi"). Further elaboration is provided in the extended commentary (*shu* 疏) to the *Book of Rites* provided by Kong Yingda 孔穎達 (574–648):

> This is because inside one's gate, among the members of the family, there is an abundance of affection and this overshadows rightness. And so, one may follow kindness and not rightness inside the family door.... "Outside one's gate" refers to the realm of government. It means that a person serving in the government must ensure that rightness checks and controls his personal affection.[31]

Mengzi also shares the view that different values may have different rankings in different domains: "There are three things that are acknowledged by the world to be exalted: rank, age, and virtue. At court, rank is supreme; in the village, age; but for assisting the world and ruling over the people it is virtue" (*Mengzi* 2B2).[32]

Another important distinction is the distinction between oneself and other people. In Confucian ethics, there is a higher standard for oneself but a much lower standard for other people. While we can urge ourselves to realize as much good as possible, we can only require others to remain above a minimal baseline. Perfectionism is only for oneself. Minimalism is what we demand from others.

In the *Zhongyong*, it is said, "The superior man governs men according to their nature and with what is proper to them, and as soon as they change *what is wrong*, he stops" (*Zhongyong*, chap. 14).[33] The expression "govern others according to the standard for others" (*yiren zhiren* 以人治人) should be contrasted with the expression "govern others according to the standard for oneself" (*yiji zhiren* 以己治人).[34] We should not require other people to live the way we think we should live. We do not try to rectify them because they are not living up to a high standard. We try to rectify others only when they have done wrong. Beyond that we stop. The spirit of this principle is that we allow people to be different. The default assumption is that they are doing fine and they don't need to justify each and every one of their actions. Only when they are clearly wrong can we require them to make some adjustment. Such a double standard for oneself and for others can easily be found in the Confucian classics. For example, in the *Analects*, we are told that a gentleman should "set a high standard for himself but have a low demand on other people" (*Analects* 15.15). One who aspires to be a gentleman should always use *yi* 義 (rightness) as the standard for one's own behavior:

> In dealing with the world's affairs, the gentleman has no absolute dos and don'ts. He is always on the side *yi*. (*Analects* 9.10)
>
> The gentleman has *yi* as his basic stuff. (*Analects* 15.18)
>
> The gentleman regards *yi* to be of highest importance. (*Analects* 17.23)

However, we are told explicitly not to use *yi* as the standard for criticizing other people's behavior. "If we use *yi* as the standard to measure people, then it is very difficult to find one person who meets the standard. If we compare people with one another, we can find out who are the good people" (*The Book of Rites*, "The Record of Example"). In judging ourselves, we should use the absolute standard. We should not congratulate ourselves just because we are doing better than other people. By contrast, we should not use the absolute standard in judging others. For other people we should use a relative standard. If a person is doing fine when compared with others, we should regard him as a good person.

There is only one person to whom we can apply the highest standard:

> Kongzi said, "In the whole world there is only one person who can be demanded to love morality without any desire of personal gain and hate immorality without any fear of personal loss. So, the gentleman keeps the *Dao* as a standard for himself and sets up laws for the common people." (*The Book of Rites*, "The Record of Example")

The expression "only one person" unmistakably refers to oneself. The gentleman applies the highest standard only to himself. The passage clearly implies that the laws for the common people are not harsh and only maintain a basic standard.

A third distinction relevant to moral thinking is the distinction between moral goals and moral constraints. According to Mengzi, the moral task consists of two parts: don't do the wrong thing, and do the right thing. The first task should have higher priority than the second task. "Mengzi said, 'Only after we don't do what we should not do can we do what we should do' " (*Mengzi* 4B8). According to his view, ethics should have a teleological and a deontological component. On the one hand, there are moral constraints that set limits to what is morally permissible. On the other hand, there are moral goals that specify what kinds of things are valuable and worth pursuing. The moral task is to pursue the moral goals within the moral constraints.[35]

Kongzi distinguishes three approaches to morality: the undisciplined (*kuang* 狂), the overcautious (*juan* 狷), and the *zhongdao* 中道 (*Analects* 13.21). The undisciplined are eager to realize moral goals, but they may go so far as to violate moral constraints. The overcautious scrupulously work within the moral constraints, but they tend to do too little to fulfill the moral goals. By contrast, those who follow *zhongdao* attempt to realize the moral goals as much as possible while keeping the moral constraints. Kongzi regards all three approaches as legitimate expressions of morality. Although Kongzi prefers the *zhongdao* approach, he sees the value of the other two approaches.

Kongzi puts forward two moral principles:

> Do not do to others what you do not want to be done to you. (*Analects* 12.2; see also 15.24)

> Help others to take a stand insofar as you wish to take your stand, and get others there insofar as you yourself wish to get there. (*Analects* 6.30)

The first principle is negative in nature (about what we should refrain from doing) while the second principle is positive (about what achievements we should try to attain). The first principle specifies the limiting condition while the second principle specifies the goals to be pursued. Putting the second principle into practice is regarded as having higher achievement. But the second principle should not be fulfilled at the expense of the first.[36]

Such a two-level morality is made up of a minimal morality and a maximal morality. Like the morality of human rights, the minimal morality specifies the limiting conditions that have to be met, even in the pursuit or fulfillment of highly valuable moral goals. Such a two-level morality can provide a framework giving some direction for handling multiple values.[37]

Conclusion

In this chapter I have presented a line of thinking in Confucian ethics for accommodating and integrating multiple values that is expressed by a set of Confucian concepts such as *zhongdao* 中道, *zhongxing* 中行, and *zhongyong* 中庸. I hope to have demonstrated one important way in which Confucian ethics remains a living ethical tradition that can provide contemporary people with insights into the nature of morality and ethical thinking.

However, I don't expect that those who are seriously interested in solving ethical problems will be entirely happy with the account that I have presented. No clear explanation has been given regarding how we can strike the right balance among multiple values.

To this I reply, following Aristotle, by saying that ethics is an art, not a science. We cannot demand greater precision than the nature of the subject allows.[38] General ethical principles are helpful in providing some direction to our ethical deliberations, but they by themselves cannot determine a clear answer and can only give rough and general guidance. There is a place for casuistry in ethical thinking.

The Handling of Multiple Values in Confucian Ethics 47

Others may object that ethical thinking involving multiple values is too complicated. It is not the case that we don't have a choice. Single-value theories are much more simple, logical, and elegant. Multiple-value ethical theories are not really theories, because they do not provide us with a problem-solving mechanism but only a checklist or general guidelines.

To this I can only reply that in spite of the various theoretical and philosophical merits of single-value theories they have one fatal problem—the right answer is just not there. It is interesting to note that in practical decision making in daily life, people take a number of factors into consideration and are quite comfortable doing so. For example, when people decide whether to change their job, they consider not only the salary, but also the nature of the job, the prospects for the future, and so on. When someone considers whether to marry another, they take into account a number of factors, such as the person's character, personality, beliefs, economic prospects, and so forth. It is quite amazing to see that many philosophers believe that in ethical thinking there is only one relevant factor that should be taken into consideration, as if ethical thinking is a more simple matter than ordinary decision making in our daily lives. Of course, we may not reach a justified decision, even if we take all the relevant factors into consideration. But we will be further away from what is right if we retain only one factor, disregard all the other complicating issues, and in this way reach our decision.

We might do well to keep in mind the following story, especially when we are tempted to prefer clarity to accuracy in the course of our ethical deliberations:

> One dark night a policeman comes upon a drunk. The man is on his knees, obviously searching for something under a lamppost. He tells the officer that he is looking for his keys, which he says he lost "over there," pointing out into the darkness. The policeman asks him, "Why, if you lost the keys over there, are you looking for them under the streetlight?" The drunk answers, "Because the light is much better here."[39]

Notes

The author is grateful to P. J. Ivanhoe, Julia Tao, and Stephen Angle for their comments.

1. The term "multiple values" as I use it in this chapter can be defined as separate and distinct values that cannot be reduced to each other or some higher values. Such

values are competing and may conflict with one another. Two common examples are equality and liberty on the one hand, and loyalty and filial piety on the other.

2. The Confucian approach to multiple values is most clearly stated in the *Zhongyong*. But there are also traces in the *Analects* (*Lunyu*). Kongzi does not seem to recognize only one form of life as good or one way of action as right. Faced with the tyrant Zhou (of the Yin dynasty), Viscount Wei chose to leave; Viscount Ji became a slave; Bi Gan remonstrated with the tyrant even though it cost him his life. Kongzi does not think that only one of them can be right, and he comments that "there were three men of *ren* in the Yin" (*Analects* 18.1). In another case, Shiyu and Qu Boyu acted in exactly opposite ways. Shiyu didn't change his behavior. He acted uprightly no matter whether the state was under good governance. Qu Boyu served in the government when the state was under good governance; otherwise, he would quit. Kongzi commended both of them (*Analects* 15.7). See also *Analects* 18.8.

3. It has been suggested to me that there is some significant similarity between the line of thinking I am proposing here and the view that people like Charles Taylor defend, in particular the "politics of recognition." Such an approach aims at recognizing and including as many people as possible, as "each of our voices has something unique to say" (Charles Taylor, *Multiculturalism and "The Politics of Recognition"* [Princeton, NJ: Princeton University Press, 1992], 30). Such an approach to political ethics can be reasonably expected to maximize solidarity within the state as well as to increase the level of harmony among citizens. I recognize some similarity between this approach and the Confucian approach I am outlining here, but I also see some important differences. The Confucian approach does not see value in the subjective opinions as such, but in the objective value that may be contained in the subjective opinions. As a result, the importance of scrutiny and the process of selection are emphasized (*Analects* 15.28, 13.24).

4. According to Duan Yucai's 段玉裁 commentary to the *Shuowen jiezi* 說文解字, the word *zhong* can contrast either with the word "external" (*wai* 外)—and mean "internal"—or the word "biased" (*pian* 偏)—and mean "appropriate" (Duan Yucai, *Shuowen jiezi zhu* [Taipei: Guangwen shuju, 1969], the "Zhong 中" entry).

5. Philosophers such as Cheng Yi and Zhu Xi are able to unify the two meanings of the term *zhong* by adopting the position of internalism. The unbiased internal state, when expressed or manifested, becomes the appropriate action (Zhu Xi, *Sishu huowen* [Shanghai: Guji chubanshe, 2001], 44). The interpretation presented in this chapter does not assume the two meanings can be unified. The interpretation is only based on the part of the *Zhongyong* that talks about *zhong* as in the sense of *zhong zhi dao*.

6. For example, in *Zhongyong*, chapter 9: "Men might refuse noble station, and the wealth that goes with it. They might trample the naked sword under foot. But the mean in action, it is impossible for them to achieve that" (E. R. Hughes, *The Great Learning and the Mean-in-Action* [London: J. M. Dent, 1942], 107). See also *Zhongyong*, chap. 4; *Analects* 13.21.

7. *Analects* 6.29: "As a virtue, *zhongyong* is indeed supreme! The people can rarely keep to it." A similar quotation can be found in *Zhongyong*, chap. 4.

The Handling of Multiple Values in Confucian Ethics   49

   8. Fan Ye, *Houhanshu* (Beijing: Zhonghua Shuju, 1965), "Duxing liezhuan 獨行列傳." All the translations contained in this chapter are mine, unless otherwise indicated.
   9. Cheng Rong, ed., *Hanwei congshu* (Changchun: Jilin daxue chubanshe, 1992), 624.
   10. Zhuangzi also points out the distinction between nature and humanity. Xunzi had definitely read the works of Zhuangzi, but it is unclear how far Xunzi might have been influenced by Zhuangzi. What I want to point out is that while Zhuangzi emphasizes the role of nature and the limitations of humanity, Xunzi emphasizes on the role of humanity and the limitations of nature. It is from this perspective that Xunzi criticizes Zhuangzi, saying Zhuangzi was "obsessed by the thoughts of Heaven [i.e., Nature] and did not understand the importance of man" (*Xunzi*, chap. 21, "Dispelling Obsession"; Watson's translation, in Burton Watson, trans., *Basic Writings of Mo Tzu, Hsün, and Han Fei Tzu* [New York: Columbia University Press, 1967], 125).
   11. Following this line of thinking, Mengzi is right to criticize the views of Yangzi and Mozi, but he is unjustified in rejecting them completely, and he is definitely going much too far in accusing Yangzi and Mozi of being beasts. Kongzi would be much more tolerant than Mengzi. Kongzi's general attitude is that a gentleman "honour[s] his betters and is tolerant towards the multitude," and he is "full of praise for the good while taking pity on the backward" (*Analects* 19.3; D. C. Lau, trans., *The Analects* [Harmondsworth, UK: Penguin Books, 1979], 153). According to the framework I am outlining here, Yangzi is somewhat like the overcautious and Mozi is somewhat like the undisciplined. Their problem is not so much that they are completely wrong but that they can only grasp a partial truth. They can only see a small part instead of the whole range of human values.
   12. *Zhongguanlun shu*, j. 1. Ji Zang, *[Commentary on] Zhonglun, Bailun, Shiermenlun*, Shanghai: Shanghai Guji Chubanshe, 1994, 86–102.
   13. Wang Fuzhi rejects the Song philosophers' view that the *zhongxing*, the undisciplined, and the overcautious are three separate paths. He thinks that the merit of the undisciplined is to do the right thing, and the merit of the overcautious is not to do the wrong thing. The way of the *zhongxing* is to do the right thing without doing the wrong thing. *Zhongxing* is defined by including, not by excluding, the undisciplined and the overcautious (See Wang Fuzhi, *Du sishu daquan shuo* [Beijing: Zhonghua shuju, 1975], 2:402).
   14. His wisdom is not great enough to generate worthwhile views out of nothing, but it is great enough to recognize what has worth when he sees it.
   15. The word *yong* has two meanings: "use" and "common." That *yong* should mean use is confirmed by this quotation. As pointed out by Zhang Dainian: "Although *yong* can mean both 'constancy' and 'what is ordinary,' it clearly ought to mean 'use' in this phrase.... From the Song dynasty onward, however, Zhu Xi's exegesis became the leading one. Most people know the definition: 'What is not biased is what [*zhong*] means; what is unchangeable is what [*yong*] means.' This definition is Cheng Yi's but it was

Zhu Xi who propagated it" (Zhang Dainian, *Key Concepts in Chinese Philosophy*, trans. Edmund Ryden [New Haven, CT: Yale University Press, 2002], 332). Zhang goes on to quote Wang Fuzhi: "In the *Book of History* the use of *yong* is never inconsistent with its meaning 'use.' Before Master Zhu no one had ever read this character as meaning 'ordinary' " (Zhang Dainian, *Key Concepts in Chinese Philosophy*, 335).

16. R. M. Hare, "Methods of Bioethics: Some Defective Proposals," reprinted in *Philosophical Perspectives on Bioethics*, eds. L. W. Sumner and Joseph Boyle (Toronto: University of Toronto Press, 1996), 18.

17. Andrew Plaks, "Means and Means: A Comparative Reading of Aristotle's *Ethics* and the *Zhongyong*," in *Early China/Ancient Greece: Thinking through Comparisons*, eds. Steven Shankman and Stephen W. Durant (New York: State University of New York Press, 2004), 197.

18. *Hanshi waizhuan*, 6.6. Qu Zongyuan, *Hanshi waizhuan iianshu* (Chengdu: Bashu shushe, 1996), 528.

19. Fang Yizhi (1611–1671) has an unorthodox commentary on this passage, which I regard as the correct interpretation: "Kongzi said, 'To attack a *duan* different from yours can do nothing but harm.' What he means is that we should let there be agreement or disagreement. This is called the Great Commonality. To attack it can only cause harm" (*Dongxijun zhushi*, ed. Pang Po [Beijing: Zhonghua shuju, 2001], "Rongdun").

20. Kanaya Osamu, "The Mean in Original Confucianism," in *Chinese Language, Thought, and Culture*, ed. Philip J. Ivanhoe (Chicago: Open Court, 1996), 86.

21. I have been inspired by the works of Pang Pu 龐樸. He has studied expressions of the forms "A 而 B," "A 而不 B," and "不 A 不 B" in the Chinese classics. See Pang Po, *Qianshuo yifenweisan* (Beijing: Xinhua chubanshe, 2004), 160–168 in particular.

22. John Knoblock, *Xunzi: A Translation and Study of the Complete Works*, 3 vols. (Stanford, CA: Stanford University Press, 1988–1994), vol. 1, 175. The last sentence, however, presents a two-value model. There are two sets of values, and both of them are affirmed—"respectful, reverent, attentive, and cautious" on the one hand and "inwardly at ease" on the other hand.

23. Translation from Lau, *The Analects*, 83.

24. Translation from ibid., 81.

25. Zhang Shuangdi, *Huainanzi jiaoshi* (Beijing: Beijing daxue chubanshe, 1997), "Fanlun xun."

26. James Legge, trans., *Confucian Analects, The Great Learning, and The Doctrine of the Mean* (New York: Dover Publications, 1971), 50.

27. Ibid., 382–383.

28. This treatise explains what the Duke of Zhou's thinking was and why he deserved the admiration of Kongzi. It also traces the basic elements of Confucianism before Kongzi. I regard it as a modern classic. For a more detailed review, see Yu Jinpo 余錦波, "Yinzhou zhiji de Zhongguo wenhua zhuanxiang," in *Wenhua zijue yu shehui fazhan*, ed. Ershiyi shiji Zhonghua wenhua shijie luntan choubei weiyuanhui (Hong Kong: Commercial Press, 2005), 498–506.

29. Wang Guowei, "Yinzhou Zhidu Lu," in Wang Guowei, *Wang Guowei Yishu*, (Shanghai: Shanghai Shudian Chubanshe, 1983), vol. 1, 465–494.

30. Legge, *Confucian Analects, The Great Learning, and The Doctrine of the Mean*, 413.

31. Shisanjing zhushu zhengli weiyuanhui (ed.), *Shisanjing zhushu* (zhengli ban), (Beijing: Beijing Daxue Chubanshe, 2000), vol. 15, 1952.

32. Translation from D. C. Lau, trans., *Mencius*, 2 vols. (Hong Kong: Chinese University Press, 1984), 77.

33. Translation by Legge, *Confucian Analects, The Great Learning, and The Doctrine of the Mean*, 394.

34. Cf. Li Zhi's 李贄 (1527–1602) commentary: "A gentleman governs others according to the standard of others and dares not to govern others according to the standard of oneself. People can basically govern themselves. Since people can govern themselves, they do not need prohibition in order to stop [from having improver behavior]. If it is desired that something is used to stop them, not allowing them to govern themselves, then it is to maltreat them" (Li Zhi, *Lizhi wenji* [Beijing: Shehui kexue wenxian chubanshe, 2000], 7:372).

35. Gordon Graham refers to a principle he calls "the rule of moral caution," which gives priority to avoiding acting unjustly over taking the chance of acting justly: "It is better to lose an opportunity of acting justly than to run the risk of acting unjustly." See Gordon Graham, *Ethics and International Relations* (Oxford: Blackwell, 1997), 121.

36. Here I make a distinction between the negative and positive formulations of the Golden Rule. My discussion here is inspired by Fung Yu-lan. See Fung Yu-lan, *A Short History of Chinese Philosophy*, ed. Derk Bodde (New York: Free Press, 1948), 43–44. For a review and critique of Fung, see David S. Nivison, "Golden Rule Arguments in Chinese Moral Philosophy," in David S. Nivison, *The Ways of Confucianism*, ed. Bryan W. Van Norden (Chicago: Open Court, 1996), 61–64 in particular.

37. For further elaboration of such a two-level morality, see Kam-por Yu, "Human Rights and Cultures," in *Menschenrechte, Kulturen, und Gewalt*, ed. Ludger Kühnhardt and Mamoru Takayama (Baden-Baden: Nomos, 2005), 65–76.

38. *Nicomachean Ethics* 1094b: "Our account will be adequate if its clarity is in line with the subject-matter, because the same degree of precision is not to be sought in all discussions.... So we should be content... to demonstrate the truth sketchily and in outline.... It is a mark of an educated person to look in each area for only that degree of accuracy that the nature of the subject permits" (Roger Crisp's translation; see Aristotle, *Nicomachean Ethics*, trans. and ed. Roger Crisp [Cambridge: Cambridge University Press, 2000], 4–5).

39. Joseph Weisenbaum, *Computer Power and Human Reason: From Judgment to Calculation* (Harmondsworth, UK: Penguin Books, 1984), 127.

Chapter 3

Humanity or Benevolence?

The Interpretation of Confucian *Ren* and Its Modern Implications

Qianfan Zhang

Introduction

If we had the fortune of inviting a sage of the Warring States period (481–256 BCE), say, Mengzi, to visit China today, he would find the landscape transformed beyond recognition. Yet to his surprise, he would also find many problems familiar to his distant age. Despite rapid economic development over the past three decades, China, like many developing nations in the world today, is still a peasant-dominant society plagued by poverty. And poverty is not the only problem; the moral standard of the whole population apparently is in decline. One need not deliberately search the Internet to read dramatic headline stories. If one needs a specific example, one only has to read the tragic story of Sun Zhigang (which did produce massive public outcries at the time), a young migrant college graduate who was falsely detained by the Guangzhou city police and died of a beating by fellow inmates.[1] Here we see both official wrongs (illegal police detainment) and private wrongs (inmates' abuses, possibly with official sanction or even encouragement). Examples of incidents as bad and worse can easily be multiplied. I suppose sages like Kongzi (Confucius) and Mengzi faced just this kind of society when they tenaciously put forward their theories in order to save the declining moral and political order from total collapse. Of course, the specific situations are necessarily different, but the nature of the problems is nevertheless the same. Were Mengzi asked to comment on Sun Zhigang's case, he would unhesitatingly point to the root cause of the tragedy, that humanity (*ren* 仁) and benevolent government (*renzheng* 仁政) have been missing. China today and China two millennia ago confront precisely the same moral and political predicaments.

The theme of this chapter concerns the Confucian concepts of *ren* and *renzheng*, for the way our government treats its people is rooted deeply in the Confucian tradition, and unless this cultural tradition is changed, the nature of our political and administrative processes will remain the same. By and large the political culture that shapes the Chinese government today is still under the influence of the Confucian tradition, a tradition that consistently identifies a good government as one that serves the best interests of the people. Yet this apparently benign starting point may end up in paternalistic despotism if care is not taken to distinguish the Confucian moral concept of *ren* from its political applications.

The purpose of this chapter is to identify the original meaning of *ren*, a concept that has occupied a central position in Confucianism. The word was of relatively late origin and found its popular use only after the *Analects* (*Lunyu*), where its meaning was articulated for the first time by Kongzi. But so many meanings have been attributed to *ren*, sometimes inconsistently by the same philosopher, that to translate it as "humanity" would be already to assume the conclusion of this chapter. The word could also be translated, for example, as "care," "love," or "benevolence."[2] However, none of these translations, taken in their ordinary senses, can properly capture the true meaning of *ren* as the highest moral ideal for every Confucian. This chapter seeks to discover a consistent development of the idea among the works of Kongzi and Mengzi and to establish the conceptual linkage between *ren* and humanity in the Kantian sense; that is, to treat a human being "always at the same time as an end and never merely as a means."[3] References to Kant are made in this chapter primarily because Kantian and Confucian ethics are humanistic ethics centered on respect for human dignity. Although there are important differences between the Confucian approach and Kant's rationalistic approach, they do seem to corroborate each other and eventually agree on major moral premises.

In the next part of the chapter I argue that, as a moral concept, Confucian *ren* goes beyond the limit of the materialistic concept of benevolence and agrees with a formulation of the Kantian categorical imperative. The original idea of humanity, as illustrated in the *Analects*, implied the requirement that one ought to respect others as ends in themselves and adopt actions that are acceptable to other human beings. More than a century later, Mengzi went further and developed an ontological theory for humanity based on the assumption that human beings are good by nature, thereby confirming the ultimate source of value inherent in man. Together with the notion of the "gentleman" (*junzi* 君子), the concept of *ren* forms the core of Chinese humanism, which takes for granted that everyone is endowed by Heaven with the moral capacity for humanity and justice. To be consistent with the moral requirement of *ren*, everyone must be treated as a moral being as such and is not to be reduced to a mere animal solely concerned with welfare needs and benefits.

Yet the Confucian concept of *ren* has not always been consistently applied. While, in the matter of personal ethics, *ren* as the highest moral ideal must be understood to mean "humanity," it was reduced to the limited significance of "benevolence" in the sphere of government. This is true for the political philosophy of all Confucian schools, which had inherited, together with merits and limitations, the early Zhou idea of the rule of virtue. Limited by the historical conditions of the time, they all took for granted the legitimacy of the existing social order and the monarchical form of government and for that reason laid great emphasis on loyalty and obedience to the kings. Under that presupposition, however, they insisted that the kingly government must work for the welfare of the common people; hence, the notion of "benevolent government" (*renzheng*). The two apparently conflicting positions were united by the underlying assumption that the common people, though endowed with moral and intellectual faculties, were nevertheless incapable of sufficiently developing themselves to take care of their own welfare, much less to resist the tyranny of their rulers. The purpose of government, then, was mainly to provide protection and nourishment for the people's physical lives and, if possible, some moral education to help them rise above the status of animals.

In the third part of this chapter, I argue that such an understanding of *ren* (as in *renzheng*) is inconsistent with the ideal of humanity originally conceived by Kongzi and Mengzi and is ultimately based on negative assumptions about people's moral and intellectual capacities, which had been taken for granted since the early Zhou dynasty (1046–771 BCE). Having misconceived the basic mission of a government, neither Mengzi nor Xunzi was able to present morally powerful arguments to their rulers. Unable to count on the people, they were compelled to rely on the goodwill of rulers and appeal to their self-interest in a benevolent government—an approach with little moral force and limited practical success in the Chinese history. Finally, I explore certain passages in the works of Mengzi that require the government to transcend mere benevolence and offer the possibility of building a new political philosophy consistent with the original moral conception of *ren*.

Ren as Humanity

The idea of *ren* expresses one of the central assumptions of Kongzi's humanistic philosophy; that is, every individual is endowed with the inner moral faculty from Heaven and is capable of self-perfection without the further aid of a transcendent divine power. As Kongzi says of himself, "Heaven produced virtue in me."[4] Mengzi goes even further to state: "All things are already complete in me. There can be no greater delight than to find sincerity upon self-examination" (7A4). Although Kongzi himself rarely talked about human nature, he did indicate that *ren*—the moral faculty that distinguishes a person from mere animals—is the very definition of a human being. Thus, "Humanity is [the distinguishing character of the] human being (*ren* 人)."[5] The mainstream of Confucianism represented by Mengzi generally assumed that the moral nature, derived directly from Heaven, is innate in every human being. Through constant learning and self-cultivation, everyone can develop his or her true nature and choose a way of life that conforms to the Way of Heaven. Thus, since the early days of Chinese intellectual history, humans have been regarded as moral beings who are able to use reason to control their needs and sensuous inclinations for pleasure and to understand the higher purpose for which they were created.

Humanity and Human Nature: The Moral Construction of Mengzi

Although Kongzi introduced the central concept of *ren* to Chinese moral philosophy, he did not elaborate on its metaphysical foundation. A more systematic theory of humanity had to await Mengzi, whose doctrine later came to dominate Confucian thought. Like Kongzi, Mengzi firmly believes in the human moral capacity for self-perfection. The ultimate source of morality is the human heart, which is naturally good. A human being possesses an innate knowledge of *ren* and has the inborn capacity to be humane, as "*Ren* is [the unique character of the] human being. When embodied in human conduct, it is the Way."[6] Human evil arises not from human nature, but from humans' failure to resist the pernicious influences of the outer world. Thus, the proper end of mankind lies in the conscious effort of learning and self-cultivation, through which one recovers his or her lost good nature.

Mengzi asserts outright that *ren* is rooted in the "heart-mind" of every person. Everyone, he says, is endowed by Heaven with four "sprouts" of the "heart-mind"; they are the sources for humanity (*ren*), justice, propriety, and intelligence (*Mengzi* 6A6). While the heart-mind for shame and distaste (for one's own bad behavior) is the origin of the feeling of justice, the heart-mind for compassion is the origin of humanity. Thus, *ren* is a moral quality with which everyone is born, which defines the essential character of a human being, and without which a person would be reduced to a mere animal. The feeling of compassion plays a key role in establishing Mengzi's theory of humanity:

> All men have something that they cannot bear. Extend that feeling to what they can bear, and humanity will be the result. All men have something that they will not do. Extend that feeling to something that they will do, and righteousness will be the result. If a man can give full development to his feeling of not wanting to injure others, his humanity will be more than what he can ever put in practice. (*Mengzi* 2A6)

Mengzi's theory appeared to plainly contradict many people's common experiences in his time, when the previous political and social order established by the Zhou dynasty was dissolving, and feudal kings and warlords preyed upon one another. In fact, it is quite possible that the lack of humanity in the actual world at that time is what prompted early Chinese sages to appeal to this very ideal. Despite the apparently cruel human reality, Mengzi insisted that the heart-mind of *ren* is still innate in every ordinary human being, and on proper occasions it even compels one to act according to the moral ideal of *ren*. Mengzi attempts to illustrate the general existence of *ren* using the human urge for actions that are based upon the natural feeling of compassion, free from all contaminations of material motives:

> Now, when men suddenly see a child about to fall into a well, they all have a feeling of alarm and distress, not to gain friendship with the child's parents, nor to seek the praise of their neighbors and friends, nor because they dislike the reputation [of lack of humanity if they did not rescue the child]. From such a case, we see that a man without the feeling of commiseration is not a man.[7]

Thus, *ren* as the defining character of the human being seems to be present in every person. We all would be urged by our natural compassion to go forward and save the child from the danger without any exterior motives; presumably even a criminal would feel the same urge within. This is precisely what Mengzi means by "Yao 堯 and Shun 舜 were the same as other men."[8] We all share the innate "moral sprouts" that will generate compassionate feelings when prompted by certain instances and, when cultivated properly, will grow into a full moral character.[9]

Of course, the example given here cannot "prove" the existence of humanity. As Kant points out, humanity as a transcendental ideal cannot truly be proved by mere experience of feelings, which always find exceptions. For however compelling this example might be to an ordinary person, some people may never feel compelled to save the baby. Nor is compassion as a natural feeling necessarily limited to human beings; many animals may act in the same way. Thus, the imaginary urge to take benevolent actions out of compassion cannot establish that *ren* is the unique moral character common to every human being. Kant may also be interpreted as objecting to the use of compassion—a natural feeling—for supporting a moral argument. To be moral, one must act not only in conformity with the moral law, but also for the sake of the moral law. In other words, the ultimate motive for a moral action must be the duty itself, not merely some kind of feeling.

Although Mengzi does differ from Kant by presupposing a transcendent heart-mind as the seat of *ren*, the objections made above are not fatal to his arguments. After all, compassion is a feeling associated with our imperfect duty—the duty to help others whenever we can. And we need not take the example to mean that compassion is the only motive that induces a moral action; rather, we can interpret it to signify the power of the inner moral faculty, just as the feeling of respect signifies the presence of the Kantian moral law. More important, compassion illustrates our consciousness of the worth inherent in the lives of others. This is probably as far as anyone can go in demonstrating the common moral presence in human nature, and we would be on the verge of obstinacy to beg for an absolute proof.

Therefore, despite Mengzi's and Kant's profound differences, it seems possible to reconcile Mengzi's theory of human nature with Kantian ethics. Kant is particularly valuable for our purpose because he developed a systematic theory on humanity and human dignity—concepts that occupy a central position of Confucian ethics. Obviously his approach is different from the Confucians' empirical or intuitionist approaches, since he is exclusively concerned with a secure, *a priori* foundation for moral principles, which he thinks are not to be derived from empirical observations or perceptions that are both predetermined and susceptible to exceptions. For Kant, moral laws, unlike the laws of nature, are laws of freedom to be grasped by reason,[10] and "freedom (independence from being constrained by another's choice), insofar as it can coexist with the freedom of every other in accordance with a universal law, is the only original right belonging to every man by virtue of his humanity."[11] Yet Kant's rationalistic approach is not without its own problems, and his exclusive grounding in reason and absolute rejection of a legitimate place for moral feelings seem to originate from outdated cosmological assumptions that are no longer tenable today. With a more plausible assumption, it is at least possible to find the two approaches corroborating and complementing each other; the rationalistic framework will be enriched by incorporating moral feelings into it. From this perspective, it seems that Mengzi is quite justified to appeal to feelings of compassion in order to demonstrate the moral "sprouts" of humanity (which Kant would think belong to the unknowable noumenal world) at work.

If we can take for granted that the natural feeling of compassion is present (albeit to different degrees) in most of us, it seems to suggest two things. First, although it does not establish the metaphysical existence of morality, it is consistent with the idea that we can act morally, beyond all selfish, reward-seeking motives. Second, it implies that the beneficiary of my moral action represents a good in itself; the beneficiary's possible suffering of a misfortune somehow compels my moral conscience. For I certainly lack the same degree of compassionate feeling for the suffering of all animals. It will not be surprising if I do not feel the same urge when it is a cat approaching the well, but it is entirely different if a human being is about to suffer from the same fate. And I have the urge to do everything within my capacity to save the child, not out of any concern for myself, not even for my natural love for a cute creature, but solely for the simple reason that the child, as a human being, is a good that, being absolute and universal, manifests worth to the entire world. Thus, compassion, taken by Mengzi to be the manifestation of *ren*, does seem to imply the intrinsic value of human life.

Toward a Notion of Dignity

Based on his theory of human nature, Mengzi developed a positive doctrine of human value. A human being may differ from other animals only slightly, yet it is precisely such a difference that makes the person unique. His or her unique value lies not in the material body—because that is something he or she shares with all other animals, but exclusively in the moral faculty as embodied in his or her heart-mind. The heart-mind, responsible for moral and rational thinking, is the noblest organ endowed to human beings and enables them to lead a meaningful moral life. Thus, Mengzi distinguishes the "noble" or "great" body (the heart-mind where humanity resides) from the "ignoble" or "small" body (the sensuous organs, which give rise to passion and desire): "While a gentleman (*junzi*) follows his great body, a petty man (*xiaoren* 小人) is driven by his small body" (*Mengzi* 6A14). A petty man knows only to satisfy his base desires and ignores the moral aspects of his nature and, as a result, leads a life not so distinct from that of a mere animal. By contrast, a gentleman takes care to cultivate his sublime moral character by pursuing *ren*, which enables him to lead a life that is worthy of his noble nature. Mengzi assumes that everyone is born with the noble body together with the capacity to develop it. Thus, "everyone possesses in himself the noble value" (*Mengzi* 6A17). True nobility lies in humanity and justice, which is endowed by Heaven and cannot be substituted by human nobility (such as high social status and a comfortable material life). While human nobility is contingent on human fortune and limited to a few, the nobility of Heaven is absolute and universal to all human beings. Mengzi recognized, behind the veil of extreme social inequality at the time, a basic human equality grounded in moral capacity. He went so far as to assert that "a sage belongs to the same type as the common people" (*Mengzi* 2A2); one becomes a sage not because she or he was born with more *ren* than others, but because she or he is able to consciously cultivate *ren* throughout his or her life.

The difference, then, lies not in what one can do, but in what one will do. Human beings always have the capacity to become *ren* and will reach the kingdom of *ren* as long as they want to—as long as they can keep their selfish desires and passions in check (*Analects* 7.30). Like Kant, both Kongzi and Mengzi believed that human beings have the freedom of will to choose how they will live their lives. Thus, "whether to be *ren* depends on oneself," not on others (*Analects* 12.1). Those who give up the effort to be *ren*, thus abandoning what is noble in their nature, are merely degrading themselves and inviting disgrace from others.[12] Endowed with reason and the freedom to choose, a person is fully responsible for his or her own moral development and thus is seen as a morally autonomous being.

Only by virtue of being a morally autonomous being is a human regarded as an end in her- or himself. A person is endowed by Heaven with the innate moral capacity for justice and humanity, an inestimable worth that distinguishes him or her from other animals. While animals are seen as instrumentally useful to mankind, a human being is an end to him- or herself and is to be respected as such. The distaste for the lack of respect is clearly expressed by Mengzi: "To feed a person without love is to treat him as a pig; to love him without respect is to keep him as a domestic animal" (*Mengzi* 7A37). To treat someone with *ren*, it is not enough to merely satisfy his or her needs or even to love him or her; she or he must be respected as an ultimate end.

There is little justification, then, to reduce Confucian humanity to mere benevolence. In other words, humanity is not benevolence in its ordinary sense; rather, it is absolute benevolence, a principle by which Heaven made a person complete in his or her physical, intellectual, and moral faculties. To follow the principle of humanity, one must treat oneself and others truly as autonomous ends who, endowed with these innate capacities, were created for a higher purpose than to serve as mere subjects of their sensuous needs and desires. This is an important point to which we will return in applying *ren* to the political realm, a point that, from the Confucian experience, can easily be forgotten. Without reference to intrinsic worth, all that is left in *ren* is pity, which would fetch us right into benevolent politics as it did for the classical Confucians.[13]

The Essence of "Benevolent Government" and Its Limitations

Mengzi was the first in Chinese history to extend the notion of humanity (*ren*) and invent the term "benevolent government." He wanted to replace the "way of the despot" (*ba dao* 霸道), or the way of force, with the "kingly way" (*wang dao* 王道), the way of moral power,[14] and he expounded on this idea systematically throughout his work. His new ideal was based on the traditional theory of the "rule of virtue," which initially provided political justification for the establishment of a new dynasty, the Zhou. Like Kongzi, Mengzi accepted the traditional legends about virtuous kings, who served as paragons for all rulers in his theory of government. It was these ancient kings, he asserted, that had brought to the people physical security, material prosperity,[15] education, and decent morals, without which the people would have led merely animal-like lives.[16]

Let me begin by acknowledging that the notion of benevolent government is not just a Confucian ideal, but one that is very much alive even in the Western world. Indeed, this ideal is gaining even more support today than it did two millennia ago, as different parts of the world are entering the welfare society. Since scientific and technological advances have made it possible to dramatically improve the social and economic conditions of mankind, there is every reason for a humanistic state to eradicate misery and poverty that have hitherto denied the opportunity for the full development of human potential to the vast majority of the human population, and Mengzi was only being prescient when he proposed the *renzheng* ideal in such an economically backward society. Having said this, though, I am still convinced that *renzheng* and *ren* are two fundamentally different notions. As I shall argue below, although they share the same word (*ren*), *renzheng* as a political ideal does not quite reach the high moral elevation of *ren*, and one cannot successfully reconstitute the basic tenets of *ren* by reading passages about *renzheng*. Just as the Western welfare society is not necessarily a "decent" society,[17] a Confucian benevolent government pursuing *renzheng* would fail to be truly *ren*.

Back to Human Nature: The Foundation of Benevolent Government

Mengzi is quite consistent in applying his theory on human nature to his moral persuasions. We all have compassion for others, and the rulers are no exceptions since humanity is also in their nature: "All men have the mind that cannot bear [to see the suffering of] others. The ancient kings had this mind and therefore they had a government that could not bear to see the suffering of the people."[18] Indeed, this is where Mengzi begins to introduce his well example to illustrate that the feeling of compassion is present in everyone, and one is to recall that even such a mediocre ruler as King Xuan of Qi would be compassionate enough to spare an ox when he happened to see its dreadful appearance before slaughtering (*Mengzi* 1A7).

Thus, just as the feeling of compassion is instrumental for illustrating the presence of humanity in everyone, it is equally important in initiating a benevolent government. It is because the benevolent sage cannot bear to see the sufferings of mankind that he brought us benevolent government: "If the sage exercises his effort and continues with the government of compassion (*buren ren zhi zheng* 不忍人之政), then humanity (*ren*) will cover the whole world" (*Mengzi* 4A1). And according to the Confucian doctrine long established, since the Zhou dynasty, the ruler's benevolence is what legitimates the enjoyment of their special powers and privileges: "The three dynasties won the title to rule the world with humanity and lost the title with inhumanity. And this is the cause by which the state prospers or declines. An inhumane emperor cannot maintain the world, and an inhumane lord cannot maintain his kingdom" (*Mengzi* 4A3).

Although Mengzi's theory on benevolent government and welfare society is "politically correct" even today, the account of its philosophical underpinning differs fundamentally from what he uses to account for individual human nature. There he did use the same well and ox examples to show that the feeling of compassion is the manifestation of humanity in every human heart, but he also made it abundantly clear that humanity, together with other beginnings of the "heart-mind," is the noble part that all humans share with the sage-kings

Yao and Shun, and that everyone is able to develop these moral beginnings with studious efforts of self-cultivation, by which he or she would eventually become like Yao and Shun. Here, however, all that is left is simply the feeling of compassion for the suffering of the poor multitude, and a philosophy about human dignity is quickly reduced to a strain of pity ethics.

The cause seems to lie at least partly in Mengzi's examples themselves. When he uses the well or ox example, his purpose is to illustrate that we as observers who imagine ourselves watching some helpless creatures (a crawling baby unaware of imminent danger or an ox being led to a slaughterhouse) about to suffer serious harm will experience a feeling of compassion. When he presents the story to the rulers to persuade them to adopt benevolent government, however, he simply has the common people take the position of these inept creatures and appeals to the rulers (who are now in the position of an observer with ability to offer some help) for compassion. From this perspective, it is easy to understand why Mengzi has been so consistent in identifying rulers with parents and people with children—indeed, sometimes domesticated animals. When he reproached an official who complained about the loss of people due to a bad harvest, he said: "In bad years thousands of the old and weak among your people wandered in ditches, and the stronger dispersed to other places. Now if someone accepts others' cattle and sheep for grazing, he must manage to develop adequate land and sources for grass. If he cannot get these, should he return the cattle and sheep to the owner, or should he instead wait and see them all die?" (*Mengzi* 2B4). To be sure Mengzi does not mean that the people are just "cattle and sheep" (though he did seem to imply that they belong to some "owner"), but it is clear that not much respect is due to them here. These examples are inherently problematic when extended to the political context because the common people are put in the naturally inferior position. Of course, Mengzi could have argued that we experience our compassion for the baby not purely for the sake of pity, but also for the respect due to her innate good (indeed, it may be argued that even an ox has some innate good), so likewise the ruler should show compassion for the people out of respect and not simply pity. But in any case Mengzi never pushed his arguments in that direction since he never explicitly argued that the ruler should practice benevolence out of respect for the people's potential goodness, and his writings leave us with a pervasive sense that the people are merely the subject for compassion even in an ideal benevolent government.[19]

Thus, while Mengzi preserves the source of nobility and potential worthiness for every human being, this aspect seems to be lost in his theory of benevolent government. At least, he appears to use different kinds of arguments in different situations: one can imagine that, when he confronts an individual person, he would exhort him to take more care of his "noble body" than his "small body" and become a morally cultivated gentleman who is worthy of respect; when he confronts a king, however, he would appeal to his compassionate feeling for the poor masses, and the arguments about innate nobleness would disappear. Benevolent government is created purely out of pity for the common people.[20] While the moral theory of *ren* is explicitly founded on innate dignity and the potential of self-perfection in every human being, the word loses this meaning when it is applied to politics, with the result that the *ren* in *renzheng* means only "benevolence" on the part of government.

Weaknesses in Mengzi's Argument

This part of the chapter provides a critique of Mengzi's theory of "benevolent government" and argues that *renzheng* is an inadequate extension of *ren* as a moral concept into the political sphere. Let me begin by acknowledging, however, that we moderns (or postmoderns) all support benevolent government, and Mengzi proves to be extremely prescient since the Chinese face precisely the same kind of predicaments today as in his time: many patients in rural areas die at home for lack of medical care, many young laborers wander into the cities and put up with an array of discriminations just to earn a living, and so forth. Are these not driving people to the "ditches" or killing them with government policies? Benevolent government is precisely what China lacks and needs today, even though I would support it more as a result of sound institutional arrangement aimed to respect human dignity than an ideal motivated by compassion for human sufferings. It is pointless to blame Mengzi or Xunzi today for not having invented a political theory that would appear more fashionable to modern eyes; any serious thinker, however imaginative or even utopian, will necessarily ground his presuppositions in the political and social reality of his time, and the monolithic political framework since the Zhou dynasty had framed the political imagination of all classical Chinese thinkers, among whom the Confucians were certainly not alone. Nor do I deny that the notion of benevolent government, imperfect as it may be, did induce some rulers in the long Chinese history to exercise moderation during their terms—for example, to reduce taxes, announce amnesties, and repeal cruel corporal punishments.[21] But I do suggest that the Confucian arguments can be made more persuasive and more consistent with their moral theory if they could draw more inspiration from the moral *ren*, without which the pursuit for benevolent government would ultimately fail.

It is entirely understandable that Mengzi appeals to the rulers' self-interest in his political persuasions. If we put ourselves in Mengzi's shoes, it is not difficult to feel the convenience (perhaps even the necessity) of the way he presents his arguments to King Hui of Liang and the like. Like all intellectuals of the classical age, Mengzi faces a dilemma set by the long-standing political institution of China: he wants to convince a ruler of mediocre moral quality to do the right thing—to stop waging wars and exploiting his people, to lower taxes to prepare for bad years, and so on. Now, for sage rulers like King Wen and the Duke of Zhou it is obviously unnecessary to persuade them to do such and such, but for mediocre rulers like King Hui, who is essentially a petty man preoccupied with personal profits (*li* 利) in maintaining his state, what kind of arguments can possibly move these self-interested rulers to practice humanity and righteousness, which would immediately benefit only their people? Naturally, Mengzi would have to appeal to their self-interest; otherwise, they would simply remain unconvinced: Why be just? Why be humane? What do these moral constraints mean to *my* concerns—more population and territory, more power, and more security in enjoying my power? These are precisely the questions that King Hui put to our intellect at the opening of *Mengzi*, and unsurprisingly Mengzi is almost obligated to answer in the affirmative: you need to follow the path of humanity and righteousness in order to keep and perhaps even enlarge your profits! If you want to maintain your state, then stop worrying about profits since that would simply be counterproductive: if your ministers and subordinate officials also begin to seek profits as you do, then your kingdom will be in danger; so at least from a long-term perspective, extol moral virtues and practice benevolent government, since that will bring security to your kingdom (*Mengzi* 1A1). If the king followed the principle of justice and benevolence, he would be able to secure his interest as some sort of byproduct. This is the crux of Mengzi's arguments in all the passages involving court persuasions, and they are probably the best arguments to be made in the political settings of his time.

Just note, however, how different the style of arguments can be in a different political framework: if the rulers were popularly elected, Mengzi would hardly need to go through all the troubles to persuade them that to practice benevolent government is good not only for the state, but also for themselves: unless they are idiots, they surely know that they will lose everything in the next election if they don't. If Mengzi is still interested in traveling to the court from afar, his role would be changed to that of a policy adviser: his job is no longer to convince the rulers *why* they must practice benevolent politics, but simply to tell them *how* to do it. Imagine how much stronger Mengzi's position would be in such a political framework, where the rulers' interests are structured in such ways that it is rational in itself for them to follow moral and political principles.

But such institutional strength was unavailable—in fact, unknown—to the classical Chinese intellectuals of Mengzi's time. When they appeared before the court, they were already assigned a weak position, from which they could not appeal to moral principles straightforwardly. This weakness is not their own but a feature of the multitude to be ruled, and it merely passes on to them when they take the role of the multitude's spokesmen before the powerful ruler. So, Mengzi is at pains to convince King Hui that he should share enjoyment with his people (*yumin tongle* 與民同樂), as that would actually increase his own enjoyment. And when he meets King Xuan of Qi, he warns against the risk of the ruler's "enjoying" his lot without his people since that usually means that the ruler would not care enough about their needs and their discontent would eventually put an end to his enjoyment (*Mengzi* 1B2).

Although these arguments are well made, the weakness of Mengzi's position dictates that they cannot be entirely effective. It was quite fortunate that King Hui agreed with Mengzi that he would enjoy more with people than enjoying alone (so that their conversation could continue), but one cannot help ask what if he turned out to be a completely depraved person, who simply did not care about enjoyment with others? Anyway, if enjoyment with the people turned out to be a plus at all for the ruler's own enjoyment, it was likely to be a minor plus to a mediocre ruler and thus insufficient to push him toward the right course against his other desires. And if the people thought that King Xuan's garden was too large and King Wen's too small, so what, as long as there was not an open rebellion? The fact that King Xuan asked this question showed his concern about the difference in the people's attitude, but we cannot be sure at all that such a difference would concern him deeply enough to make him change his mind.

There are inherent limits in the type of naturalistic causal arguments that Mengzi makes. After all, humanity and righteousness are to be pursued for their own sake, and pursuit of them may well be neither necessary nor sufficient for bringing about worldly successes. As Kant points out, only the moral law contains necessity and universality; the rule of prudence is always met by an indefinite number of exceptions in experience. Without a necessary connection between moral worthiness (benevolence) and material rewards (status and power), there is a serious risk that the notion of benevolent government can be reduced to a mere fiction, hardly producing any incentive for or deterrence to bad rulers.

In the course of Chinese history, many evil rulers might simply enjoy their reigns unpunished, at least in "this life," and good rulers might never get due rewards. An oppressive regime could last long, provided that it could maintain forceful control over the helpless people, and a benevolent government might be quite short-lived. So, the Legalists could jeer at the Confucians in the example of King Yan of Xu, who lost his kingdom while practicing benevolent government.[22] When a ruler looks at mixed results and realizes the lack of a definite connection between virtue and rewards, he may simply take Mengzi's story about the "invincible humane person" (*renzhe wudi* 仁者無敵) as some sort of "noble lie" conjured up to coax him into sparing alms. Even though Mengzi might be quite correct about the overall correlation between benevolence and the stability of the empire, and even though he could perfectly predict that such violent regimes as the Qin 秦 dynasty would quickly come to ruin, a willful and capricious ruler might still ignore this prudent advice, jeopardize his own long-term interest, and take stupendous measures that would seriously harm the welfare of his people.

Mengzi's arguments are predestined in a sense because they are based on his evaluation of the moral and political realities of his time. If the people are inept as a matter of fact and must rely on a benevolent government for sustaining basic livelihood, then Mengzi would have no alternative but to appeal for the goodwill of the rulers. On the subject of *renzheng*, the *Mengzi* did convey a pervasive sense that the people are incapable of providing for their own material well-being, thus making the rulers responsible for their survival, just as parents are responsible for their children; that it was those cultural heroes (e.g., the Great Yu) who provided for them the food, clothing, shelter, and everything else necessary for material survival; that the people were too ignorant even to understand that it was their rulers' wise policy that had improved their well-being; that when the government became oppressive, the people were utterly helpless and defenseless against oppression except to wait for another benevolent ruler; that the people are ultimately material animals, hardly capable of any higher pursuit than basic material life, would be "wholly satisfied" if the means to peaceful survival was provided for them, and would have no regret even when they died.[23] Regrettably, nothing in these parts of his work ever suggests that the common people have the moral capacity for self-government. And his remark that "the difference between humans and animals is slight; the common people lose it, but the gentlemen keep it" (*Mengzi* 4B19), if taken literally, further identifies the people with inferior creatures since they failed to cultivate the unique virtues that would set human beings apart from animals.

Having taken for granted that the ordinary people were essentially uncultivated animals—weak, incompetent, and dependent, Confucian scholars of all generations lost a bulk of their moral ground for demanding that the rulers respect humanity. They did not say, "Treat your people with humanity because, like you, they are human beings endowed with potential for humanity and righteousness and ought to be treated as such"; instead, they said, "Treat your people with benevolence because they rely on you in order to survive (and, incidentally, doing so will also help to make your rule more stable)." Had Mengzi stopped with condemnations of government excesses as Mozi did and refrained from too many negative remarks on the capacities of the common people, he would have been able to develop more powerful arguments for practicing benevolent government and, more importantly, to ground this notion on a more solid moral basis. Benevolent—or more precisely, humane—government is not just about providing benefits and welfare to the people; it is also about the provision of enough opportunities for people to fully develop their innate virtues, the full development of which would ultimately enable them to govern themselves and provide for their own needs. Although the social reality at Mengzi's time was not favorable to self-government, Mengzi could have advocated for other alternatives. Perhaps the proper solution was not taking the people's weakness for granted and appealing to the ruler's compassion, but holding the state responsible for developing the people's moral and intellectual qualities. Perhaps the state should busy itself not so much with the provision of welfare as with the establishment of a fair education system, which would provide equal opportunity for moral and intellectual development to all children, irrespective of their family backgrounds in status and wealth. Although Mengzi did talk about education and the establishment of schools (*Mengzi* 3A3), a new point of departure firmly rooted in his moral theory of humanity would have moved his political persuasion to a fundamentally different and morally more forceful direction, and the unnecessarily negative view of the capacities of the common people apparently prevented Mengzi from taking that direction.

The root of the problem, then, lies in the inconsistency between the two conceptions of *ren* applied in Confucianism. While Confucian scholars, in their ethical theory, endorsed the ideal of humanity, they reduced it to the narrow notion of benevolence in political theory, where they gave up their recognition that everyone is born with sufficient capacity to lead a unique human life. In effect, they renounced in the practice of government what they had defended in the theory of human nature. Having believed that the common people were low and helpless, they were left without any ground on which they could build a sound moral foundation for the state; all they could rely upon was the benevolence of a kingly government, which was necessarily beyond the people's control. Unable to transcend the limits of historical conditions, Confucian scholars mistook the existing form of government to be the invariable law of nature and found themselves in a position where the only hope was to persuade the kings by appealing to their self-interests. Having allowed the ultimate purpose of government to deviate from the original ideal of humanity, no wonder they failed to establish a valid political theory.

Beyond Benevolence

The Chinese political tradition has been one of *renzheng* without *ren*. While the theory of *ren* recognizes that everyone can reach moral perfection through self-cultivation, the theory of *renzheng* presupposes that the ordinary people are incapable of governing themselves, so that a government must be imposed on them in order to provide them with basic goods. It is difficult to reconcile the two notions of *ren* since they are based on dramatically different emphases on the aspects of innate human capacities. The ability for moral cultivation implies an ability for self-government and, correspondingly, a version of minimal government, but this has not been the working assumption of Chinese political practice throughout history, in which the government, (supposedly) benevolent and omnipotent, always retains its moral superiority by providing goods and benefits to its subjects. The "three-represents" doctrine (that the ruling CCP is supposed to represent the "advanced productive force," the "advanced culture," and "the most basic interests of the most people") is only the latest recapitulation of the benevolent government tradition, as it still stands for a government *for* the people, but decidedly not *by* the people,[24] and not surprisingly the main reason for this is that the people are not morally and politically mature enough to govern themselves.[25] Up to this day, direct election of the representatives of the People's Congress is still limited to the lowest levels of government, since the social conditions for general elections, especially those in the "backward" rural areas, is "not yet ripe." We still live in the shadow of *renzheng*, a political tradition that is far from *ren* and has been preventing us from improving our political and moral conditions. As I argued earlier, this confusion of two conceptions of *ren* was not the result of deliberate or ignorant misreading of Mengzi's teachings, but it has been with us since the very beginning of Confucian scholarship.

For these reasons I believe that it is time now to take more seriously the Confucian moral conception of *ren* and to reconstruct Chinese political philosophy on the basis of this moral foundation. At a minimum, to take *ren* seriously means, obviously, to take human life seriously and at least avoid causing harm to oneself and others. It is true that Confucians would have strongly condemned the official misconduct in the Sun Zhigang case. Not only was it legally wrong to confine Sun, but the local officials also committed a moral crime by showing reckless disrespect for his life. The problem with traditional Confucians is that they failed to recognize the root cause of this tragedy. The incident was not an isolated mistake; it was a reflection of the customary mode of handling the common people (especially the lowest class to which Sun was mistakenly categorized), to whom the imperious rulers routinely showed scorn and contempt. Having assumed their moral inferiority, Confucians might feel justified in such contemptuous treatment of the uncultivated masses, as long as they themselves were given enough material goods and a peaceful environment for living, since this was quite close to the political ideal of *renzheng*. Yet the Sun Zhigang case and those like it show clearly that *renzheng* is not to be achieved without *ren*. So long as the people are not trusted in their moral and intellectual abilities, the government will assume too much power, which is bound to be abused, and it will bring damage to the people's welfare.[26] Without *ren*, the pursuit of *renzheng* will only condone if not positively inculcate tyranny. To avoid such a self-defeating loop, we must take issue with the fundamental aspects of the Confucian political culture and formulate a new relationship between the people and the government based on a fuller understanding of *ren*.

Thus, to take *ren* seriously means to trust and respect the people's innate abilities, usually sufficient for attaining a decent life, and leave them free to deal with most matters that affect their welfare. This implies a demand for implementing and adhering to a list of basic rights and freedoms to be respected and protected by the government.[27] Under normal circumstances, the government is not to interfere with the people's beliefs, speech, publications, assemblies, associations, or freedom of pursuing economic activities, nor should it restrict the people's freedom of movement, unless such restriction is supported by genuine public needs. These requirements seem to be implied by the traditional notion of *ren*, even though "rights" and "freedoms" are absent in the traditional Chinese vocabulary. And this is not to say a government based on *ren* should abstain from providing material goods, as *ren* does mean to provide material support in needy circumstances; indeed, even Western liberal governments are deeply committed to welfare provisions today. And the government is certainly instrumental in providing the proper institutional environments (e.g., protection of property rights, which is also part of the existing Chinese constitution through the most recent amendments) as well as a sound education system (especially compulsory education for children), which is a precondition for developing innate human potentialities. This essay argues only that the mere provision of material benefits is not enough to meet the moral requirements of *ren*. If benefits are distributed without respect for people's innate abilities, from which rights and freedoms are derived, then we are back to the state of *renzheng* without *ren*.

Notes

1. See "The Sun Zhigang Case Has Achieved a Breakthrough," *Xinhua Daily*, 14 May 2003. One can easily find relevant news and comments by searching "孫志剛" on www.baidu.com.

2. The ideographic structure of the word *ren* interestingly illustrates its implication. The word is composed of two parts. The left half represents a person standing aside; the right half stands for "two," indicating the plural form of the left half. Taken together, *ren* is understood to express the moral principle that governs human relationships.

3. See Immanuel Kant, *Grounding for the Metaphysics of Morals*, trans. J. W. Ellington (Indianapolis: Hackett, 1993), 429. This (second) formulation of the categorical imperative is logically related to the first (universal law) and the third (autonomy) formulations.

4. *Analects* 7.22; see Wing-tsit Chan, *A Source Book in Chinese Philosophy* (Princeton, NJ: Princeton University Press, 1963), 32.

5. *Doctrine of the Mean*, chap. 20; Wing-tsit Chan, *A Source Book in Chinese Philosophy*, 104.

6. *Mengzi* 7B16; see Chan, *A Source Book in Chinese Philosophy*, 81.

7. *Mengzi* 2A6; trans. Chan, *A Source Book in Chinese Philosophy*, 65.

8. *Mengzi* 4B32; see Chan, *A Source Book in Chinese Philosophy*, 77.

9. Philip J. Ivanhoe, *Confucian Moral Self Cultivation*, second edition (Indianapolis, IN: Hackett, 2000), 34.

10. Immanuel Kant, *The Metaphysics of Morals*, trans. Mary Gregor (Cambridge: Cambridge University Press, 1996), 214–216.

11. Ibid., 237.

12. *Mengzi* 2A8, 2A10.

13. As Margalit points out in *The Decent Society*, compassion may well arise out of pity rather than respect for the indigents—"The poor are given charity out of pity" (Avishai Margalit, *The Decent Society*, trans. Naomi Goldblum [Cambridge, MA: Harvard University Press, 1996], 231)—and the feeling of pity is premised on the inferior status of those who receive assistance.

14. Chan, *A Source Book in Chinese Philosophy*, 50.

15. The word "material" refers broadly to all things related to the satisfaction of human needs and pleasure or avoidance of pain.

16. *Mengzi* 3A4, 3B9.

17. Margalit, *The Decent Society*.

18. *Mengzi* 2A6; see Chan, *A Source Book in Chinese Philosophy*, 65.

19. Even Mengzi's famous notion of people being "nobler" than the king (*junqing mingui* 君輕民貴) is to be understood as taking the people's welfare as the basis of the state, which is essentially the same notion as benevolent government. It simply expresses the idea that the people's welfare is a higher priority than the king's.

20. Since the notion of benevolent or compassionate government is metaphysically founded on the heart-mind for compassion (*buren ren zhi xin* 不忍人之心), one wonders whether it is better to take the Golden Rule as the primary interpretation of *ren*. After all, compassion is so closely associated with pity that once one begins one's arguments along that direction, it is too easy to end with an ethics of pity and forget about the true source giving rise to compassion. This is partly why I used the Golden Rule to argue that Confucian moral philosophy is really centered on human dignity and leave out compassion altogether when interpreting humanity. See Zhang Qianfan, "The Idea of Human Dignity: A Reconstruction of Confucianism," *Journal of Chinese Philosophy* 27, no. 3 (September 2000): 299–330.

21. Guo Jian, "*Ren* in Confucianism and the Chinese Legal Culture," in Research Committee on Chinese Confucianism and Legal Culture, eds., *Confucianism and Legal Culture* (*Ruxue yu falu wenhua*), (Shanghai: Fudan University Press, 1992): 102–107.

22. *Hanfeizi*, "Five Vermin," sec. 49.4.

23. *Mengzi* 1A3, 2A5, 3A4, 3B9, 7A13, 1A5, 3B5, 7A23, 7A12.

24. Theoretically, the current regime is one *of* the people, since the 1982 Constitution stipulates that "all powers belong to the people" (art. 1). But without adequate mechanisms for the people to exercise their powers, such statements remain empty.

25. The immaturity thesis, of course, has been taken for granted throughout Chinese political history, but only in the late Qing dynasty, when the imperial government was forced to undertake institutional reforms, was it put forward as a theory by such prominent scholars as Liang Qichao and others as an argument against immediate democratization. Since then both the supporting and opposing arguments were repeatedly raised during the Nationalist government, see, for example, Hu Shih, "The Question of Constitutionalism," *Independent Review* (*Duli pinglun*) 1 (1932): 2–3. For an argument against the conventional wisdom that elections require high levels of education and literacy, see Cai Dingjian, ed., *A Survey Report of the Chinese Elections* (Beijing: Law Press, 2002).

26. Of course, the whole enterprise of traditional Confucianism is to reduce official abuses to an absolute minimum, mainly through moral education, but Chinese history shows at most mixed success in this grand political project. This is a broad topic by itself, and I discuss it in more detail elsewhere.

27. It is noteworthy that the new amendment to the 1982 Constitution, ironically together with the "three-represents" doctrine, stipulates that "the State respects and protects human rights." What is lacking so far is an effective mechanism to protect concrete rights and freedoms.

Chapter 4

East Asian Conceptions of the Public and Private Realms

Chun-chieh Huang

Introduction

Mengzi 7A35 records the following dialogue between Mengzi (371–289? BCE) and Tao Ying 桃應:

> Tao Ying asked, "When Shun was Son of Heaven, and Gao Yao was his Minister of Crime, if 'the Blind Man' [i.e., Shun's father] had murdered someone, what would they have done?"
> Mengzi said, "Gao Yao would simply have arrested him!"
> Tao Ying asked, "So Shun would not have forbidden it?"
> Mengzi said, "How could Shun have forbidden it? Gao Yao had a sanction for his actions."
> Tao Ying asked, "So what would Shun have done?"
> Mengzi said, "Shun looked at casting aside the whole world like casting aside a worn sandal. He would have secretly carried his father on his back and fled, to live in the coastland, happy to the end of his days, joyfully forgetting the world."[1]

In the above dialogue, Tao Ying asks Mengzi a hypothetical question. The core sense of his question is what should Shun do when his *si* 私 (private responsibility)—as son of "the Blind Man," Shun ought to protect his father—conflicts with his *gong* 公 (public responsibility)—as Son of Heaven,

Shun ought to obey the law of the land? Should he ignore the law and protect his father or should he obey the law of the land and forsake familial affection in order to preserve righteousness? It comes down to whether being filial to his father or being loyal to his state has the higher priority. The key to this question lies in distinguishing and sorting out the differences between the public and private realms.

During the late Warring States period (403–222 BCE), before this discussion between Mengzi and Tao Ying had ever taken place, a discourse about the concepts of *gong* (public) and *si* (private) already had a developed history in ancient China. Subsequent to this dialogue between Mengzi and Tao Ying, Chinese, Japanese, and Korean Confucians suggested different explanations regarding the implications of this dialogue, and these can be taken as reflections of the intricate transformation of the concepts of "public" and "private" in the history of East Asian thought. And so, the following, second section of this chapter begins by examining changes in the concepts of public and private that occurred during the Western Zhou (1045?–771 BCE), down to the Warring States period, and how these were manifested in the concrete situations of life. The third section analyzes different East Asian Confucian interpretations of *Mengzi* 7A35, in order to observe the transformation of the concepts of public and private within modern East Asian thought. The last section presents my conclusions.

The Development of the Concepts *Gong* and *Si* in Ancient Chinese Thought

Between the Western Zhou and the late Warring States period, the meanings of the words *gong* and *si* evolved from referring to concrete human beings or things into abstract standards of value judgment. Moreover, they came to have a strong connotation of moral judgment. Let us cite some textual evidence to further clarify this point.

In his early dictionary, the *Shuowen jiezi* 說文解字, Xu Shen 許慎 (30–134 CE) explains the meanings of the words *gong* and *si* in the following way:

> *Gong* is to distribute evenly. [The character *gong* 公 (public) is formed] by combining the elements *ba* 八 (opposed to) and *si* 厶 (private). The meaning of *ba* is equivalent to *bei* 背 (to oppose). Han Feizi said, "What opposes the private is public."
>
> *Si* (private) is wicked and deviant. Han Feizi said, "When Cang Jie composed characters, he took *si* 厶 (private) to mean centering on oneself."[2]

But the origin of the two words *gong* and *si* probably is related to ancient Chinese agricultural life. Xu Zhongshu 徐中舒 once said, "*Si* 私 (in its original form: 厶) depicts the shape of a plough used in farming." He continues, "A plough is a farm tool, which is an item a person uses in daily life. So it has to be claimed as something one owns. Thus, a plough is a possession and came to be glossed as "mine." *Si* 厶 and *si* 私 should be understood as extensions of and derived from the word 'plough.'"[3] Katō Jōken 加藤常賢 believed that the word *gong* originated from *gong gong* 公宮 (patriarch's residence), the place where, in antiquity, the clan leader lived. Over time, the clan leader came to be called *gong* 公.[4]

In ancient texts and records, the two words *gong* and *si* both indicate concrete persons or things. The "Punishments of Lu" chapter of the *Shangshu* 尚書 (The Book of History) contains the sentence "Do not seek private advantage for yourselves by pleading both sides."[5] Here, the word *jia* in the term *sijia* 私家 perhaps should be the word *hun* 圂, miswritten due to their similar shapes.[6] Nevertheless, it is certain that the word *si* refers to people who listen to a lawsuit. Examples of *gong* and *si* being used to refer to concrete persons or things are often seen in the *Shijing* 詩經 (The Book of Odes). For example, *si* appears in the ode "Getan" 葛覃 of the "Zhounan" 周南 section, "I will wash my private clothes clean; And I will rinse my robes."[7] Here, *si* means *yanfu* 燕服 (the everyday clothes one wears at home). The ode "Shiren" 碩人 of the "Weifeng" 衛風 section contains the following lines: "The daughter of the marquis of Qi; The wife of the marquis of Wei; The sister of the heir-son of Qi; The sister-in-law of the marquis of Xing; The viscount of Tan also her brother-in-law (*si* 私)." The commentary says, "The husband of one's younger sister is called *si* 私."[8] In the ode "Qiyue" 七月 of the "Binfeng" 豳風 section, "The boars of one year are for themselves; Those of three years are for our prince,"[9] *si* and *gong* are used to mean "one's own family" (i.e., "themselves") and "the prince's family" (i.e., "our prince"), respectively. The word *si* in the following line from the ode "Dadong" 大東 from the "Xiaoya," 小雅 "The sons of the poorest families, form the officers in public employment,"[10] refers to "people from lower-class (*si*) families." The *gong* and *si* that appear in the following lines from the ode "Datian" 大田 in the "Xiaoya," "May it rain first on our public fields; And then come to our private [fields]!"[11] mean "public farmland" and "private farmland," respectively. There are many similar examples, more than we can point out here. All of the examples of *gong* and *si* that appear in the *Shijing* and *Shangshu* refer to concrete persons, affairs, or things and particularly emphasize their social and political significance. Just as Nishida Taichirō 西田太一郎 says, prevalent use of the word *si* began in the late Western Zhou period. This term usually indicates the personal affairs, things, or behavior of a minister, officer, or scholar-officer; *si* contrasts with *gong*, which specifically refers to a ruler's personal affairs, things, or behavior.[12]

In the Spring and Autumn period (722–404 BCE), the two words *gong* and *si* still often referred to concrete humans, affairs, or things. In the *Zuozhuan* 左傳 (Zuo's Commentary [to the Spring and Autumn Annals]), *gong* and *si*, in the realm of politics, often refer to the "house of the lord" and the "personal clans," respectively; both of these have a concrete reference. The entry for the Ninth Year of Duke Xi of Lu (650 BCE) mentions, "Doing to the extent of my knowledge whatever will be advantageous to your House (*gongjia* 公家) is loyalty."[13] Here, *gong* refers to the ruler of Lu. In the Sixth Year of Duke Wen of Lu (621 BCE), Yu Pian 庾駢 says, "To injure the public service for my private ends would not show loyalty."[14] In these lines, "private" refers to personal resentment and "public" refers to the killing of Jia 賈 in order to take precautions against Zhao Dun 趙盾. In the Twenty-fifth Year of Duke Xiang of Lu (547 BCE), Yanzi 晏子 says, "who excepting his private associates (*sini* 私暱), would presume to bear the consequences with him?"[15] Here, *sini* refers to a person held dear. Since in the Spring and Autumn period *gong* and *si* often refer to concrete objects, they often appear as part of a compound reference term paired with concrete things or affairs. For example, in the *Zuozhuan* for the Third Year of Duke Zhao of Lu (539 BCE), Shu Xiang discusses the disarmament of the ruling house of Jin 晉 in terms of the "ducal house" (*gongshi* 公室), the "duke's commands" (*gongming* 公命), and the "ducal clans (*gongzu* 公族)."[16] When Nu Shuqi 女叔齊 discusses the political situation with the marquis of Jin in the Fifth Year of Duke Zhao of Lu (537 BCE), he says, "The duke's house is divided into four parts, and [like one of] the people he gets his food from others. No one thinks kindly of him."[17] The sense is that the people no longer favor Lu Gong. In the Twentieth Year of Duke Zhao of Lu (522 BCE), the *Zuozhuan* says, "Oppressive duties are levied on the private [baggage of travelers]."[18] Here, *si* refers to personal possessions. In the Fifth Year of Duke Ai of Lu (490 BCE), it says, "Private enmities should not interfere with public [duty]."[19] Du Yu 杜預 (222–284 CE) adds the following commentary: "It is a public affair."[20] Each of these examples uses *gong* and *si* to indicate some concrete affair.

In various texts of the Warring States period, the sense of the two words *gong* and *si* gradually developed from having concrete references to involving abstract concepts. They often referred to virtuous character in the abstract, and the *gong* came to be advocated over the *si*. This trend of thought reached full maturity in the "Guigong" 貴公 (In praise of the public) and "Qusi" 去私 (Eliminating the private) chapters of the *Lüshi chunqiu* 呂氏春秋 (Master *Lü*'s

Spring and Autumn Annals).²¹ In the course of this process of transforming their sense from concrete references to abstract meanings, Xunzi 荀子 (ca. 298–238 BCE) was one of the first to clearly advocate *gong*'s having priority over *si*.²² Hanfeizi 韓非子 (280–233 BCE) carried forth what Xunzi had begun and brought the conceptual world into the concrete political world, promoting the absolute priority of *gong* in the realm of politics. A comprehensive view of Warring States period texts reveals that *gong* and *si* often are used in ways that are related to some abstract moral idea. For example, in the *Mozi* 墨子 the senses of *gong* and *si* never stray from the central theme of "impartial caring." The chapter "Impartial Caring" says: "This describes the extensiveness of King Wen's impartial care for the world. It compares his impartiality to the way the sun and the moon impartially illuminate the entire world without showing any favoritism. This was King Wen's impartial care."²³ In the chapter "The Proper Model," we find:

> "What then is the proper model for managing the government?"
> "For the reasons [given above]," I [Mozi] say, "nothing is better than modeling oneself on Heaven. The actions of Heaven are broad and impartial; it bestows abundance but without thought of return; its illumination endures without fading."²⁴

None of these examples use the word *si* to refer to particular concrete affairs or things; rather, they indicate a personal preference for ethical conduct. The "Five Vermins" chapter of the *Hanfeizi* says, "Whatever was opposed to the private was public."²⁵ Daoist texts such as the *Laozi* 老子 and the *Zhuangzi* 莊子 even use the principle of the transformations of the natural world to stress the superiority of *gong* as a moral standard over *si*. For instance, the "Zeyang" 則陽 chapter of the *Zhuangzi* says:

> The four seasons have different characteristics; Heaven shows no preference among them, and so the year comes to completion. The five bureaus have different duties; the ruler shows no preference among them, and so the state is well ordered. The great man shows no preference for civil or military affairs, and so their different excellences are perfected. The myriad things have different principles; the *Dao* shows no personal favorites (*busi* 不私), and so they remain nameless.

This passage emphasizes the moral goodness of having no "personal favorites."²⁶

In the late Warring States period, the great Confucian Xunzi had an especially significant role in the developmental history of the concepts *gong* and *si*. In the *Xunzi*, the words *gong* and *si* often have abstract meanings; they are placed in opposing positions within the guiding themes of Xunzi's moral theory, with *gong* being superior to *si*. In this way, the two words *gong* and *si* often become combined with concepts that have universal moral implications, such as "the Way," "fairness," "righteousness," "desire," or "injustice."[27] For instance, Xunzi believes that only "after one can train one's intentions to overcome the concern for personal interest can one be righteous,"[28] and only then can one become a great Confucian. Moreover, Xunzi emphasizes the thought that only a "gentleman" is able "to use a sense of the public and righteousness to overcome private desires."[29] The ideal ruler must "clearly define duties, order all affairs and enterprises, determine the ability of officials, and assign positions according to each person's ability. When everything is properly ordered, the public path prevails and private access is blocked off. Then, public righteousness flourishes and private affairs are terminated."[30] So-called *cuanchen* 篡臣 (usurping ministers) are those "who have no concern for public affairs or universal righteousness, who collude with others and form cliques in order to surround the ruler, with the aim of promoting their personal interests."[31] The ideal scholarly official should be "enlightened, universally minded, and public spirited."[32]

Xunzi drew out the abstract implications of *gong* and combined *gong* with *yi* 義 righteousness); he emphasized using "a sense of the public and righteousness to overcome private desires."[33] This reflected a new trend of thought that developed during the late Warring States period. For example, *Mozi* raised "public righteousness" over and in opposition to "personal resentment," saying, "promote public righteousness and prevent private resentment."[34] Han Feizi also frequently championed "public righteousness."[35] The "Collection of Illustrations: Outer Group" chapter of the *Hanfeizi* says, "No private feud should be brought into public office."[36] These examples reveal a consensus that can be found among many thinkers of the Warring States period: in the realm of value, *gong* has priority over *si*, and *si* should not be allowed to harm *gong*.

Now, let us look at how conceptions of *gong* and *si* from the world of thought were manifested in the concrete world. What we see in the historical sources of ancient China is that the ancient Chinese regularly used suicide as a way to escape from situations in which there was an irresolvable conflict between *gong* and *si*. In the Spring and Autumn period, during the Fourth Year of Duke Xi of Lu (656 BCE), Duke Xian of Jin took Li Ji 驪姬 as his wife and wished to establish her son as the crown prince. This generated a conflict at the royal court, and Duke Xian's elder son found himself in a deep dilemma—he was unable to fulfill both the demands of "loyalty" (as a subject) and "filial piety" (as a son). And so, he committed suicide in order to resolve this dilemma.[37] In the Ninth Year of Duke Xi of Lu (651 BCE), Li Ke 里克 of Jin killed Xi Qi 奚齊 and Gongzi Zhuo 公子卓. Xi Qi's teacher Xun Xi 荀息 killed himself in order to make clear his view of these events.[38] In the Second Year of Duke Xuan of Lu (607 BCE), Duke Ling of Jin commanded Chu Ni 鉏麑 to kill Zhao Xuanzi 趙宣子. Chu Ni confronted a moral dilemma: " 'to murder the people's lord would be disloyalty, and to cast away from me the marquis's command would be unfaithfulness. Either alternative is worse than death.' With these words, he dashed his head against a cassia tree and died."[39] During the Spring and Autumn period, Bu She 不奢, the minister of justice assigned by King Zhao of Chu, chased after a murderer. When he caught up with him, Bu She discovered that the culprit was his own father. So, he returned to the palace and spoke to the king of Chu:

> The murderer is my father. To serve a political end by using my father would not be filial, but to fail to obey my lord's law would not be loyal. To be lenient toward this crime and abandon the law, showing favor to enhance my father's well-being, this is what I, as a minister, must guard against.

Then, he bent over the chopping block and asked King Zhao to have him executed. King Zhao of Chu decided to release him. However, Bu She said,

> This cannot be. Not favoring my father is to be unfilial. Not obeying my lord's law is to be disloyal. Remaining alive while condemned for a capital offense is to be dishonest. Your majesty's wish to pardon me is the kindness of a superior. My inability to forego punishment is the righteousness of a subordinate.

He then cut his own throat and died in the palace hall.[40]

In the Spring and Autumn period, when Tian Chang 田常 confronted a moral dilemma in which he had to either "abandon my ruler in order to be filial but disloyal or discard my parents in order to complete my lord's business but be unfilial,"[41] he committed suicide in order to resolve his dilemma. In the Spring and Autumn period, during the rebellion of Duke Bai of Chu, there was a minister who sacrificed his life for his ruler who said, "Fearing for my life is a personal good; dying for my lord is a public good. I have heard that a gentleman will not allow personal good to harm public good."[42] Suicide is the way that many ancient Chinese sought to free themselves from irresolvable conflicts between the realms of the public and private.

The ancient Chinese practice of committing suicide in order to free oneself from irresolvable conflicts between *gong* and *si* suggests the following three implications. First, within the ancient Chinese world of thought, one's death was regarded as an integral part of one's life. The primary reason the ancients chose suicide as a way to escape from irresolvable conflicts between their obligations to the public and private realms is that they believed the moment when a person's biological life ends is also the day their cultural life is made manifest. They used ending their biological lives as a way to concretely embody the cultural values to which they were committed.

Second, the above cases of suicide show that the choices that ancient Chinese people made in an effort to fulfill public or private duties were deeply intertwined in a complex network of social and political relationships. In other words, the ancient Chinese did not deliberate about "public" and "private" as abstract categories or universal concepts. On the contrary, their reflections on the division between public and private and the ethical distinctions between them have a strong sense of *situatedness*. They were like spiders, suspended from a dense network of social and political relationships, arduously struggling to fulfill their most cherished values.

Third, the many cases in which ancient Chinese people used suicide to resolve the conflict between public and private show that in their scheme of values deontological ethics had priority over utilitarian ethics. Moreover, the former often appears as a consideration within the latter's primary mode of reasoning. So-called deontological ethics presents a kind of absolute value that remains unchanged despite the agent's external conditions, such as his or her identity, position, or vocation. Deontological ethics does not appeal to any end other than an absolute value. In contrast, utilitarian ethics stresses consequences; its aim is to achieve various utilitarian goals. Deontological ethics makes judgments according to the essential nature of the matter at hand, while utilitarian ethics measures the value or expected benefits or utility of the matter at hand. On the ancient Chinese view of utilitarian ethics, the most important issues to be considered when making judgments of value were the agent's role and position within the network of social and political relationships. Among the various relationships in ancient Chinese society, the relationship between father and son was regarded as primary, most natural, and most important. All other social relationships were developed on the model of the relationship between father and son. This is why the ancient Chinese often drew an analogy between fathers and rulers, teachers, elder brothers, and husbands. The ancient Chinese ethic of rulers and ministers required rulers to treat their people as their children. This perfectly reflects the idea that the relationship between rulers and ministers was an extension of the relationship between fathers and sons. In those cases discussed above in which there was an irresolvable conflict between fulfilling obligations of filial piety and loyalty, filial piety almost always had priority over loyalty. And so, in ancient Chinese texts when we see historical cases of children murdering their fathers, these always receive extremely harsh condemnation.

To sum up the above discussion, we have seen that in the world of ancient Chinese thought, the meanings of the concepts *gong* and *si* developed from the Western Zhou period, when they referred to concrete people or things, to the Warring States period, when they indicated abstract moral values, and the value of the realm of *gong* had higher priority over the realm of *si*. Nonetheless, in actual practice, if there was an irresolvable conflict between the realms of the public and the private, then the ancient Chinese might chose to commit suicide as a way to escape from the dilemma. It is precisely because of the irreconcilable conflicts that sometimes occur between one's obligations in the public and private realms that the legal practices of modern societies (such as the United States) employ the principle of a "conflict of interests." This allows one to refuse to serve as a witness to the purported crimes of one's family members (such as husbands and wives or fathers and sons testifying against one another) and avoids the conflict between the public and private realms.

East Asian Confucian Perspectives on the Relationship between the Public and Private Realms Based on Interpretations of *Mengzi* 7A35

Now that we have reviewed the development of the conceptions of public and private from the Western Zhou to the late Warring States periods, let us return to an examination of the implications of the dialogue between Mengzi and Tao Ying and the opinions of later Chinese, Japanese, and Korean Confucians in order to make clearer the ways in which modern East Asian Confucians handle the relation between the realms of the public and the private.

Premodern East Asian Confucian perspectives on the relation between the realms of the public and private can be characterized in terms of the following two major lines of thought:

First, during the pre-Qin period (prior to 221 BCE), although Kongzi (551–479 BCE) and Mengzi emphasized the boundaries between the public and private, they never separated them into two distinct poles. Moreover, they regarded the realm of the public as an expansion and extension of the realm of the private and its fulfillment or completion. In the Spring and Autumn period, Kongzi responded to She Gong's 葉公 question about the stealing of a sheep (*Analects* 13.18) by saying that it is not considered "upright" for a son to testify against his father. This implies that the "uprightness" practiced in the public realm actually does not conflict with the affection one has in the private realm.[43] Mengzi emphasized that "the foundation of the world is the state; the foundation of the state is the family; the foundation of the family is the person" (*Mengzi* 4A5). He believed that the realm of the private was an equally valuable part of a process of development that led to the realm of the public—seeing this process as an expanding series of concentric circles—and that there was no conflict between the public and private realms. Kongzi and Mengzi regarded the public and private realms as unified and continuous; therefore, they considered an obligation to obey the law or carry out political affairs to be an extension of one's ethical affairs. Within this unified and continuous public and private realm, Kongzi and Mengzi always used parental kindness to accommodate and nurture the rigid political and legal order, in order to transform them into lively living beings. Therefore, in answering Tao Ying's question, Mengzi pointed out that if Emperor Shun confronted the dilemma of having to watch his father go to prison for killing someone, he would give up the world (i.e., renounce his throne). The solution Mengzi proposed implies that the "principle of kinship" is the basis for resolving difficulties involving "mutually irreconcilable obligations" between the public and private realms.[44] In Mengzi's philosophy, humans are integrated beings. Whether as ethical agents or law-abiding agents, human beings are unified wholes, and the person as a law-abiding agent is deeply informed by the person as an ethical agent.

Kongzi's and Mengzi's suggestion that the public realm is an expansion and extension of the private realm was challenged by Xunzi during the late Warring States period. When Xunzi discussed the way of the minister, he warned rulers to take precautions against those "who have no concern for public affairs or universal righteousness, who collude with others and form cliques in order to surround the ruler, with the aim of promoting their personal interests"—the *cuanchen*—and their attempts to seize power.[45] Xunzi emphasized that the ruler who has perfect moral integrity necessarily will "use a sense of the public and righteousness to overcome private desires."[46] He clearly differentiates between the realms of "public" and "private" and insists that rulers must "work for the public" rather than be "corrupted by private interests."[47] When Xunzi discusses the principle of filial piety, he suggests that to be "filial when at home and respectful to one's elder brother outside the home are minor forms of behavior.... To follow the *Dao* rather than one's ruler and follow righteousness rather than one's father are great forms of behavior."⁴⁸ In the "Way of the Son" chapter, he makes clear that the distinction between "great filial piety" and "petty filial piety" is precisely the same as the difference between public and private. This shows that, by the late Warring States period, Xunzi already was questioning Mengzi's approach to the issue of public and private.

By the eleventh century and thereafter, Northern Song Confucians began to differentiate the realms of public and private even more rigorously. Cheng Yi 程頤 (1033–1107) said, "Righteousness and [personal] profit are just the [issues] of public and private"⁴⁹ and "The Duke of Zhou was extremely concerned with public rather than private [good]. He performed or abstained from acting in accordance with the *Dao* and without being in any way obscured by the desire for [personal] profit."⁵⁰ After the Cheng brothers, many Northern Song Confucians clearly differentiated the public and private realms; they emphasized the priority of the public over the private and the idea that the public is more important than the private. As a result, they began to express profound reservations and doubts about Mengzi's response to Tao Ying. The most remarkable example of this tendency is the thought of Sima Guang 司馬光 (1019–1086).

Sima Guang's criticisms of Mengzi in his essay "Doubts about Mengzi" in fact are directed against and evoked by Wang Anshi 王安石 (1021–1086), who highly recommended Mengzi' views. "Doubts about Mengzi" was written between 1082 and 1085.⁵¹ At that time, even though Wang Anshi was no longer active on the political stage, he was still using his influence to promote Mengzi as worthy of being worshipped in the Confucian temple. Sima Guang's "Doubts about Mengzi" is obviously directed against Wang Anshi and evoked by his new policies.⁵² Sima Guang criticizes Mengzi's response to Tao Ying by saying:

> The Blind Man already had been arrested by Gao Yao. How could Shun rescue and hide him with the intention of carrying him on his back and fleeing to the coast! Although Gao Yao arrested him in accordance with the law, secretly he harbored the intention of releasing him to Shun. This is nothing but a case in which ruler and minister conspire together to deceive the world.⁵³

Sima Guang's criticism of Mengzi emphasizes the importance of the public over the private in order to criticize Mengzi's discourse.

Slightly later than Sima Guang, Su Che 蘇轍 (1039–1112) also criticized Mengzi's response to Tao Ying's question. Su Che wrote "Explaining the *Mengzi*" in order to express his doubts about Mengzi's response that Shun would rescue his father and flee to the coast, saying such a view is worthy of a barbarian rather than a gentleman. He said, "If the parents of the ruler commit a crime, one should launch criticism against it. Who can say that if the ruler's father murders someone, he won't be exempt from execution?"⁵⁴ Su Che's opinion happens to agree completely with Sima Guang's. They both use the ideas of not letting the private harm the public and not allowing personal favor to abolish state law in order to criticize Mengzi.

During the Southern Song dynasty (1127–1279), Yu Yunwen 余允文 (ca. 1163) rose up and refuted Sima Guang's criticism of Mengzi. He argued that

> Mengzi's point is that even all the wealth in the world and the honored position of the ruler cannot change one's filial obligation to serve his father. And so, he replied that the world can be forgotten but fathers cannot be forsaken even for a moment in order to illuminate the way of father and son. How can one say that this is but a minor contribution to Confucian teachings!⁵⁵

Yu Yunwen restated Mengzi's original point of view. Although he cannot eliminate Sima Guang's doubt, Yu Yunwen's opinions on the issue of public and private are of particular historical significance. Yu Yunwen says:

> Tao Ying's view is that the law is the greatest expression of public good in the world. Shun is one who makes the law. Gao Yao is one who guards the law.... Shun does not dare to prevent Gao Yao from carrying out his duties, because he will not allow personal favor to abolish the public law of the world.... Now the laws were established by the former kings and publicly shared throughout the world. Scholar-officials who received the laws from the former kings cannot, on someone else's behalf, use them to pursue private [interests].⁵⁶

Yu Yunwen's main point appears to be different from Sima Guang's, but their views actually are the same. They both advocate the principle of not allowing the private to abolish the public.

By the time of the Southern Song dynasty, Zhu Xi 朱熹 (1130–1200) integrated concepts such as "Heavenly principle" and "human desire" into the discourse about public and private. In his commentary on *Mengzi* 1A1, he says:

> Benevolence and righteousness are rooted in the innate human heart-mind, which is publicly shared, Heavenly principle. The

inclination to pursue [personal] benefit arose with the emergence of physical objects and the self; these are selfish desires. If one follows Heavenly principle, one will not seek [personal] benefit; as a result, everything proves to be beneficial. If one follows human desires, then even before one begins to seek benefit, one already has suffered harm.[57]

Zhang Shi 張栻 (1133–1180), in his "Explaining the *Mengzi*," adopted Zhu Xi's connection between the concepts of "Heavenly principle" and "human desires" and the concepts of "public" and "private" and upheld "the public nature of principle" in contrast to "the private nature of human desires."[58] He said: "The senses of propriety and righteousness originate from Heaven and are manifested in the human heart-mind. Each has its principle, which cannot be broken. They are shared publicly by the world rather than privately owned by me."[59] When Zhang Shi discussed Mengzi's teachings about how official positions should be assigned on the basis of virtue, he suggested that official positions and salaries are all paths open to the public, rather than the private possessions of a ruler.[60] When he discussed Gaozi's 告子 theory that righteousness is external, he pointed out that Gaozi argued for the externality of righteousness because he mistook the universal principles of the world to be personal viewpoints.[61] Both Zhu Xi's and Zhang Shi's opinions stress the priority of the public over the private.

From the pre-Qin thought of Kongzi and Mengzi, in which public and private are understood as interpenetrating and interrelated, through Xunzi's challenge, raised in the late Warring States period, and down to Song dynasty Confucians, who advocated the priority of the public over the private, we can see the submerged tension between the public and private realms. In the eleventh century, this issue started to receive more and more attention within the Chinese intellectual world. In the seventeenth century, Ogyū Sorai 荻生徂徠 (物茂卿; 1666–1725), a Japanese master of the Ancient Learning School, clearly differentiates between *gong* and *si*. In "Distinguishing Terms," he says, "Public is the opposite of private. What everyone shares in common is called public. What one controls individually is called private. The path of a gentleman involves both what is shared in common and what is controlled individually."[62] This view had a profound and enduring influence in the history of Tokugawa thought.[63]

The second line of thought that East Asian Confucians advocated (in regard to the relationship between public and private) is the idea that if there is a conflict between the public and private realms, the ideal is to find a compromise that preserves both. If this cannot be attained, then "principle,"

"Heavenly principle," or "the heart-mind [shared by all] the world" is used as the standard for deciding.

In the Southern Song dynasty, when Yang Shi 楊時 (1053–1135) commented on the dialogue between Tao Ying and Mengzi, he said:[64]

> [The relationship between] a father and son concerns the exercise of private favor. The law concerns the world's publicly shared righteousness. Both of these are important, and neither can be upheld in a partial manner. And so, if [private] favor is given higher priority over righteousness, then the law has to be bent in order to fulfill such favor. If righteousness is given higher priority over private favor, then such favor has to be obscured in order to obey the law. When the importance of favor and righteousness do not triumph over each other, then both are fulfilled to the utmost. When Shun was the ruler of the world, the Blind Man killed someone, and Gao Yao arrested him instead of setting him free. As Shun, how could he not forgive his father? Now, releasing the murderer is to abandon the law, while executing his father is to harm private favor. The implication is that the world cannot be without the law even for a day; nor can a son be without his father even for a day. The people do not worry about having no ruler. So [Shun] preferred to abandon his throne in order to uphold the public righteousness of the world. Rescuing his father and fleeing with him on his back, Shun was able to fulfill his private favor. This was how Shun was able to preserve both principles.

However, in actual life the goal of "being able to preserve both principles" often is difficult to achieve. In such cases, how is one to settle conflicts that arise between one's obligations in the public and private realms?

When more recent East Asian Confucians are faced with conflicts between the public and private realms and are not able to reach the ideal described by Zhu Xi—"Gao Yao acknowledges the law but not the ruler's father. Shun acknowledges his father but not the world. Each of them exhausts the obligation of their respective ways without opposing one another"[65]—they often rely on universal concepts such as "Heaven" or "Heavenly principles" to resolve the tension between the realms of the public and the private. In the *Zhuzi yulei* 朱子語類 (Classified Conversations of Master Zhu), there is the following dialogue:[66]

> Question: "When the Blind Man killed someone, Gao Yao only acknowledged the law but not the ruler's father. Shun only acknowledged his father but not the world. This shows that the heart-minds of sages or worthies are calm and direct. Is it that when confronted with some affair their attention is focused and there is no need to consider side issues?"
>
> Answer: "Mengzi is just describing the heart-mind of a sage or worthy. The heart-minds of sages or worthies respond immediately like this. There is no need for them to engage in evaluation. However, in extreme circumstances where one cannot but act, one must be flexible in order to work things out. Now, the law is the shared public possession of the world; there is nothing for Gao Yao to do but arrest him [i.e., the Blind Man]. If the heart-minds of the people do not allow Shun to abandon the world and leave, then this is Heaven's [will]. How could even Gao Yao disobey Heaven! Law and principle are embedded in the core of every person's heart-mind. But the heart-mind has to respond immediately in this way, in order to make the proper evaluation. People today respond immediately to affairs without this core heart-mind; from the very beginning, they engage in evaluation. This is not proper.

Zhu Xi recognizes that the law is "the shared public possession of the world." When the father of the ruler kills someone, according to the law, he should be arrested and sent to prison. Nevertheless, if one is able to preserve one's heart-mind with "Heavenly principle," then one will be able to make the right decision. Zhu Xi, in his "Combined Commentaries on the *Mengzi*," says:

> This chapter discusses how if one is a scholar-official, one will only acknowledge the law and not the honor due to the ruler's father. If one is a son, he will only acknowledge his father and not the importance of the world. Now the heart-mind is nothing other than the acme of Heavenly principle, the highest good regarding human relations. Those who consult it will attain understanding; there will be no need to wait for calculation or evaluation, and yet no situation will prove difficult [to resolve].[67]

Zhu Xi believes that if one can attain an understanding of "the acme of Heavenly principle," one will be able to put into proper order "the highest good regarding human relations." Because "Heavenly principle" is universal and transcendent principle, it is not in the least constrained by thoughts of private or even the state's interests. This is just what Wang Fuzhi 王夫之 (1618–1692) says: "If one only talks about the great fault of familial relationship from the perspective of overturning ancestral and social norms, then in evaluating greater and smaller gains and losses, one will distort the natural rules of Heavenly principle."[68]

Zhu Xi's use of the concept of "Heavenly principle" to ease the tension between conflicting obligations in the public and private realms made a deep impression on Korean Confucians of the Chosŏn dynasty (1392–1910), and they adopted and elaborated on this idea. In the sixteenth century, Cho Ik 趙翼 (1579–1655) further developed Zhu Xi's views, saying:

> Law holds sway throughout the world; it cannot be suppressed. If it is suppressed, it cannot perform [its function] as law. So, the only thing for Gao Yao to do is to arrest him [i.e., the Blind Man]; there is no other way for him to proceed. Nothing is more pressing than for a son to save his father from misery. How can the world decide the importance of this? So, the only thing for Shun to do is to flee; there is no other way for him to proceed. Tao Ying's question is asked from the perspective of everyday human feelings, and so there seems to be a difficulty. This is why he has doubts and needs to ask this question. However, the appropriateness of principle is just like this. It is only when humans are in the grip of selfish thoughts that they find this a difficult situation. The sage sees things from the perspective of Heavenly principle, which is perfectly correct, and so he knows that things must be like this. Moreover, his words are clear, resolute, and in general not problematic. How could anyone who lacks a deep understanding of the perfect correctness of righteousness and good order, in the way that the heart-mind of the sage understands, ever be like this?[69]

Of course, the explanation given by the Korean Confucian Cho Ik is convincing, but still there remains the question of how one is to decide what constitutes the "perfect correctness of Heavenly principle." Who determines the "perfect correctness of Heavenly principle?" If a number of different "Heavenly principles" conflict, how does one decide which kind of "Heavenly principle" determines what is correct? These questions are appropriately directed against any proposal that uses the concept of *tianxia* 天下 (all under Heaven) in order to resolve the conflict between the public and the private. So, let us continue by discussing the views of the Korean Confucian Yi Ik 李瀷 (1681–1763):[70]

> The dialogue in this chapter has not been followed through to its conclusion. Let us follow the implications of Mengzi's ideas and elaborate their hidden meanings. If Tao Ying had asked, "In that case what should Gao Yao do?" Mengzi definitely would have replied, "Murder is a crime in the world; the law is the law in the world. Using the law in the world to punish a crime in the world, this is the duty of a scholar-official. Nonetheless, the ruler is both mother and father of the world. If the mother and father of the world were to carry his father on his back and flee, then the world would lose its parents. The world then would cry like a baby and search for where its parents had gone. Where would it have the leisure to think about the crime of murder? Gao Yao only is led by and follows the heart-mind of the world." If [Tao Ying] had asked, "In that case what should Shun do?" [Mengzi] definitely would have replied, "Shun ruled the world but would rather not have participated in it. He did not originally think [of ruling the world]. He abandoned the world happily but with concern. [Later,] when the world would turn to him [again], it would be as if he had served as ruler all along." If [Tao Ying] had asked, "If [the crime is committed] by his father, he can be pardoned; if [the crime is committed] by the people, they must be punished. If this is how it works, is there still the law?" [Mengzi] definitely would have replied, "The pardon is a pardon given by the world; the punishment is a punishment given by the world. Shun would not be involved in either. The sage is sincere and reverent, and thereby the world is pacified. There has never been a case of following the heart-mind of the world that led to the law failing to reach completion."

Yi Ik advocates allowing "the world" to resolve the conflict Shun faced between his obligations to the public and private realms. Although this seems to be a feasible proposal, one wonders how the public opinion of "the world" could be expressed under the autocratic political systems of East Asian countries in premodern times? Who represented the public opinion of "the world"? When we consider these questions within the context of the autocratic political systems of East Asian countries in premodern times, (it is clear that) neither transcendental

"Heavenly principle" nor the universal concept of "the world" could overcome the conflicts that arose between the public and the private.

In premodern East Asian societies, the authority to interpret concepts like "principle" or "Heavenly principle" was in the hands of those who controlled political power. This is why many conflicts regarding different interpretations of "principle" were reduced to conflicts of political power. For this reason, conflicts over various interpretations of "principle" could only be resolved in the arena of political power, according to who had more or less power. In the eighteenth century, Dai Zhen 戴震 (1723–1777), responding to this kind of unprincipled understanding of principle, raised trenchant objections. Dai Zhen said:[71]

> The honored reprove the lowly on the basis of "principle." Elders reprove juniors on the basis of "principle." The noble reprove the humble on the basis of "principle." Even when they are wrong, they claim that they simply are following principle. The lowly, juniors, and humble challenge such treatment by appealing to principle, but even when they are right, they are said to be acting against principle. This is why those in inferior positions are unable to use the feelings that all share and the desires that all have in common to reach those in superior positions. When those in superior positions use "principle" to reprove those in inferior positions, [we find that] there are countless "crimes" being committed down below.

Dai Zhen clearly points out that "principle" cannot transcend the problem of stronger people oppressing and controlling the weak, which is a product of the power structure.

We can further reflect on this question by placing it within the history of the Chinese legal system. In a Han dynasty (BCE 206–221 CE) legal work, there is a so-called inappropriate acts clause. The Tang dynasty (618–906) *Tanglu* 唐律 (Laws of the Tang) has an "acts that are crimes simply because they should not be done" clause, which refers to criminal actions that are not explicitly stipulated in the written legal code but that should not be done based simply on normal feelings and common sense. A judge relies on his sense of "principle" in order to arrive at a verdict on such matters. After the Tang dynasty, the "inappropriate acts" clause remained a feature of Chinese legal codes, appearing in the *Song xingtong* 宋刑統 (The compendium of Song punishments), *Minglu* 明律 (Laws of the Ming), and *Daqing luli* 大清律例 (Collection of law of Great Qing). This clause was only abolished in 1910. The extensive influence of this code even reached Japan, where it was not abolished until the fifteenth year of the Meiji period (1882).⁷²

Ideally, this "inappropriate acts" clause would offer considerable latitude in legal practice, the goal of which is to preserve the ideal of substantial justice. However, in the course of actual practice, a judge who can appeal to "principle" in order to decide what is an "appropriate" or "inappropriate" action often relies upon "free intuitive testimony" and drifts into the misuse of power. The actual experience of Chinese legal history tells us that using "principles" or "normal feelings and common sense" offers a highly ineffective foundation for judging whether a crime has or has not been committed. Zhu Xi suggested using "Heavenly principle" to overcome the conflict between public and private; the difficulties encountered by his view are similar in nature to those faced by this traditional Chinese idea of "acts that are crimes simply because they should not be done."

Because Zhu Xi's conception of "Heavenly principle" could not overcome the conflict between public and private, modern Confucians who came after Zhu Xi often criticized Zhu Xi's Lixue 理學 (Learning of Principle). In the seventeenth century Itō Jinsai 伊藤仁齋 (1627–1705), a Tokugawa Confucian who was a member of the Ancient Learning School, said, "It is not the case that principle existed first and later gave rise to this *qi* 氣 [vital force]. To the contrary, so-called principle is just the orderly pattern of the vital force."⁷³ Itō Jinsai criticized the notion of "principles that are without sound or odor," advocated by Zhu Xi and Song Confucians, and insisted that "principles" appear in the daily life of human relations. He stressed the spatial and temporal qualities of "principle" and opposed the transcendent principles established by Song Confucians. His position happens to agree completely with that of the eighteenth-century Chinese Confucian Dai Zhen,⁷⁴ which to a considerable extent embodies a general trend of thought among modern East Asian Confucians.⁷⁵ From the seventeenth century, intellectuals such as Huang Zongxi 黃宗羲 (1610–1695), Gu Yanwu 顧炎武 (1613–1682), and others advocated the idea of bringing together all of the world's "private" (aspects) in order to form a (single) "public" world. With this suggestion, the understanding of the relationship between public and private entered a new phase.⁷⁶ Nevertheless, before this concept of a (worldwide) covenant fully spread and penetrated deeply into peoples' way of thinking in premodern Chinese society, the innovative suggestion of bringing together all of the world's "private" (aspects) in order to form a (single) "public" world that Huang Zongxi and others had suggested still faced challenges that proved difficult to resolve.

Concluding the discussion in this section, modern East Asian Confucian reflections on the dialogue between Mengzi and Tao Ying and on the enduring indivisible character of and mutual tension between the public and private realms display a profound depth of understanding. In an effort to ease the conflict between humans beings as ethical agents and humans beings as political agents, modern East Asian Confucians proposed using conceptual tools with universal qualities, such as "Heavenly principle" or "the world," to resolve the problem. However, such conceptual tools often are monopolized by the powerful, and so the issue of the conflict between the public and private realms has yet to be settled or resolved.

Conclusion

The realms of the public and the private are highly relative and continuously generate multiple levels of meaning that form expanding sets of concentric circles. Relative to a family, an individual is considered as the "private"; the family is considered the "public." Relative to a particular "private" family, society or the state is considered the "public." Relative to a specific "private" state, the international community is the "public." Located within this developing process of multiple levels and concentric circles of meaning, an individual often faces conflicts among multiple identities and responsibilities. The dialogue between Mengzi and Tao Ying recorded in *Mengzi* 7A35 is an extremely lucid way to set out the problem of Shun's incompatible roles in and responsibilities for the realms of the public and the private, and so it elicited many comments and discussions by East Asian Confucians and constituted an important problem in the history of East Asian thought.

In the second section of this chapter, in the course of tracing the origins of the concepts of *gong* and *si*, we discovered that in the transition from the Western Zhou to the Warring States period the meaning of the two words changed: originally referring to something concrete, they both came to imply something abstract. Moreover, in the course of this process of abstraction, the concepts *gong* and *si* came to imply a value judgment. Among thinkers in the late Warring States period, it was widely recognized that the "public" had priority over the "private." However, in reality the "public" and "private" had always been incompatible. A large volume of historical material from the Spring and Autumn period onward shows that the ancients at times chose to end their lives in order to escape from situations in which the "public" and "private" were in irreconcilable conflict.

Since the tenth century CE, East Asian Confucians have offered innumerable theories concerning the dialogue between Mengzi and Tao Ying. Their explanations are—like stars in the summer sky—simply too numerous to count. The third section of this chapter sums up these discussions, pointing out that East Asian Confucians were deeply impressed with the recognition that virtuous activity in either the public or the private realm can only be fully manifested in the public realm. Yet they also recognized the constant, irresolvable tension between the public and private realms. They attempted to use the concepts of transcendental *tianli* 天理 (Heavenly principle) or universal *tianxia* 天下 (all under Heaven) as conceptual tools to reconcile the conflict between public and private. Unfortunately, under the autocratic social conditions that existed prior to the modern age, the authority to determine the meaning of either *tianli* or *tianxia* was monopolized by those who were dominant in power. They usurped the transcendental or universal characteristics of these two concepts and transformed them into tools to suppress the people. This is one of the reasons why, beginning in the seventeenth century, in various East Asian countries, thinkers from the Ancient Learning School such as Itō Jinsai and Dai Zhen criticized the Cheng-Zhu School for constructing their core philosophical system on "principle."

Notes

Thanks to Cindy Wing-yan Choi for translating the original essay from Chinese into English.

1. Translation by Bryan W. Van Norden in Philip J. Ivanhoe and Bryan W. Van Norden, eds., *Readings in Classical Chinese Philosophy*, second edition (Indianapolis, IN: Hackett, 2005), 153–154.

2. *Shuowen jiezi xizhuan tongshi*, *Sibu congkan chubian suoben*, 3.24 (lower part).

3. Xu Zhongshu, "Leisi kao," *Zhongyang yanjiuyuan lishi yuyan yanjiusuo jikan* 2 (1930): 1.

4. Katō Jōken, "Gongsi kao," *Lishixue yanjiu* 96 (February 1942): 1–13.

5. "Lu-xing," *Shangshu* (Taipei: Yiwen yinshuguan yingyin shisanjing zhushuben, 1993, 19:29, 33 [upper part]).

6. Qu Wanli, *Shangshu jinzhu jinyi* (Taipei: Taiwan shangwu yinshuguan, 1969), 184.

7. "Getan," "Zhounan," vol. 1.2 of *Maoshi zhushu*, 2 (upper part). Translation by James Legge, *The She King*, vol. 4 of *The Chinese Classics* (Reprint, Taipei: Southern Materials Resource Center, 1983), 7.

8. "Shiren," "Weifeng," vol. 3.2 of *Maoshi zhushu*, 15 (lower part). Translation by Legge, *The She King*, 94–95 (with minor modification).

9. "Qiyue," "Binfeng," vol. 8.1 of *Maoshi zhushu*, 16 (lower part). Translation by Legge, *The She King*, 230.

10. "Dadong," "Xiaomin zhi shi," vol. 13.1 of *Maoshi zhushu*, 10 (lower part). Translation by Legge, *The She King*, 355.

11. "Datian," "Beishan zhishi," vol. 14.1 of *Maoshi zhushu*, 16 (lower part). Translation adapted from Legge, *The She King*, 381.

12. See Nishida Taichirō, "Kōshi kannen no tenkai to shijin no igi," *Shinagaku* 9, no. 1 (July 1937): 87–106, particularly 94–95. Also see Liu Ji-yao, *Gong yu si zhong de lunli neihan*, in *Tiandao yu rendao*, ed. Chun-chieh Huang (Taipei: Lianjing chuban shiye gongsi, 1982), 179.

13. Yang Bojun, *Chunqiu zuozhuan zhu* (Taipei: Yuanliu chubanshe, 1982), 1:328. Translation by James Legge, *The Ch'un Ts'ew with the Tso Chuen*, vol. 5 of *The Chinese Classics* (Taipei: Southern Materials Research Center, 1983), 154.

14. Yang Bojun, *Chunqiu zuozhuan zhu*, 2:553. Translation by Legge, *The Ch'un Ts'ew with the Tso Chuen*, 245.

15. Yang Bojun, *Chunqiu zuozhuan zhu*, 2:1098. Translation by Legge, *The Ch'un Ts'ew with the Tso Chuen*, 514.

16. Yang Bojun, *Chunqiu zuozhuan zhu*, 2:1266–1337. Translation adapted from Legge, *The Ch'un Ts'ew with the Tso Chuen*, 589.

17. Yang Bojun, *Chunqiu zuozhuan zhu*, 2:1266. Translation adapted from Legge, *The Ch'un Ts'ew with the Tso Chuen*, 604.

18. Yang Bojun, *Chunqiu zuozhuan zhu*, 2:1417. Translation by Legge, *The Ch'un Ts'ew with the Tso Chuen*, 683.

19. Yang Bojun, *Chunqiu zuozhuan zhu*, 2:1630. Translation by Legge, *The Ch'un Ts'ew with the Tso Chuen*, 806.

20. Yang Bojun, *Chunqiu zuozhuan zhu*, 2:1630.

21. Nishikawa Yasuji, *Kō no shisō: Ryoshisyunjū ni okeru tōitsu genri ni tsuite*, *Chūgoku gakushi* (1988): 1–14.

22. See Sawada Takio, *Senshin ni okeru kō shi no kannen*, *Tōkai daigaku kiyō bungakubu* 25 (1976): 1–8, esp. 5.

23. Mozi, *Jian'ai*, vol. 4 of *Sibu congkan chubian suoben*, 16:36 (lower part). Translation by Philip J. Ivanhoe; see Ivanhoe and Van Norden, *Readings in Classical Chinese Philosophy*, 72.

24. Mozi, *Fayi*, vol. 1 of *Sibu congkan chubian suoben*, 4–5.

25. "Wudu," *Hanfeizi*, vol. 19 of *Sibu congkan chubian suoben*, 49.97.

26. Guo Qingfan, *Jiaozheng Zhuangzi jishi* (Taipei: Shijie shuju, 1974), vol. 8 (lower part), *Zeyang* 25, 909.

27. Kurita Naoya, "Kō to shi," in *Chūgoku shisō ni okeru shizen to ningen*, by Kurita Naoya (Tokyo: Iwanami shoten, 1996), 188–206.

28. Wang Xianqian, *Xunzi jijie* (Taipei: Shijie shuju, 1969), "Ruxiao," chap. 8, 92.

29. Xunzi says, "He does not take too much when angry nor give away too much when happy. This is because the proper model takes precedence over personal feelings. The *Book of History* says, 'Do not innovate for the sake of personal preferences; follow the way of the kings. Do not innovate for the sake of personal aversions; follow the way of the kings.' This describes how the gentleman is able to use a sense of the public and righteousness to overcome private desires." See Wang Xianqian, *Xunzi*, vol. 2 (upper part) of *Shisanjing zhushuben*, "Xiushen," chap. 2, 22. Yang Liang 楊倞 adds the following comments, "Law overrides the private," and "the public is used to extinguish the private so that rewards and punishments can be upheld." The mutual interconnection between the "public" and the "law" reveals the special spirit of Xunzi's school of thought.

30. Wang Xianqian, *Xunzi jijie*, "Jundao," chap. 12, 157.

31. Ibid., "Chendao," chap. 13, 164.

32. Ibid., "Qiangguo," chap. 16, 202.

33. Ibid., 23.

34. Mozi, *Shangxian shang*, vol. 2 of *Sibu congkan chubian suoben*, 8.12.

35. "Shixie," *Hanfeizi*, vol. 5, 19.9.

36. "Waichushuo zuoxia," *Hanfeizi*, vol. 12, 23.64.

37. Yang Bojun, *Chunqiu zuozhuan zhu*, 1:295–299.

38. Ibid., 1:328–330.

39. Ibid., 1:658. Translation by Legge, *The Ch'un Ts'ew with the Tso Chuen*, 290.

40. *Hanshi waizhuan*, *Sibu congkan chubian suoben*, 2:14.

41. Ibid., 6:62.

42. Ibid., 1:7.

43. Since the May Fourth Movement, some Chinese and foreign scholars have often used Kongzi as an example of one who lacks respect for the law and denies people their independent wills; for instance, Sizukuisi Kōkichi, "Chichi wa ko no tame ni kakushi ko wa chichi no tame ni kakusu," in *Uno Tetsuto sensei hakuju shukuga kinen Tōyōgaku ronsō* (Tokyo: Uno Tetsuto sensei hakuju chukuga kinenkai, 1975), 511–527, promotes such a view. However, further discussion of this issue is needed.

44. See Chun-chieh Huang, *Mengxue sixiangshi lun* (Taipei: Dongda tushu gongsi, 1991), 1:106–107.

45. Wang Xianqian, *Xunzi jijie*, "Chendao," chap. 13, 164.

46. Ibid., "Xiushen," chap. 2, 22.

47. Xunzi says, "Testing tallies and throwing lots is the way to ensure that public interest is preserved. If those above are fond of deviousness and pursue private interests, then the ministers, down to the most minor officials, will follow along and show prejudice" (Wang Xianqian, *Xunzi jijie*, "Jundao," chap. 12, 51). In this chapter, in order to promote the idea that the ruler is the root of order in the state, Xunzi says: "There are rulers [who produce] chaos; there are no [inherently] chaotic states. There are people who can produce order; there is no model that [alone] will produce order.... The model is the first blossom of order; the ruler is the source of the model" (151). "The ruler is the source of order.... The ruler nurtures the source. If the source is pure, the stream

will be pure; if the source is muddy, the stream will be muddy" (152). Xunzi wanted the ruler to maintain public standards and shun private interest. Then, the ministers, down to the most minor officials, "will maintain the public good without the need to test tallies or throw lots" (152). At the same time, "The enlightened ruler provides his personal favorites with gold, gems, pearls, and jade but never by appointing them to office or granting them official duties. Why is this? I say, because personal favor should never be the source of such benefits" (160). Here, too, Xunzi is clearly distinguishing the public and private realms; this advice is of greatest benefit to states and rulers.

48. Ibid., "Zidao," chap. 29, 347. The entire text reads: "Filial when at home and respectful to one's elder brother outside the home are minor forms of behavior. To be compliant to one's superiors and devoted to one's subordinates are mid-level forms of behavior. To follow the *Dao* rather than one's ruler and follow righteousness rather than one's father are great forms of behavior."

49. *Ercheng ji* (Beijing: Zhonghua shuju, 1981), 17:176.

50. Wing-tsit Chan, *Jinsilu xiangzhu jiping* (Taipei: Xuesheng shuju, 1998), 10:456.

51. Kondō Masanori, "Ōanseki ni okeru Mōsi sonsū no tokushoku ichigenhō no Mōsi haikyō to Mōsi shōninron o chūshin toshite," *Nippon chūgoku gakkai hō* 36 (1984): 34–147.

52. Bai Ting 白珽 of the Yuan dynasty notes that people of that time recognized that Sima Guang wrote the *Yi Meng* "for a particular reason. At that time, Wang Anshi was using Mengzi's discourse in order to gain respect for himself. [Sima Guang] believed that Anshi's claims should not be fully trusted" (*Zhanyuan jinyu, Zhibuzuqi congshu ben*, 2:14).

53. Sima Guang, *Wenguo wenzheng Sima Gongwen ji*, 73:532–533, in *Zunmengbian*, by Yu Yunwen (Shanghai: Shangwu yinshuguan ju shoushange congshuben paiyin, 1937), 1:10.

54. Su Che, *Mengzijie*, in *Shoushan'ge congshuben*, vol. 1 of *Zhihai*, 13. This book has other editions, for example the *Ming wanli dingyou 25 nian bishi kan liangsu jingjie ben* (now compiled in *Zhongguo zixue mingzhu jicheng zhenben chu bian* (Taipei: Zhongguo zixue mingshu jicheng bianyin jijinhui yinxing, 1978) and the *Sikuquanshu ben*).

55. Yu Yunwen, *Zunmengbian*, 1:11.

56. Ibid.

57. Zhu Xi, *Mengzi jizhu*, in *Sishu zhangju jizhu* (Beijing: Zhonghua shuju, 1982), 1:202.

58. Zhang Shi, *Nanxuan xiansheng mengzi shuo*, vol. 1 (lower part), 2, vol. 1 (upper part), 10.

59. Ibid., vol. 4 (upper part), 33.

60. Ibid., vol. 5 (upper part), 27.

61. Ibid., vol. 6 (lower part), 6.

62. Ogyū Sorai, *Benmyō*, in *Nihon shisō taikei* (Tokyo: Iwanami shoten, 1982), 36:230.

63. See Maruyama Masao, *Nihon seiji shisō shi kenkyū* (Tokyo: Tokyo daigaku shuppankai, 1952), 80.

63. Yang Shi, *Zhoushizong jiarenzhuan*, vol. 9 of *Guishan ji* (Taipei: Taiwan shangwu yinshuguan, 1973), 23–24.

64. Zhu Xi, *Mengzi huo wen*, in *Sishu huo wen* (Shanghai: Shanghai guji chubanshe, Anhui jiaoyu chubanshe, 2001), 13:500.

65. Li Jingde, ed., *Zhuzi yulei* (Beijing: Zhonghua shuju, 1986), 60:1450. The *Zhuzi dayu* 朱子答語 contains the following sentence: "The law is the shared public possession of the world." The earliest occurrence of this expression is found in the Western Han, when Zhang Shizhi 張釋之 said to King Wen of Han, "The law is the shared public possession of both the king and the world." See *Shiji, Zhangshizhi fengtang liezhuan* 42, vol. 102 of *Xinjiao biaodian ben*, 2754.

66. Zhu Xi, *Mengzi jizhu*, in *Sishu zhangju jizhu*, 13:360.

67. Wang Fuzhi, *Dusishu daquan shuo* (Taipei: Heluo tushu chubanshe, 1974 photocopy), Fourth Year of Tongzhi, *Xiangqing zengshi kanben*, vol. 10 (upper part), 49.

69. Cho Ik, *Maengcha chŏnnsŏl*, in *Han'guk kyŏnghak jaryŭ jipsŏng* (Seoul: Sŏnggyun'gwantaehak taedongmunhwa yŏn'guwŏn, 1988), vol. 35, *maengcha* 1, 602–603.

68. Yi Ik, *Maengchajilsŏ, Songhojilsŏ*, in *Han'guk kyŏnghak jaryŭ jipsŏng* (Seoul: Sŏnggyun'gwantaehak taedongmunhwa yŏn'guwŏn, 1988), vol. 39, *maengcha* 5, 433–434.

69. Dai Zhen, *Mengzi ziyi shuzheng*, in *Daizhen quanshu* (Beijing: Qinghua daxue chubanshe, 1991), vol. 1, part 1, *li*, 161.

70. See Huang Yuancheng, *Tanglu buyingdezui di dangdai sikao*, in *Dongya chuantong jiaoyu yu fazhi yanjiu (II)—Tanglu zhuwenti*, ed. Gao Mingshi (Taipei: Taida chuban zhongxin, 2005): 3–66.

71. Itō Jinsai, *Go-Mo jigi*, in *Nihon rinri ihen*, ed. Inoue Tetsujirō and Kanie Yosimaru (Tokyo: Ikuseikai, 1901), vol. 5, *Kogakuha no bu* (middle), 12.

72. See above for Dai Zhen's criticisms of Song conceptions of principle as a standard for moral criticism.

73. Chun-chieh Huang, "Dongya jinshi ruxue sichao de xindongxiang—Dai Dongyuan, Itō Jinsai, yu Ding Chashan dui Mengxue de jieshi," in *Ruxue chuantong yu wenhua chuangxin* (Taipei: Dongda tushu gongsi, 1986): 77–108.

74. See Mizoguchi Yūzō, *Chūgoku no kō, shi*, in Mizoguchi Yūzō, *Chūgoku no kō to shi* (Tokyo: Kenbun shuppan, 1995): 42–90.

Chapter 5

Trust Within Democracy
A Reconstructed Confucian Perspective

Julia Tao

Introduction

In this chapter, I examine the question of the relation between trust and democracy in the governance of modern society. In particular, I focus on one specific question: Is trust necessary for democratic governance? When Kongzi (Confucius) was asked about government by his disciple Zigong more than two thousand years ago, he said that three things are needed for government: weapons, food, and trust. If a ruler can't hold on to all three, he should give up the weapons first and the food next. Trust should be guarded to the end: without trust we cannot stand (*Analects* 12.7). Are Kongzi and his advice still relevant today?

The relationship between trust and democracy is receiving increasing attention in the literature because of two main reasons. First, many studies have shown a decline of trust in democratic countries in recent decades; second, the decentering of the state and the disaggregation of government functions have resulted in an increasing reliance on civil society to achieve the tasks of governance.[1] This has led to interesting debates about the foundations of civil society and the role of trust in democratic governance. Important questions are being raised: For example, is trust necessary for democracy? Does democracy generate or erode the culture of trust? What are the moral foundations of trust? Is trust attainable within democracy?

Strategic Trust: Trust as Encapsulated Interest

To try to explore these questions, I begin by examining the thesis on trust developed by Russell Hardin. According to Hardin, trust in government is *not necessary* and is *impractical*. He challenges the view that "without normative commitments by citizens, government cannot gain obedience from citizens."[2] He further maintains that "any claim that government requires citizen trust is conspicuously false."[3]

Hardin cites in support of his thesis the old Greek understanding of the relationship between trust and government. According to the Greek tradition "The Anonymous Iamblichi," obedience to the law can be motivated by compelling incentives of self-interest even when there is no trust.[4] What is being emphasized is that the law itself is sufficient to guarantee social cooperation among self-directed individual agents motivated entirely by incentives of self-interest. It is believed that where there is lawfulness, there will also be trust, since even self-serving individuals will realize that it is in their interest to obey the law and to comply with contracts and agreements that in turn will lead to the common benefit of all. The basic argument runs like this: "The first result of lawfulness is trust, which greatly benefits all people and is among the greatest goods. The result of trust is that property has common benefits, so that even just a little property suffices, since it is circulated, whereas without this even a great amount does not suffice."[5]

Hardin's approach to trust in government follows the Greek tradition. His account is premised on the assumption that the primary motivation for compliance with the law and obedience to government is the maximization of personal interests and preferences. It emphasizes the instrumental or strategic reasons why one should trust another. The individual is conceived as the profit-making individual who occupies center place in current economic exchange theories. As Hardin observes: "We are concerned with trust and trustworthiness because they enable us to cooperate for mutual gain and benefit. Cooperation is the prior and central concern."[6] On this account, trust itself has no moral content. Trust is a fundamentally cognitive notion. To trust or to distrust others is to have some presumption of knowledge about them. Trust is a matter of mere rational expectations about the behavior of others. It is grounded in the truster's assessment of the trusted's interest in fulfilling the trust. My trust in you is typically encapsulated in your interest in fulfilling my trust. One should trust when it is in one's interest to do so by knowing the motivations of the trusted. This explains why Hardin defines trust as "encapsulated interest." From such a perspective, trust is always strategic and instrumental in nature and outcome.

Relationships of trust are no more than mere expectations grounded in the interests of the trusted to fulfill the trust. Hardin therefore argues that it is impossible to have a meaningful account of trust in government because most citizens do not have the information they need to decide to trust. Notwithstanding the general assumption that government requires public-spirited people to make it work well, in practice most political institutions are staffed by people whose motives are heavily, if not entirely, self-interested.

Hardin therefore argues that if public officials and their institutions are to be trusted, they must have interests in fulfilling trusts placed in them. The implication is that any account of trust in government will have to be based on the truster's assessment of the trusted's incentive to be trustworthy. We may depend on government. We may find government reassuringly predictable. It is impossible to have a meaningful account of trust in government because most citizens do not have the information they need to decide to trust. To gain our trust, government has to work in our interest.

To a large extent, Hardin's account of trust as "encapsulated interest" can be explained in terms of the logic of rational choice and its underlying assumption of self-interested individual agents who are mutually disinterested. His claim that trust in government is not necessary also underscores the paradoxical relationship between democracy and trust. Democracy is often regarded as being premised on the distrust of authority.[7] This is demonstrated in the way that most of the principles constitutive of the democratic order assume the institutionalization of distrust.

As Sztompka explains, under the principle of legitimacy, for example, democracy requires justification of all power. The principle of periodic elections and terms of office assumes distrust in the willingness of the rulers to surrender their power voluntarily and to subject their performance to periodic scrutiny. The principle of division of powers, checks, and balances clearly implies the suspicion that institutions will tend to expand, monopolize decisions, and abuse their powers. The same can be said of the principle of the rule of law, the principles of constitutionalism and judicial review, due process, and so forth. They are all intended to provide a kind of backup or insurance for those who would be ready to risk trust, a disincentive for those who would contemplate breaking trust, or a corrective for actual violations of trust, if they occur.[8] One of the significant outcomes of the institutionalization of distrust in modern democracy is "audit explosion," analyzed by Michael Power,[9] coupled with excessive accountability that in turn undermines autonomy.[10]

The important insight of Hardin's strategic approach to trust is his drawing attention to the fact that trust is risky, that trust has a cost, and that it is not always warranted. A similar point about the moral risk of trust was made by Annette Baier.[11] In drawing attention to the risks and vulnerabilities in trust, Hardin reminds us that trust is a function of the rational monitoring of risks by individuals. For Hardin, the decline of trust in political institutions is not a problem. Indeed, it may even be a sign that citizens are becoming increasingly sophisticated about the conditions of trust. He believes that the answer to the problem of the paradoxical relationship between trust and democracy is to focus on "merely institutionalizing government and the implementation of policies," which "should lead to greater stability of expectations, and hence to greater trust."[12] On Hardin's account, there is no need for value commitment to each other between the government and the people in a modern democracy. Neither is such a value commitment a necessary moral requirement to fulfill the purpose of government. Hardin's views on trust and democracy are opposed by those who argue that democratic practices require a measure of trust.[13] This is especially true in an age of the decentering state, risk society, and multiculturalism. The opponents maintain the view that a society that fosters robust relations of trust is probably a society that can afford fewer regulations and greater freedom, deal with more contingencies, tap the energy and ingenuity of its citizens, limit the inefficiencies of rule-based means of coordination, and provide a greater sense of existential satisfaction. Hardin's account of strategic trust as "encapsulated interest" is considered to be too impoverished an account of trust to be able to support the practice of democratic governance. It cannot provide the basis for a robust civil society and an active citizenry who are mutually committed instead of being mutually disinterested, and who have the capacities for taking collective actions to achieve self-government. Critics argue that there is something profoundly wrong with, naive about, and reified in Hardin's proposed "institutionalist" way out of the trust dilemma.[14] Their main concern is that democratic institutions cannot be a source of trust where institutions are driven by the purpose to institutionalize distrust in order to protect expectation and to support the practice of probabilistic expectation.

Moralistic Trust: Trust as a Moral Good

The second perspective on trust that I want to examine is the account developed by Eric Uslaner.[15] Instead of seeing trust as rational probabilistic expectation, Uslaner's account focuses on the normative meaning of trust. He argues that there are different types of trust and maintains that it is important to distinguish between *moralistic* trust and *strategic* trust. The former values trust as a moral good; the latter defines trust as a strategy in social and political life.

According to Uslaner, putting faith in strangers is moralistic trust; having confidence in people you know is strategic trust. The latter depends on our experiences, whereas the former does not.[16] Confidence in government is strategic trust. Trust in strangers, however, is largely based on an optimistic view of the world and a sense that we can make it better. Our personal experiences—including how well-off we are—have minimal effects on whether we trust strangers.

This sets moralistic trust apart from strategic trust, which is not primarily based on personal experiences. Moralistic trust is not about having faith in particular people or even groups of people. This is trust in people whom we don't know and who are likely to be different from ourselves. It is a general outlook on human nature and is an essential foundation of a civil society. Trusting strangers means accepting them into our "moral community." Strangers may look different from us, and they may have different ideologies or religions, but we believe that there is an underlying commonality of values. We have obligations to one another. We take others' moral claims seriously. Moralistic trust provides the rationale for getting involved with other people and working toward compromises. It connects us to people who are different from ourselves, not to people we already know or folks just like us. Trust is a moral resource. The capacity for developing such a moral resource is innate to human beings. Baier cites the case of infant trust and dependence to remind us that some degree of innate trust seems to be a necessary element in the experience of any surviving creature whose first nourishment comes from another.[17] This innate trust is important for an understanding of the very possibility of trust. It leads to a sense of connectedness with the world. Such a sense of connectedness stands at the heart of moralistic trust. It supports a sense of shared humanity. It provides the moral grounding for altruistic concern and commitment to take the interest and the well-being of the other person seriously as a fellow member of the same moral community.

Beyond the distinction between strategic and moralistic trust, Uslaner also proposes that there is a continuum from *particularized* trust to *generalized* trust. Generalized trust is the perception that most people are part of your moral community. Its foundation lies in moralistic trust. It is based on morals and our collective experiences. Generalized trust is a measure of the scope of our community. Particularized trust is the notion that we should only have faith in people like ourselves, and this restricts the size of our moral community.

Though not based on knowledge about each person, particularized trust has an informational foundation. Generalized trust, however, cannot be based on such knowledge.

The significant difference between particularized trust and generalized trust is that particularized trusters may help their friends, their family, and people like themselves, but generalized trusters will reach out to others. Generalized trust expresses the belief that others share your fundamental moral values and therefore should be treated as you would wish to be treated by them. The values they share may vary from person to person. What matters is a sense of connection with others because you see them as members of your community whose interests must be taken seriously. Moralistic trust is a commandment to treat people *as if* they were trustworthy.

Where does moralistic trust come from? Levi, Offe, and others have argued that a state, and particularly a democratic state, can produce trust in people.[18] Levi holds that "the trust-worthiness of the state influences its capacity to generate interpersonal trust."[19] But Uslaner challenges this view. He argues that "you may write any type of constitution that you wish, but statutes alone won't create generalized trust. Generalized trust does not depend upon contracts. Seeking to instill generalized trust from the top down (by reforming the legal system) misses the mark in most cases." If courts, or government more generally, can build up any type of trust at all, it is strategic trust. For similar reasons, you can't produce trust in people through institutional reforms.[20] Uslaner is of the view that democratic institutions cannot generate moralistic trust. At best, reform of our political institutions can only help to build up strategic trust. But he does not rule out that public institutions in the form of redistributive policies to achieve higher economic equality will lead to a higher level of trust in society.[21]

Uslaner also argues that there is no evidence that civic engagement creates trust. When we socialize with friends or attend group meetings of civic associations, we congregate with people like ourselves. We don't expand the scope of our moral community. We might learn to trust our fellow club members more, but we are merely reinforcing *particularized* trust (in our own kind) rather than *generalized* trust, the idea that "most people can be trusted."

Another major difficulty with particularized trust, in contrast to generalized trust, is that it may lead to situations where in-groups pursue policies that harm out-groups.[22] Or, it may lead to a civic dead end, where people participate only with their own kind, neither contributing to nor taking away from trust in the larger society. Moreover, voluntary associations do not necessarily work as producers of civic values and attitudes, such as generalized trust. Membership in voluntary organizations can involve participation in networks that produce distrust toward others, for example, criminal or racist organizations, as well as networks that potentially produce trust, such as parent-teacher associations or the Boy Scouts. This leads Uslaner to conclude that civic engagement often cannot and does not generate moralistic trust.

To the question "Where does our moralistic trust come from?" Uslaner's answer is that it mostly, though hardly exclusively, comes from our parents.[23] Our parents are our first moral teachers. We develop our dispositions to trust or distrust early in life.[24] By the time we get involved in either formal civic groups or even most of our adult socializing, our fundamental worldview has been largely set. He agrees with the research findings of the renowned psychologist Erik Erikson that "the amount of trust derived from earliest infantile experience [depends] on the quality of the maternal relationship. Mothers create a sense of trust in their children."[25] As human beings, we need trust to survive and to thrive. As Sissela Bok observes, "Whatever matters to human beings, trust is the atmosphere in which it thrives."[26] The maternal bonding creates a reciprocal trust relationship. It provides a bridge for reaching out to others and to the outside world. It generates faith in other people. It is in this sense that the maternal relationship is the source of moralistic trust.

But what is the relationship between horizontal trust in interpersonal relationships and vertical trust in government and political institutions? Why are some nations more trusting than others? On these two questions, Uslaner agrees with the conclusion drawn by Inglehart and his research team based on two World Values Surveys carried out during the periods from 1990 to 1991 and from 1995 to 1997 on more than sixty societies around the world and representing more than 70 percent of the world's population. Their analysis reveals that there is a strong correlation between economic development and interpersonal trust. The people of rich societies show higher levels of interpersonal trust than the publics of poorer ones.[27] This seems to confirm the thesis of Banfield, Putnam, and Fukuyama that interpersonal trust is essential to the cooperation with strangers that is a prerequisite for large-scale economic organizations.[28]

The World Values Survey data also show, in particular, that those with relatively high levels of education and those with postmaterialist values show high levels of interpersonal trust. This reflects the fact that these groups contain the relatively secure members of a society. But culture also matters. Although the people of richer societies are indeed more trusting than those of poorer societies, the cross-cultural differences also reflect the society's cultural heritage. Protestant- and Confucian-influenced societies consistently show higher levels of interpersonal trust than do historically Roman Catholic or Islamic societies.

Of the eighteen societies in which more than 35 percent of the public believes that most people can be trusted, thirteen are historically Protestant, three are Confucian-influenced, one is predominantly Hindu, and only one (Ireland) is predominantly Catholic. Of the ten lowest-ranking societies, *none* is historically Protestant or Confucian. These cross-cultural differences in interpersonal trust persist in multivariate analysis that controls for gross national product per capita. Furthermore, in both the 1990 and 1996 World Values Surveys (carried out by two different organizations), China shows about the same level of interpersonal trust as Japan. These findings seem to suggest that Fukuyama might be mistaken in characterizing China as a low-trust society.[29]

Uslaner is right to distinguish between moralistic trust and strategic trust in his account and to argue that moralistic trust is a moral good. He is also right to point out the difference between generalized trust and particularized trust and to remind us that particularized trust does not necessarily lead to generalized trust. Important also is his alternative account of the moral foundations of trust. He argues that the sources of trust lie in our culture and our disposition, not in our institutions. Unlike Hardin, he sees the human subject as someone whose behaviors are driven not only by the desire to seek and advance his or her individual self-interest, but more importantly perhaps also by a shared commitment and benevolence toward others. Of course, in real life, no one is completely individualistic, just as no one is entirely benevolent. Trust can also be unwarranted, misplaced, and misused; Baier has poignantly reminded us of the moral risks of trust.[30]

Uslaner's important insights show that trust in government and faith in other people are both essential to democratic life, although they have different roots. Confidence in government is based on your experiences. Trust in other people is not. Good government doesn't generate trust, but trust in others helps make governments work better. Trust is more the cause than the effect of good government, perhaps because trusting people are more likely to endorse strong standards of moral behavior. Trust enables groups and whole societies to accomplish various purposes. Among others, Kenneth Arrow implicitly and P. Dasguta explicitly[31] characterize trust as a public good. Sissela Bok also says that trust is a "social good ... and when it is destroyed, societies falter and collapse."[32]

This is echoed by Uslaner, who argues that trust matters: societies with higher levels of trust in turn have institutions that function better. Trust leads to better institutions—not the other way round. According to Uslaner, the roots of trust are not institutional. They lie in the deeper values societies hold—and in the distribution of resources. Societies do not become more trusting because they are more democratic. They become trusting because they distribute their resources more equally. Trust is neither a prerequisite for nor a consequence of democracy.

To the questions "Can the state produce trust?" and "Are certain types of state structures more likely to be associated with high levels of trust?" Uslaner's answer is that "democracy does not make people become more trusting."[33] He argues that state structures cannot produce trust, but state redistributive policies can. Trusting societies have bigger governments that redistribute wealth from the rich to the poor, spend more on education, and pursue policies that will stimulate economic growth. In particular, trusting societies are more likely to devote a higher share of their national wealth to transfer programs that assist the poor. Trusting societies are also more willing to reach out to outsiders: high trust goes hand in hand with open economies and fewer restrictions on trade. And trade promotes economic growth.

Uslaner also agrees that support for the rule of law depends on trust. He reminds us that trusters are also critical supporters of the legal system. They do not give blanket endorsements to upholding laws under all circumstances. Trusters believe that law must be based on justice. They are also more likely to say that protest demonstrations should be permitted. This reminds those in government that we must enforce just laws, and people must be permitted to protest statutes that they believe are wrong.

Uslaner's conclusion is that "governments that redistribute income, spend money on education, transfer wealth from rich to poor, have large public sectors, and maintain open economies do not generate trust. Trust seems to come first."[34] Economic equality is a strong determinant of trust, and trust leads to policies that create wealth and reduce inequalities. One can increase trust indirectly by pursuing policies that reduce economic inequality. But one can also adopt these policies without a trusting citizenry. Government cannot produce trust in people. People can provide government officials with the latitude to work on major social problems and thereby indirectly increase trust in government. Uslaner's account of trust brings much new insight to the debate on the moral foundations of trust and the relationship between trust on the one hand and democratic institutions and governance on the other hand. However, his account does not explain whether, and how, development from particularized trust to generalized trust is possible, or whether their relationship is one of mutual exclusion or mutual reinforcement. Although Uslaner has made an important distinction between strategic trust and moralistic trust, his account offers no philosophical analysis of the importance of moralistic trust for the purpose of government or for the ideal of democratic governance, except to point out that high-trust societies tend to achieve higher economic growth while making it more possible for governments to act in a trusting environment. Importantly, his account has left unanswered the following question: "What is the philosophical justification for claiming that trust is necessary for democratic governance?" Should we adopt the stand taken by Kongzi, who argues that trust is a fundamental virtue constituting the very foundation of government?

A Third Account of Trust: The Confucian Approach

A third perspective of trust I examine is the Confucian perspective. In Confucian moral and political philosophy, trust is also valued as a moral good rather than as a strategy in social life. It is a good because it is one of the foundational virtues of human relationships, including familial relationships in the private world, civic relationships in the social world, and political relationships in the public world. Trust is a familial virtue, a civic virtue, and a political virtue. It is believed that families, societies, and governments that are characterized by the virtue of trust can provide the best environment for the thriving of human beings, who are altruistic and relational by nature. In this regard, Confucian moral and political philosophy is grounded in a different understanding of the nature of the self, a different perspective on the relationship between self and others, and a different ideal for the purpose of government, which sets it apart from mainstream liberal theories of the self and of the relationship between the self and society that have become dominant in the West.

In the remaining part of this chapter, I elaborate on each of these key aspects of Confucian moral and political philosophy to show how they might offer insights to help us get out of the paradox of trust by putting trust back into democratic governance. I want to argue that the Confucian account of trust grounded in its philosophy of *ren* 仁 can provide useful intellectual resources to further enrich the account developed by Uslaner.

Confucian Trust: Trust as Moral Virtue

The cardinal concept in Confucian philosophy is the concept of *ren*. *Ren* can be translated as altruistic or benevolent regard for others. It is the defining characteristic of human beings in Confucian philosophy. It grounds an understanding of human nature that is essentially altruistic rather than egoistic in character. A person who is not *ren* cannot be called a human being. The realization of *ren* is the passage to true humanity. The concept appears more than one hundred times in the *Analects* (*Lunyu*). In his reply to one of his disciples, Kongzi says, "*Ren* is to love people" (*Analects* 12.22). It is love in the notion of caring and respecting.

On a deeper level of analysis, the concept of *ren* has two senses. As a particular virtue, it refers to the virtue of benevolence and altruistic concern for others. As a general virtue, *ren* stands for perfect virtue, goodness, the *Dao*, or morality itself. *Ren* as perfect virtue provides the overarching, unifying ethical framework in Confucian ethics, encompassing all the other particular virtues, such as benevolence, propriety, courage, filial piety, and loyalty, and so it is the virtue of virtues.

According to Mengzi (Mencius; 391–308 BCE), the source of this first sense of *ren* can be traced to the natural heart that is sensitive to the sufferings of others. He wrote, "The reason why I say all men have a sense of compassion is that, even today, if one chances to see a little child about to fall into a well one will be shocked and moved to compassion, neither because he wants to make friends with the child's parents, nor because he hates to hear the cry of the child.... The sense of compassion is the beginning of benevolence" (*Mengzi* 2A6).[35]

Compassion is important because it signifies attentiveness to and engagement with others. It is the sprout or potential of *ren*. It enables us to know about others and to be other-directed. The development of one's heart of compassion is the route to becoming a person of humaneness, or *ren*, which is the passage to humanity. The way to achieve this ideal is through a process of constant self-cultivation and moral transformation to realize our moral nature.

Our potential to develop into moral persons constitutes the source of our natural nobility and dignity. It is a natural endowment that all human beings share. It constitutes the basis of our equal moral worth. Mengzi further distinguishes between "natural nobility" and "human nobility" in this way:

> There is the nobility of Heaven [or natural nobility (*tianjue* 天爵)] and the nobility of man [*renjue* 人爵]. Humaneness, rightness, loyalty, and truthfulness—and *taking pleasure in doing good, without growing weary of it*—this is the nobility of the Heavens. The ranks of duke, minister, or high official—this is the nobility of man. (*Mengzi* 6A16; my emphasis)

From the Confucian perspective, human beings are understood as mutually interested in one another rather than mutually disinterested. They are connected through a relational perspective grounded in a common humanity. It is this shared humanity, binding us to one another, that makes moralistic trust possible. Moralistic trust is the foundational virtue in the state-society relationship, family relationship, and civic relationship. It is essential to our human thriving.

Confucian Trust: Trust as Familial Virtue

Confucian *ren* philosophy argues that as human beings, we can act morally, beyond self-centered or benefit-seeking motives. The nobility of our human nature lies in our potential to develop general love for others.

Ren is the basis of our shared humanity that binds us to one another. It is the highest moral principle that pervades all human relationships, including state-society relationships, family relationships, and civic relationships. On this understanding, human beings are mutually interested in one another rather than mutually disinterested.

The notion of general love, however, does not mean universal love. It is not a requirement to love everyone equally or a demand to assume the same caring responsibility for all people at all times. The requirement of general love is to be actively concerned about the well-being of others *in addition to one's own*.

Moreover, the notion of "general love" means more than the mere provision of benefits. What is being emphasized is an underlying attitude of respect and caring for the humanity in the other person. To treat someone with *ren*, it is not enough merely to satisfy his or her basic needs. There must also be love and respect for the other person, which Mengzi puts in this way: "To feed a person without love is to treat him as a pig; to love him without respect is to keep him as a domestic animal" (*Mengzi* 7A37).

Both Kongzi and Mengzi advocate the practice of *ren*'s starting within the family: "Filial piety and brotherly respect are the root of benevolence" (*Analects* 1.2); "It is benevolence to love one's parents" (*Mengzi* 7A15). Family ethics is central to Confucianism, and this makes some scholars such as Bertrand Russell uphold the mistaken view that filial piety is the weakest point of Confucian ethics because it prevents the growth of public spirit.[36] Confucianism actually advocates people's extending the practice of *ren* from within the family to other people. Mengzi is well known for this principle of "care by extension" (推己及人, *tui ji ji ren*). Under the principle of extension, a benevolent person should "extend his love from those dear to him to those he does not love" (*Mengzi* 7B1). By the same principle, we should extend respect and caring for our own family members to those who are unrelated to us. The ideal is expressed by Mengzi in this way: "Treat the aged of your own family in a manner befitting their venerable age and extend this treatment to the aged of other families; treat your own young in a manner befitting their tender age and extend this to the young of other families, and you can roll the Empire on your palm" (*Mengzi* 1A7).

Ren is a radiating process of love that starts naturally from within one's family and extends to more remote social relationships, to include friends, members of the society, and strangers in general. Kongzi himself had said that he had three goals in life: respect for the old, care for the young, and trust between friends (*Analects* 5.26).

The family is the starting point for developing the capacity for relationships of mutual trust, caring, and respect, but the final destination is the extension of trust, caring, and respect to the generalized other in the wider society.

Confucian Trust: Trust as Civic Virtue

From the Confucian perspective, human society and civic life are possible because of human beings' capacity for mutual trust, caring, and respect. John Cooper has also pointed out that civic relations involve mutual goodwill, trust, and well-wishing.[37] The mutual interest that fellow citizens have in one another's character and development is part of that goodwill and well-wishing. It provides the motivation for taking common action to achieve the common good. Civic friends have and do things in common, just like members in a family. From the Confucian *ren* perspective, moralistic trust as a civic virtue can be viewed as an extension to the whole community of the kinds of psychological bonds that tie together a family and that make possible the participation by each member in the good of the others.

Moralistic trust is essential to civic relations and political life because they are different from mere commercial relations or mere associations for economic cooperation. In commercial relations, people are bound by treaties for mutual commerce, and they are only concerned that no one covered by the trade and business agreements be unjust. But they do not concern themselves about what kind of people the others ought to be. They are only concerned that they do nothing unjust to one another. By contrast, in civic relations, people living together in a community are bound by a common enterprise that goes beyond not wanting to be cheated or treated unjustly in commerce or in other activities. More importantly, they also care about what kind of people their fellow citizens are and what kind of community they want for themselves. This creates a mutual concern of each citizen for each other citizen, whether they know one another personally and indeed whether they have had any direct and personal dealings with one another whatsoever. This mutual concern of fellow citizens for one another's good character and development is a crucially important feature of civic life. It is also similar to what Aristotle conceives as *civic friendship*.[38]

In Confucian *ren* philosophy, there are two basic principles for developing this kind of mutual concern and bonding among fellow human beings in a community: the principle of *zhong* 忠 (sincerity) and the principle of *shu* 恕 (empathy). *Shu* is expressed by Kongzi in the *Analects* as follows: "Do not do unto others what you do not want others to do unto you" (15.28). It implies taking a relational perspective and recognizing a reciprocal relationship between oneself and others. It enlarges our moral sensibility and enables us to develop an empathetic point of view of the needs and interests of others.

Zhong is expressed as follows: "Help others to be established the way you wish to be established, and help others to advance the way you wish to advance yourself" (*Analects* 15:28). It involves assuming a positive virtue of active concern about the welfare of others *in addition to one's own*. *Zhong* and *shu* together constitute the rule of reciprocity in Confucianism.

The Confucian rule of reciprocity emphasizes a relational point of view of human needs and interests that is not merely self-directed, but is also other-directed. The moral basis of such a notion of reciprocity is neither a social contract nor based on calculations for mutual gain and benefit. Reciprocity in the Confucian moral tradition is based on the notion of equal humanity. It implies empathy and altruistic concern for others, rather than quid pro quo or "fair exchange." It is not the same kind of reciprocal relationship embedded in Hardin's notion of "encapsulated interest" based on exchange theories. Neither is it a moral duty based on some kind of Kantian categorical imperative. It is a commitment to generalized altruism that is the foundation of moralistic trust—the reason for taking others' well-being and moral claims seriously.

Moralistic trust as a civic virtue is constituted by this kind of generalized altruism and reciprocity. It creates the specific sort of connectedness that grounds the interest in and concern by each citizen for the well-being of his or her fellow citizen. It provides the motivation for common action for the common good in the community. In short, it is what makes civic life possible and sustainable.

Confucian Trust: Trust as Political Virtue

Confucian political philosophy understands the purpose of government and the goal of political life to be securing the best conditions for the development of the altruistic character of human beings. This requires setting exemplary models and designing public institutions by those in government to build trust, to uphold the moral ideal of *ren*, and to support the common good of the citizens.

An important implication is that caring for all others is not to be only a personal excellence to be nurtured in individuals alone; it is also to be institutionalized. The demand for institutionalization was expressed explicitly by Xunzi (298–234 BCE), in the "Wangzhi" ("Regulations of a king") chapter in this way:

> In the case of the Five incapacitated groups, the government should gather them together, look after them, and give them whatever work they are able to do. Employ them, provide them with food and clothing, and take care to see that none are left out.... Look after widows and orphans, and assist the poor.[39]

As Henry Rosemont observes, here Xunzi is clearly advocating the establishment of basic welfare institutions in ancient China that would be the modern Western functional equivalent of job training programs, Aid to Families with Dependent Children, welfare, and Medicare for the needy. But what is all the more impressive about this advocacy is that "it requires the state to provide many goods and services to groups of people who cannot possibly pose a threat to that state's power: Machiavellian it is not."[40]

From the Confucian perspective, the purpose of government is the welfare of the people. Such a view is in sharp contrast to Machiavelli's doctrine of government in the West. The welfare of the people stands at the heart of the Confucian political doctrine of *renzheng* 仁政 (benevolent government). According to this doctrine, "The people are the most important; the goods of the land and grain is the next; the ruler is of the least importance" (*Mengzi* 7B14).

To practice the governance of *ren* (benevolence) is to look after the well-being of the common people. If a ruler can take good care of the people, they will trust him and he can then maintain his political legitimacy; so, being caring is the way of becoming a wise ruler. Kongzi himself reminded those in government: "In guiding a state of a thousand chariots, approach your duties with reverence and be trustworthy in what you say; avoid excesses in expenditure and love your fellow men; employ the labor of the common people only in the right seasons" (*Analects* 1.5).[41]

As a political virtue under the Confucian moral ideal of *ren*, trust is grounded in the duty of government agents to serve the interests of citizens. Trust in government is important because Kongzi recognized that it is the moral duty of those who are in government to be committed to the welfare of the people, and they should not inflict hardships on the people. To a certain extent, this interpretation is similar to the view of Locke, who had also argued that the justification of trust lies in those agents "whom society hath set over it self, with this express or tacit Trust, That it shall be imployed for their good, and the preservation of their Property."[42]

The business of government is not only to protect survival and security; it also involves the important duty of maintaining the material conditions of political and economic security to enable the practice of trust and its flourishing among the populace. It is therefore not surprising that on numerous occasions, both Kongzi and Mengzi emphasized the importance of the duty of government to provide for food and to provide security from war, in short, to provide for the basic needs and well-being that are the necessary conditions for the general populace to practice trust, to honor obligations, and to uphold the law. The Confucian understanding of the conditions of trust is in this sense different from those defined earlier by Hardin. As Mengzi observed, "a wise ruler will decide on such a plan for the people's means of support as to make sure that they can support their parents as well as their wives and children, and that they have enough food in good years, and are saved from starvation in bad" (*Mengzi* 1A16). He firmly believed,

> that is the way of the common people. Those with constant means of support will have constant hearts, while those without constant means will not have constant hearts. Lacking constant hearts, they will go astray and get into excesses, stopping at nothing. To punish them after they have fallen foul of the law is to set a trap for the people. (*Mengzi* 3A3)

But benevolent government requires more than the mere provision for needs and the lending of help to the people; benevolent government also demands the practice of equitable distribution of resources and the protection of interests, as Mengzi further observed:

> Benevolent government must begin with land demarcation. When boundaries are not properly drawn, the division of land according

to the well-field system and the yield of grain used for paying officials cannot be equitable.... Once the boundaries are correctly fixed, there will be no difficulty in settling the distribution of land and the determination of emolument. (*Mengzi* 3A3)

Protecting the welfare of the people is important; however, this is not the final goal of government. Caring in Confucian ethics does not only refer to the provision of benefits and service; the final goal of government is aiding the people to develop their moral character and to achieve their full humanity. This explains the following observation made by Mengzi:

According to the way of man, if they are well-fed, warmly clothed, and comfortably lodged but without education, they will become almost like animals. The Sage emperor Shun worried about it and he appointed Xie to be minister of education and teach people human relations.... Emperor Yao said, "Encourage them, lead them on rectify them, straighten them, help them, aid them, so that they discover for themselves [their moral nature], and in addition, stimulate them and confer kindness on them." (*Mengzi* 3A:4)

In order for trust to develop and to be sustainable, certain conditions have to obtain to make the practice of honesty, lawfulness, and constancy a possibility among the common people. To make these conditions obtained for the development of trust as a civic virtue among the populace is the duty of those in government when they fulfill their duties of care and honor the political virtue of trust by instituting fair laws, clear rules, and the practice of humane government.

Moreover, the notion of "benevolent government" means more than the mere provision of benefits. What is being emphasized is an underlying attitude of respect and caring for others. To treat someone with *ren*, it is not enough merely to satisfy his or her basic needs. There must also be love and respect for the other person. Mengzi further explained:

If your Majesty wants to run a benevolent government, why not turn to what is of fundamental importance? Let mulberry trees be planted about each homestead to five *mu* of land, and those who are fifty will have floss silk garments to wear. Let fowls, pigs and dogs be raised without neglecting their breeding season, and those who are seventy will have meat to eat. Let farm work be done without interference in a hundred *mu* of land, and a family of eight mouths will not go hungry. Let careful attention be paid to education in local schools, where the significance of filial and fraternal duties is stressed repeatedly and grey haired people will not be carrying loads on the roads. In a state where old people are clothed in floss silk garments and have meat to eat, and the masses do not suffer from hunger and cold, what prince can fail to unify the whole world? (*Mengzi* 1.7)

A good ruler ensures that the people do not miss their farming seasons, have good harvests in good years, and are prepared for bad years. In contrast, a despotic ruler is someone who does not care about the well-being of his people, and Mengzi believed that "there is a duty not just to oppose but also to *depose* any unjust ruler."[43]

Can Generalized Trust and Particularized Trust Be Reconciled?

Confucian *ren* philosophy argues that as human beings, we can act morally, beyond self-centered or benefit-seeking motives. *Ren* is the basis of our shared humanity that binds us to one another. It is the highest moral principle that pervades all human relationships, including state-society relationships, family relationships, and civic relationships. The promotion of private interest is not conceived to be necessarily in competition or in conflict with supporting the common good, from the Confucian perspective.

Drawing on the moral principle of extension, Mengzi more than two thousand years ago articulated a vision of how institutions can harmonize the relationship between one's private interest and the collective's common good, when he put forward a proposal for the *jingtian* 井田 system of land allocation, commonly translated as the "well-field" system. It is a system that divides a piece of land into nine plots. When a piece of land is divided in this way, it looks like the Chinese character *jing* 井 (well):

> If those who own land within each *jing* befriend one another both at home and abroad, help each other to keep watch, and succor each other in illness, they will live in love and harmony. A *jing* is a piece of land measure one *li* square, and each *jing* consists of 900 *mu*. Of these the central plot of 100 *mu* belongs to the state, while the other eight plots of 100 *mu* each are held by eight families who share the duty of caring for the plot owned by the

state. Only when they have done this duty dare they turn to their own affairs. (*Mengzi* 3A3)

Mengzi's well-field system tells a story of supporting the common good while cultivating one's private interest, of extension from particularized care to generalized care. The reconciliation has expressive, practical, and experiential meaning. It instantiates a much broader symbolic meaning of a nonindividualistic self-understanding that is relational in its perspective and communal in its orientation, being committed to both cultivating one's own private interests and to the broader concerns of sustaining the common good beyond one's immediate, private interest. It generates altruism for the nurturance of trust and reciprocity in the community at the same time as it generates food and sustenance for the satisfaction of human needs and interests.

Being able to see oneself as part of a shared humanity, being able to develop a relational view of the relationship between the self and others, and being able to extend one's caring from those who are naturally related to oneself to those who are unrelated or are strangers through taking action to support the common good, these are the key insights of a Confucian *ren*-based moral philosophy. They provide the moral commitments to establish well-designed institutions for both the promotion of the common good and the enhancement of private interests and well-being that stand at the heart of any account of good governance.

Are Moralistic Trust and Strategic Trust Mutually Exclusive in Democratic Governance?

On the basis of Hardin's analysis, we seem to have no choice but to accept that high degrees of insurmountable distrust and suspicion are the necessary moral condition within a democracy. Trust is not essential to democracy because moralistic trust is not attainable within such a model of democracy. What is achievable is a kind of liberal procedural democracy founded on self-directed (often irresponsive and irresponsible) individualism. The price is a deficit in civic virtues because of difficulty in generating commitment to any shared vision of the common good.

I would, however, like to suggest that if democracy is to be stable, sustainable, and well-functioning, it needs a strong bellystock of civic virtues to sustain a more expansive view of democracy, which emphasizes civic responsibility as much as the rights of the individual. I also suggest that a reconstructed

Confucian perspective can offer us some of the intellectual resources for reenvisioning trust within democracy. Although Uslaner does emphasize the moral foundation of trust, and that the root of trust lies in our culture and dispositions, he offers no suggestions on how such a culture or dispositions are to be cultivated or sustained.

As pointed out earlier, the Confucian account of trust is grounded in the moral ideal of *ren*. One first learns benevolence, or *ren*, in the family. But *ren* is not only about developing particularized care or particularized trust. The highest ideal of *ren* requires the extension of care, respect, and trust to those who are outside the family to reach the "generalized" other, to include those who are distant, unrelated, or strangers.

It is in this sense that the state is the family writ large in the Confucian ideal of government, whereby everybody is related by concern or *ren* (benevolence) through the moral principle of extension, which penetrates the boundary between particularized trust and generalized trust, bridging at the same time the private world and the public world in which the human being thrives.

Such an understanding of the relationship between public and private virtues in Confucian ethics can provide a theoretical link between particularized trust and generalized trust through the principle of "extension of care." Confucian emphasis on the inner life of the moral agent as the basis of morality can also lend support to the claim that the sources of moralistic trust lie in our culture and disposition. In this way, it can provide a healthy counterbalance to the overreliance on institutions and the overemphasis on distrust of all authority, which are major causes for the erosion of a culture of trust in democracy. It draws attention to the importance of cultivation of virtues for the building of trust and for sustaining a culture of trust instead of adopting a deceptively simple and easy way out of the structural scarcity of trust. Governments should not abandon trust as the principle of governance, and they also have the positive duty to create the material conditions and institutional arrangements necessary for the people to be able to honor trust and to fulfill their commitments of care to one another.

A Reconstructed Confucian Model of Trust within Democracy?

What is clear from the Confucian perspective is that the way out of the dilemma of trust in democracy will have to be negotiated through embracing a different perspective on the fundamental nature of the human agent, a different approach to ground the moral foundation of trust, and a different model of civil society underpinned by strong civic virtues. Kongzi's ethical insights can help to build a robust civil society modeled on the familial principles of care, respect, and trust, the same set of principles we learn in the family. It can provide the moral resources for creating an active citizenry in an age when more and more nations and countries in the world, whether liberal or illiberal, are surrendering themselves to the seduction of the market and the merciless forces of globalized capital. We need a civil society underpinned by strong civic virtues where citizens are committed to the common good and to protecting the vulnerable as much as they are committed to counting their rights and maximizing their individual interests.

There is certainly no notion of autonomy in the sense of self-determination and self-government in the Confucian moral and political tradition. But there is in Confucian philosophy a strong belief that human beings have the potential and obligation to develop into autonomous agents capable of making critical moral judgments. Such a view of common humanity is premised on Mengzi's theory that all human beings are born with the four sprouts, or potentials, for the four basic virtues of benevolence, righteousness, propriety, and wisdom. And it is this belief that provides Chinese people with their own Chinese sources for the moral conviction that it is everyone's duty to dissent when government is wrong. Although loyalty is an important value in the Confucian moral system, numerous stories of "loyal disobedience" have been told in Chinese history. In fact it is well accepted that a loyal official is expected to follow only the mandate of heaven, or *Dao*, that is, morality, and to resist and correct any policy or decision considered to be in conflict with it, whatever the personal cost. It is a duty of ministers to remonstrate with sovereigns who are doing wrong. Long before Rousseau, Mengzi, without any backing of the law, promoted the notion of *minyi* (民意 popular will), which was believed to be able to check a failing and unjust rule and, whenever necessary, to mobilize the populace to remove it (4A10, 5A5).

It is therefore not surprising that in Confucian political philosophy, although trust is an important political virtue, it is not the ultimate value in political life. As Mengzi pointed out, "A great man need not keep his word nor does he necessarily see his action through to the end. He aims only at what is *yi* 義 [right]" (*Mengzi* 4B11). Political pacts and agreements that are not right command no moral force. Only "when agreements are made according to what is right, [can] what is spoken . . . be made good" (*Analects* 1.13). What is being clearly asserted is that the foundation of trust is morality. Laws, contracts, agreements, and promises that do not comply with the standard of morality do not have binding force, including any pact made between rulers and the ruled. The ultimate standard of morality and the moral imperative to follow what is right in all human relationships offer important safeguards against abuse of trust and abuse by trust in democracy.

When Kongzi replied to his disciple that no government can stand when trust is lost, he was referring to moralistic trust as a political virtue. The loss of trust in this sense implies the loss of commitment to a set of common ideals, loss of a common bond, which connects the individual with the collective, and loss of a common morality, which harmonizes the private good with the common good. Should there be a deficit in weapons, the state may survive, even if there is a deficit in food, the state is still likely to survive, but when there is a deficit in the political virtue of moralistic trust, the state will become ungovernable and collapse.

In a country like China, in particular, where such huge disparities exist between the rich and the poor, between the cities and the villages, we need a robust sense of citizen responsibility that is not just based upon noninterference, mutual tolerance, and maximization of preferences. We need the mutual engagement and mutual concern emphasized in the Confucian vision of trust to remind us of our shared fate and mutual responsibility at all levels of our human connectedness, at both the local level and the global level.

Notes

1. See, for example, R. D. Putnam, "Bowling Alone: America's Declining Social Capital," *Journal of Democracy* 6 (1995): 65–78.
2. R. Hardin, "Trust in Government," *Trust and Governance*, eds. V. Braithwaite and M. Levi (New York: Russell Sage Foundation, 1998), 10.
3. Ibid.
4. "The Anonymous Iamblichi," in *Early Greek Political Thought from Homer to the Sophists*, translated and edited by M. Gagarin and P. Woodruff (Cambridge: Cambridge University Press, 1995).
5. R. Hardin, "Trust in Government," in *Trust and Governance*, eds. V. Braithwaite and M. Levi (New York: Russell Sage Foundation, 1998), 9.
6. R. Hardin, *Trust and Trustworthiness* (New York: Russell Sage Foundation, 2002), 173.
7. P. Sztompka, *Trust: A Sociological Theory* (Cambridge: Cambridge University Press, 1991).
8. Ibid.
9. M. Power, *The Audit Explosion* (London: Demos, 1994).
10. O. O'Neil, *Autonomy and Trust in Bioethics* (Cambridge: Cambridge University Press, 2002).

11. A. Baier, *Postures of the Mind: Essays on Mind and Morals* (Minneapolis: University of Minnesota Press, 1985).

12. R. Hardin, "Trusting Persons, Trusting Institutions," in *The Strategy of Choice*, ed. R. J. Zeckhauser (Cambridge, MA: MIT Press, 1991), 204.

13. See, for example, C. Offe, "How Can We Trust Our Fellow Citizens?" in *Democracy and Trust*, ed. M. Warren (Cambridge: Cambridge University Press, 1999).

14. Ibid., 65.

15. E. M. Uslaner, *The Moral Foundations of Trust* (Cambridge: Cambridge University Press, 2002).

16. Ibid., 4.

17. A. Baier, "Trust and Anti-Trust," *Ethics* 96 (1986): 242.

18. M. Levi, "A State of Trust," in *Trust and Governance*, eds. M. Levi and V. Braithwaite (New York: Russell Sage Foundation, 1998); Offe, "How Can We Trust Our Fellow Citizens?"; A. Pagden, "The Destruction of Trust and Its Economic Consequences in the Case of Eighteenth-Century Naples," in *Trust*, ed. D. Gambetta (Oxford: Basil Blackwell, 1988), 139; B. Misztal, *Trust in Modern Societies* (Cambridge: Polity Press, 1996), 198; J. L. Cohen, "American Civil Society Talk," College Park, MD: National Commission on Civic Renewal, Working Paper no. 6, 1997, 19–20.

19. Levi, "A State of Trust," 87.

20. Uslaner, *The Moral Foundations of Trust*, 47.

21. E. M. Uslaner, "Trust, Democracy, and Governance: Can Government Policies Influence Generalized Trust?" in *Generating Social Capital: Civil Society and Institutions in Comparative Perspective*, eds. M. Hooghe and D. Stolle (New York: Palgrave Macmillan, 2003), 171–72.

22. Baier, "Trust and Anti-Trust," 31–32; Levi, "A State of Trust."

23. Uslaner, *The Moral Foundations of Trust*, 26.

24. E. Erikson, *Identity: Youth and Crisis*, (New York, W.W. Norton, 1968), 103.

25. E. Erikson, *Childhood and Society*, second edition (New York: W.W. Norton, 1963), 249.

26. S. Bok, *Lying: Moral Choice in Public and Private Life* (New York: Pantheon, 1978), 31.

27. R. Inglehart, M. Basznez, and A. Moreno, *Human Values and Beliefs: A Cross-Cultural Sourcebook* (Ann Arbor: University of Michigan Press, 1998).

28. E. Banfield, *The Moral Basis of a Backward Society* (New York: Free Press, 1958); R. D. Putnam, *Making Democracy Work: Civic Traditions in Modern Italy* (Princeton, NJ: Princeton University Press, 1993); F. Fukuyama, *Trust: The Social Virtues and the Creation of Prosperity* (New York: Free Press, 1995).

29. Fukuyama, *Trust*.

30. Baier, "Trust and Anti-Trust."

31. K. Arrow, *The Limits of Organization* (New York: Norton, 1974), 23; P. Dasgupta, "Trust as a Commodity," in *Trust: Making and Breaking of Cooperative Relations*, ed. D. Gambetta (Oxford: Basil Blackwell, 1988), 64.

32. Bok, *Lying*, 28.
33. Uslaner, "Trust, Democracy, and Governance," 170.
34. Ibid., 185.
35. *Mengzi* translations are from D. C. Lau, trans., *Mencius* (London: Penguin, 1970), unless otherwise noted. On regicide, see 1B8; on the moral hierarchy, 7A14.
36. B. Russell, *The Problem of China* (London: Allen & Unwin, 1922).
37. J. M. Cooper, "Political Animals and Civic Friendship," in *Friendship: A Philosophical Reader*, ed. N. K. Badhwar (London: Cornell University Press, 1993).
38. *Aristotle*, D. Ross (London: Methuen, 1949).
39. Burton Watson, trans., *Hsun Tzu: Basic Writings* (New York: Columbia University Press, 1963), 34–37.
40. H. Rosemont Jr., "Whose Democracy? Which Rights? A Confucian Critique of Modern Western Liberalism," in *Confucian Ethics: A Comparative Study of Self, Autonomy, and Community*, eds. K. L. Shun and D. B. Wong (Cambridge: Cambridge University Press, 2004), 61.
41. Translated by D. C. Lau, *Analects* (Hong Kong: Chinese University Press, 1992).
42. J. Locke, *Two Treatises of Government*, ed. Peter Laslett (1690; Cambridge: Cambridge University Press, 1988), 381.
43. D. Hall and R. Ames, *The Democracy of the Dead: Dewey, Confucius, and the Hope for Democracy in China* (Chicago: Open Court, 1999), 171.

Chapter 6

A Defense of *Ren*-Based Interpretation of Early Confucian Ethics

Shirong Luo

Virtue ethics, especially that of the Aristotelian strain, has been described as a type of "agent-centered" in contrast to "act-centered" moral theory. But as contemporary virtue ethics matures and differentiates, a finer distinction becomes necessary.[1] According to Michael Slote, virtue ethical approaches are to be divided into three categories: agent-focused, agent-prior, and agent-based. All virtue ethical theories are at least agent-focused, meaning that one's ethical theory gives pride of place and emphasizes the centrality of the actions of virtuous individuals. In addition to being agent-focused, agent-prior theories insist that the moral worth of actions depends on and derives from the agent's character traits. All agent-based theories are agent-prior, but the difference is that the former derive the value of good actions directly and exclusively from admirable qualities internal to the agent.[2]

Slote argues that among these three alternatives, only agent-based theories are pure and freestanding forms of virtue ethics because they base ethical assessment entirely on the admirableness or reprehensibility of the inner qualities of the agent. Slote's own theory is agent-based because it elects the virtue of empathic caring as the basis of moral evaluation. He maintains that the goodness of caring is intuitively clear, and therefore there is no need for it to be further explicated in terms of other value concepts. By contrast, Aristotelian ethics, David Hume's moral sentimentalism, and Nel Noddings's ethics of caring can only be characterized as "agent-prior" because the value of virtue has to be further explained by the desirability of *eudaimonia*, utility, or the caring relationship—notwithstanding the fact that they all place the ethical assessment of the agent prior to the evaluation of his or her action.

Anyone who is adequately conversant with the *Analects* cannot help but be impressed by the centrality of *ren* 仁 in Kongzi's ethical teachings.[3] Kongzi declares that once we set our hearts on *ren*, we will be free from immorality (*Analects* 4.4). He also maintains that a person who is fond of *ren* cannot be surpassed (4.6). Since *ren* is rendered into English as "caring," "benevolence," "humanity," or "compassion," it is natural to see the connection between Kongzi's ethics and the agent-based virtue theory advocated by Slote.

We live in an increasingly connected world in which a general concern for human beings has become a central issue for contemporary moral philosophy. I believe that early Confucian ethics has ample resources to address such concern. A recasting of Kongzi's moral teachings in agent-based virtue ethics terms enables us to make cogent arguments for its relevance to many issues within as well as beyond the purview of ethics. For early Confucians, a general concern for humanity is not paying lip service or offering help to the needy in a perfunctory manner. On the contrary, it should be a manifestation of one's inner moral force *de* 德 (virtue).[4] Western virtue ethics tends to focus more on the issues of what it means to be virtuous and how we can best justify our concerns for others, but less on how we should acquire virtue, in other words, the issue of moral self-cultivation. It is in this area that the strength of early Confucian ethics is manifest. If virtue is the sole basis of ethical judgment in Confucian morality, then early Confucians' preoccupation with moral self-cultivation makes a great deal of sense. Kongzi's teachings, however, like those of many other great thinkers, leave room for more than one interpretation. There is resistance in various forms to recasting early Confucian ethics in agent-based terms. For instance, among contemporary commentators there has been a debate about whether the notion of ritual (*li* 禮) in early Confucian ethics is more basic than *ren*.[5] The notion of way (*dao* 道) also seems to be a strong candidate to compete with *ren*.[6] As I indicate below, there are serious difficulties with reading early Confucian ethics as based in ritual or the *dao*. My main focus, however, is on presenting arguments against a more formidable challenge by D. C. Lau who claims that no moral virtue can be the sole basis of ethics. Lau thinks that Confucian ethics rests ultimately on propriety (*yi* 義) rather than *ren*.[7] This view is classified as *yi*-based interpretation in my discussion.

The phrase "early Confucian ethics" can be understood in both a broad and a narrow sense. In the narrow sense, it refers to the ethical teachings of Kongzi (551–479 BCE), who is commonly regarded as the founder of Confucianism; in the broad sense, it means the moral views held by Kongzi as well as his two successors, Mengzi (385–304 BCE) and Xunzi (310–219 BCE). In this chapter, I use the phrase "early Confucian ethics" primarily in the narrow sense.

It should also be pointed out that there is a distinction between agent-basing and *ren*-basing. Agent-basing requires that the moral status of the agent's character traits be the basis of ethical assessment, but the notion of agent-basing in itself does not specify any particular inner quality as the ultimate source of moral value. It is possible therefore for the virtue of justice or some other virtue to be identified as most fundamental. The notion of *ren*-basing, however, concentrates on a specific moral quality, namely the virtue of *ren*. In light of this distinction, it may be said that *ren*-basing is a special form of agent-basing, but agent-basing is not necessarily *ren*-basing. Consequently, the specific thesis that I defend is that early Confucian ethics is *ren*-based.

Most of Kongzi's remarks support the reading that his moral system is *ren*-based, although a few of his remarks allow room for different interpretations.[8] In general, Kongzi's extremely terse and aphoristic style makes the task of interpretation difficult. A good case, nevertheless, can still be made in favor of the thesis that Kongzi is a *ren*-baser. A certain level of ambiguity in his sayings should come as no surprise because he was not so much preoccupied with theory construction as with political and social activism: he attempted to put his ethical and political ideas into practice; he taught students that they could implement those ideas if they become government officials. My task is to identify the overall thrust of his ethics based on the majority of the teachings attributed to him rather than on one or two isolated remarks.

A common complaint against virtue ethics is that it is incomplete.[9] As I indicated earlier, Lau claims that no moral theory can be solely based on moral virtue and early Confucian ethics is no exception. Lau identifies *yi* rather than *ren* as the ultimate basis of early Confucian morality. For Lau, *yi* as the ultimate moral standard is not a virtue, but rather the relationship between an action and the circumstances under which the action is performed or omitted. Thus, the disagreement between his *yi*-based interpretation and my *ren*-based reading is not between two agent-based accounts. My main task in this chapter is to defend an agent-based reading of early Confucian ethics against Lau's nonagent-based account. However, in addition to Lau's *yi*-based interpretation, there are other nonagent-based views concerning early Confucian ethics such as *dao*-basing and *li*-basing. I begin by first disposing of them because they, like Lau's, pose a challenge to *ren*-basing by relegating *ren* to a less fundamental role in ethical assessment.

Dao-Basing

The *dao* is a strong contender for the ultimate basis of classical Confucian morality because of its crucial importance as a Confucian concept. Its significance for

Kongzi is political and ethical rather than metaphysical or cosmological, because he refuses to speak of transcendental entities.[10] Although in general the meaning, connotation, and nuance of the term *dao* may vary with context, in some passages the use of the term gives the impression that the speaker is referring to a state of affairs on the basis of which the "gentleman" (*junzi* 君子) makes crucially important decisions such as whether he should participate in politics. Kongzi, for example, advises his disciples to seek governmental appointments when the *dao* prevails in the state (*bangyoudao* 邦有道). And he advises against being employed by the government when the *dao* does not prevail in the state (*bangwudao* 邦無道).[11] *Youdao* means therefore that desirable or auspicious state of affairs in which the gentleman official is able to exercise his talent, ability, and judgment for a good cause, whereas *wudao* refers to that inauspicious state of affairs in which it is unlikely for the gentleman to do good in the capacity of a government official. It seems that the question of whether a state is characterized by *youdao* or *wudao* is an important matter in the gentleman's decision-making process. According to this construal, *ren* may be defined as a quality of the individual that is in conformity with or conducive to the *dao*. One might say, for example, that a *ren* person is someone whose actions are conducive to the attainment and maintenance of the *dao*. The official who works diligently for a corrupt and venal government cannot be regarded as a *ren* person. As a matter of fact, Kongzi thinks that such a person should be ashamed of himself for attaining wealth and distinction in a *wudao* state. It seems plausible to characterize a *ren* person in terms of the *dao*. I contend, however, that *ren* as a virtuous characteristic is independent of the *dao* because the state could change from *youdao* to *wudao* or vice versa but a person's disposition would not necessarily change accordingly, for instance, from "gentleman" to "petty person" (*xiaoren* 小人). For one thing, the gentleman can shield himself from bad influences by refusing to be employed by a corrupt administration. In fact, that is one of the main reasons Kongzi thinks the gentleman should refrain from seeking governmental positions in a morally corrupt state.

That early Confucian ethics does not exemplify *dao*-basing may also be seen in *Analects* 1.2, where the disciple Youzi says, "The gentleman devotes his efforts to the roots, for once the roots are established, the 'Way' (*dao*) will grow therefrom. Being good as a son [i.e., displaying 'filial piety' (*xiao* 孝)] and obedient as a young man is, perhaps, the root of a man's character."[12] Here Youzi spells out in unequivocal terms the relationship between the genesis of the *dao* and the cultivation of *ren*: *ren* is primary and fundamental, while the *dao* is derivative and secondary; it is the natural outgrowth of *ren*. So, it is incorrect to assume that the *dao* is more basic than *ren*.

Dao, construed as the overall political and ethical milieu of a state, can be changed by human agency. This point is clearly shown in passage 15.29, where Kongzi remarks, "It is Man who is capable of broadening the Way. It is not the Way that is capable of broadening Man."[13] A virtuous ruler and his officials create, maintain, and improve a *youdao* society. The crucial importance of a *ren* ruler in creating a *youdao* state lies in the fact that such a ruler issues decrees and edicts out of consideration for the welfare of his people. The conduct of a ruler is just as important, if not more so, as his decrees and policies, for, to a large extent, we all learn how to behave through emulation and practice. A *ren* ruler makes a great contribution to the formation of the *dao* by setting an example through his virtuous behavior for his officials as well as his people. In contrast, a vicious ruler and his cohorts, through their wicked conduct and policies, bring about a *wudao* state and its further deterioration. The root of their vileness and corruption lies in the fact that they place their own satisfactions and sensuous pleasures above the interests of the people. It is clear therefore that different motivations on the part of the people in power lead to different conduct and attitudes, which in turn engender different overall social environments.

In light of the reasons mentioned above, early Confucian ethics is not *dao*-based.

Li-Basing

Among contemporary scholars, there is a debate about whether *ren* in Kongzi's ethical teachings is more fundamental than "rituals," which designate the body of practices and norms that dictate appropriate behavior in a variety of social contexts. According to Kwong-loi Shun, there are two main positions on the issue. One is what Shun refers to as "the instrumentalist interpretation" according to which *ren* has evaluative priority over *li*; on this view, it is *ren* alone that has ultimate value. In contrast, there is "the definitionalist interpretation," according to which the *ren* ideal is defined in terms of the general observance of the *li*; on this reading, the concept of *li* has evaluative priority over *ren*.[14] The instrumentalist interpretation is compatible with agent-basing, where the definitionalist interpretation falls into the category of nonagent-based interpretations. Scholars such as Tu Wei-ming, Homer Dubs, and D. T. Suzuki have dealt with this issue from different perspectives, but it appears that they all regard the *li* as various manifestations or externalizations of *ren*.[15] Thus, their views provide support to the agent-based interpretation of Kongzi's ethical teachings that I defend. Shun tries to strike a balance between the instrumentalist and definitionalist interpretations by insisting that *ren* is the ultimate driving force behind revisions of the *li*, yet, at the same time, acknowledging the pivotal role of the *li* in moral cultivation. In my view, Shun's reading is essentially *ren*-based. It may be possible to construct an even stronger case on behalf of *ren*-basing in defense of modern versions of Confucianism, but that is beyond the scope of this chapter. The resolution of this issue will not definitively solve the problem that is our central concern. For even if it can be established that *ren* is more basic than *li*, we still do not have an across-the-board argument against other views, such as Lau's, according to which *yi*, rather than *ren*, is most fundamental.

Li-basing is a powerful contender to vie with *ren*-basing. If *li* refers to a collection of practices and norms that dictate propriety in all aspects of social life, then *li*-basing is essentially rule-basing according to which moral norms alone are the ultimate criteria for all ethical evaluations. For instance, a righteous person is someone whose behavior is in conformity with moral rules. The *li*-based reading of early Confucian ethics requires that *ren* be defined or explained in terms of *li*.

However, there is a passage in the *Analects* that forcefully discredits the *li*-based interpretation yet lends great support to the *ren*-based reading. Kongzi in 3.3 is recorded as saying, "If a human being is not *ren*, what is the point of *li*?"[16] I submit that Kongzi is suggesting that *ren*, as the best quality of an individual, stands in a specific relation to the *li* as a set of practices and norms for propriety. If *ren*, as Kongzi explains, is loving others, not imposing on others what we do not want, helping others share what we value, and so forth, then it would not seem inappropriate to describe *ren* as the general disposition to live and let live, or to coexist harmoniously with others. This construal of *ren* leads to two questions.

First, what is the most effective way to cultivate the virtue of *ren* in a student who is beginning moral cultivation? Kongzi's answer is clear: learning and practicing the *li* can efficaciously help instill and cultivate virtuous attitudes and patterns of behavior.[17] Often, however, it is easy to lose sight of the purpose of practicing the *li*, which for the most part is to shape the character of those who practice them, and when this happens, learning and practicing the *li* becomes pointless and perfunctory. So, it is quite natural for Kongzi to warn his disciples not to fall in a rut of much ado about nothing.

Second, do those who have already acquired the virtue of *ren* to a substantial degree still need to practice the *li*? We must realize that in addition to forging one's disposition or character, the *li* also express, reinforce, and further refine the virtue of those who know them well. We all know that practice makes perfect;

even a virtuoso needs to practice his instrument on a regular basis. Similarly, a *ren* person still needs to practice the *li*; a good character tends to atrophy if its possessor discontinues practicing what has helped the formation of it in the first place. Even those people in the advanced stages of moral cultivation still need to practice the *li*.

The *li* also function as a means to express our various feelings and emotions in ways that will be understood by others. For example, the *li* dictate that during the period of mourning, one should don somber clothing and refrain from luxury food and attire. Such a practice not only serves as a vehicle for expressing the principal emotional state, such as sadness, depression, and longing, but also tends to invoke empathetic and sympathetic responses from other community members. Kongzi himself disapproved of "being unsorrowful in the conduct of mourning." He was sympathetic toward those in mourning dress.[18]

If we understand that the virtue of *ren*, as the Chinese character 仁 suggests, is constitutive of the ideal harmonious relationship, it is not hard to realize that the making of a virtuous character facilitated by the *li* invariably leads to a harmonious society.[19] "Of the things brought about by the rites, harmony is the most valuable" (6.1).[20] Society is, in a sense, like an orchestra that achieves harmony through reading the same musical score and playing in a well-coordinated fashion. Any member's playing out of sync with others will disrupt the concord. The *li*, which may be likened to a musical score for the orchestra, are essential not only to the formation of a virtuous character, but also for the harmonious coexistence of all members of society.[21]

Based on the earlier discussion, I conclude that the *li*-based interpretation is mistaken because for Kongzi, *ren*, which signifies both a virtuous character and the ideal human relationship, is the end to the achievement of which the *li* function as a means. It is in this sense that *ren* is more fundamental than *li*. Clearly the *ren*-based reading seems more defensible.

Yi-Basing

Now I examine the interpretation suggested by Lau, who defends the view that Kongzi's ethics is *yi*-based. Lau's basic thesis entails a denial of *ren*'s foundational status in moral evaluation. He acknowledges that *ren* is the most important virtue[22] and that Kongzi is more interested in the moral virtues of men than in the moral qualities of their acts,[23] yet he claims:

> No moral system can be solely based on moral virtues, and Confucius' system is no exception. . . . Although Confucius does not state

> it explicitly, one cannot help getting the impression that he realizes that in the last resort *yi* is the standard by which all acts must be judged while there is no further standard by which *yi* itself can be judged. After all, even benevolence (*ren*) does not carry its own moral guarantee. "To love benevolence without loving learning is liable to lead to foolishness" (XVII.8). As we shall see, the object to be pursued in learning, in this context, is likely to have been the rites, and the rites, as rules of conduct, can, in the final analysis, only be based on *yi*. We can say, then, that in Confucius' moral system, although benevolence occupies the more central position, *yi* is, nevertheless, more basic.[24]
>
> *Yi* is a word which can be used of an act in which case it can be rendered as "right," or it can be used of an act an agent ought to perform in which case it can be rendered as "duty," or it can be used of an agent in which case it can be rendered as "righteous" or "dutiful." When used in a general sense, sometimes the only possible rendering is "moral" or "morality." . . . Rightness is basically a character of acts and its application to agents is derivative. A man is righteous in so far as he consistently does what is right. The rightness of acts depends on their being morally fitting in the circumstances and has little to do with the disposition or motive of the agent . . . Although benevolence occupies the more central position, *yi* is, nevertheless, more basic. . . . Rightness (*yi*) is the standard by which all acts have, in the last resort, to be measured.[25]

My critique of Lau's argument focuses on its three constitutive claims: (1) that no moral system can be solely based on moral virtues; (2) that *ren* does not carry its own moral guarantee; (3) *yi* is the ultimate standard of ethical assessment. It seems that these three claims stand in relation to one another in the following way: if *ren* as the most important and all-encompassing virtue does not carry its own moral guarantee, it is hard to imagine that any other virtue does. If no virtue carries its own moral guarantee, then two consequences seem to follow: (a) that their moral guarantee has to come from an external source; (b) that no ethics can be solely based on moral virtues, which is (1).

Consequence (a) paves the way for (3)—that *yi* is the ultimate guarantor of moral value; consequence (b) entails a denial of agent-based freestanding virtue ethics.

Lau's sweeping generalization that no moral system can be based solely on moral virtues poses a challenge to the attempt at interpreting early Confucian ethics as being agent-based, and also to the idea of agent-basing and the viability of virtue ethics as a distinct type of moral theory. Lau's dismissive attitude toward the possibility of a freestanding virtue ethics is shared by a number of contemporary ethicists of deontological or consequentialist persuasion, but this comes as no surprise and does not represent a serious challenge. Lau's claim is in effect a variant of a major objection to virtue ethics, that is, "the problem of incompleteness."[26] We do not, however, engage this kind of objection in a broad fashion within the confines of this chapter. Instead, we focus on what undergirds this sweeping generalization, for if it can be shown that the claim that *ren* does not carry its own moral guarantee is not justified by textual evidence, then Lau's assertion that no moral system can be solely based on virtues may be undermined.

Let us now examine Lau's claim that *ren* does not carry its own moral guarantee to see whether or how well it is substantiated by textual evidence. The passage cited by Lau in support of this claim is 17.8, in which Kongzi remarks that being fond of *ren* without love of "learning" (*xue* 學) is liable to lead to foolishness.[27] Lau seems to think that if *ren* carried its own moral guarantee, it could never lead to foolishness. Foolish actions are not morally praiseworthy. If *ren* alone can at times lead to foolishness, it cannot guarantee the morality of an action. Notice, however, that prudence and morality do not always coincide. Stupidity is different from immorality. A foolish act, for example, does not have to be immoral or wicked, whereas an immoral act can be intelligently executed. Notice also that Kongzi did not say that being fond of *ren* without love of *xue* was liable to lead to *immorality* (*e* 惡). Furthermore, the notion of *ren*-basing does not entail that whatever the gentleman does is a morally praiseworthy act, for even a paragon of virtue still has to eat and brush his teeth like everyone else.

But suppose prudence and morality coincide, which means that foolishness and immorality entail each other. I want to contend that Kongzi does not mean that possessing the virtue of *ren* without love of learning is likely to lead to immorality, because the key phrase in what Kongzi says is "being fond of *ren*." It seems that there is a distinction between being fond of *ren* and being in possession of *ren*, for *ren* is a stable and entrenched disposition or character trait, and if so it cannot be acquired by liking or being fond of it alone. The cultivation of *ren* requires a lifelong commitment, arduous effort, and extensive learning. To be sure, Kongzi did say figuratively (*Analects* 7.30) that *ren* was not far away; as soon as one desired it, it would arrive. It is possible, however, that when Kongzi made that remark, what he had in mind was the beginning phase of moral cultivation. At the initial stage it does not seem to be difficult to do a few good deeds out of genuine other-regarding concerns (*ai ren* 愛人), especially when one is in a good mood. But, the hard thing is to be this way over the long term. It is hard to establish *ren* as the dominant motif in the music of one's life in the midst of temptation, fatigue, self-centeredness, and other contrasting notes. Being able to devote one's heart to *ren* for three months was considered to be an outstanding achievement (6.7). Thus, liking, desiring, or being fond of *ren* may be sufficient for the first few steps of a lifelong journey, but it is not enough to sustain the development of a good character. In addition, we do not know for sure the context in which Kongzi made that remark. It is possible that it was intended to give hope to some of his new disciples who thought of *ren* as being out of their reach, so they were reluctant to take the plunge, so to speak.

Let's summarize the difference between liking *ren* and possessing *ren* this way: possessing *ren* implies being fond of *ren*, but the converse is not true. *Ren* is a virtue, but is a fondness for *ren* also a virtue? It is hard to say. Even if it is, it is a virtue of a different kind. If I say, "I love music," that does not necessarily mean that I am a musician. Similarly, "I love *ren*" does not entail that the speaker is a *ren* person already. This point is borne out by the fact that when Kongzi made the remark, he was speaking to his disciples, none of whom had attained the virtue of *ren* in the full sense of the word. If this is correct, the statement "Being fond of *ren* but without love of learning is likely to lead to foolishness" is not the same as "Possessing *ren* yet without knowledge is likely to lead to foolishness." Given the distinction between being fond of a virtue and having that virtue, it seems unwarranted to draw the conclusion, as Lau does, that *ren* does not carry its own guarantee, on the basis of *Analects* 17.8.

Lau might reply that the reason Kongzi emphasizes the importance of learning is because the object of learning, for the most part, is the *li*; the rightness of the rules of conduct in turn is determined by *yi*. If so, obviously *ren* alone is not sufficient to ensure the rightness of an act. If it were, then why bother with the *li*? I think that this objection involves a misconception of *ren*. Although *ren* is the most important and overarching virtue, it is not a substitute for everything. To borrow what Immanuel Kant says of "a good will," *ren* "need not be the sole and complete good, but it must still be the highest good and condition of every other."[28] To illustrate, even if you are virtuous, you still have to familiarize yourself with traffic laws and pay attention to stop signs and speed limits.

But in spite of the fact that *ren* is not a substitute for everything, it invariably motivates its possessor to learn what needs to be done in order to effectively help the needy. Those who claim to be fond of *ren* but never bother to augment their knowledge and experience cannot be said to be genuinely so. They are indeed fools if they throw good things around or give them to the first person they encounter.[29] Their foolishness may also manifest itself in their being taken advantage of or falling prey to all sorts of machinations and fraudulent schemes. A wealthy person, for example, may be reduced to penury due to his ignorance and thereby loses his resources to help others. But a *ren* person is not a fool. On the contrary, choosing *ren* as one's lifelong pursuit is a manifestation of wisdom (4.1). Obviously, some students of Kongzi's do not seem to have a solid grasp of this aspect of *ren*. For example:

> [Zai Wo] asked, "A benevolent man, though it be told him, 'There is a man in the well,' will go in after him, I suppose." [Kongzi] replied, "Why should he do so? A superior (*ren*) man may be made to go to the well, but he cannot be made to go down into it. He may be imposed upon, but he cannot be deceived."[30]

Zai Wo appears to have assumed that the benevolent person would embark on a rescue mission at the drop of a hat. But Kongzi makes it clear that *ren* includes cognition and wisdom. What he says here is consistent with his caution against being fond of *ren* without love of *xue*. On both occasions the master tries to correct a common yet erroneous conception that *ren* pertains only to the heart by highlighting the intellectual aspects of *ren*. A truly *ren* person is also an intellectually competent and worldly person. He is eager to learn all the rules that make social living possible; he is eager to acquire the factual information in order to make his assistance to the needy more efficacious; he knows a crook when he sees one. Kongzi's idea that a *ren* person is also a worldly person and is clearly inherited and developed by Xunzi, as evidenced by the following quotation:

> [One] who is humane (*ren*) is always respectful of others. There is a way for behaving with strict reverent care toward others. When a man is worthy, one should honor him as well as respect him. [Not to respect a worthy man is to act like a dumb beast.] When he is unworthy, one should be fearful of him while showing respect. [Not showing respect for an unworthy man is to treat a tiger with contempt.] When he is worthy, one should endeavor to be close to him while paying him respect. When he is unworthy, one should keep him at a distance while showing him respect.[31]

In addition, wisdom conditioned by *ren* is also valuable outside the moral domain. After all, we are not constantly living in the ethical dimension as the utilitarian would want us to believe. *Ren* is inclusive of altruistic sacrifice but it is not exclusive of self-concern. We have our personal projects and hobbies, and there is nothing wrong with having a certain amount of self-concern; nor is there anything wrong with pursuing one's own projects or hobbies as long as doing so does not infringe on the welfare of others. Kongzi himself liked singing and enjoyed music in the midst of his campaign for a peaceful and harmonious society. Besides the virtue of *ren* we need other virtues as well, but just because we need other virtues it does not mean that *ren* lacks intrinsic value within the moral sphere.

It may be noted that our disagreement about whether *ren* carries its own moral guarantee may stem from the fact that *ren* is quite widely recognized as having two senses. When construed in the narrow sense, *ren* refers to the single virtue of compassion or humaneness, whereas in the broad sense it pertains to the all-encompassing virtue. If *ren* is the all-inclusive virtue or complete goodness, it should by definition include all other good qualities in addition to the core virtue of compassion. It seems that when Kongzi says that a benevolent man is sure to possess courage (14.4), he is using the word *ren* in the broad sense. There are other occasions on which Kongzi uses *ren* to refer to moral perfection as well. For instance, he maintains that a man who is fond of *ren* cannot be surpassed (4.6). Only when *ren* means the highest ethical ideal can such a remark make sense. In contrast, when he says that to love benevolence without loving learning is liable to lead to foolishness, he seems to use *ren* in the narrow sense, because loving *ren* would imply loving learning if *ren* included learnedness as a constitutive virtue. It makes perfect sense to say that when Lau claims that *ren* does not carry its moral guarantee, it is the narrow sense of *ren* that he has in mind, whereas when I insist that it does, I am thinking of the broad sense of the word. While this certainly helps clarify and elucidate our disagreement, it does not resolve it, for Lau does not believe that a moral system can be solely based on *any* virtue, single or otherwise. His view is that early Confucian ethics is ultimately based on *yi*. It is to this claim that we now turn.

Lau's assertion that *yi* is the ultimate criterion by which all actions as well as rules of conduct are to be evaluated is closely related to the claim that "*ren* does not carry its own moral guarantee," because if *ren* does not possess intrinsic moral value, its worth must come from something else that does. And according to Lau, this "something else that does" is *yi*.

But the question is: What is *yi*? According to Lau, the word *yi* has three meanings. It can be used to refer to a specific property of an action, that is, its rightness. It also designates a particular quality of the agent, namely the virtue of *yi*.[32] And finally, it means the moral fitness of an action in the circumstances. *Yi* in this sense is not a character trait but a relationship between an action and the circumstances in which the action is performed. Lau maintains that *yi* as the relationship rather than the property of an act or the virtue of an agent is the criterion by which all acts have, in the last resort, to be measured.[33] Again, our main concern is whether or how well the assertion that *yi* is the ultimate standard is really corroborated by Kongzi's remarks. The passage Lau quotes in support of his claim is *Analects* 17.23:

> [The disciple] Zilu said, "Does the gentleman (*junzi*) consider courage (*yong*) a supreme quality?" The Master said, "For the gentleman it is morality (*yi*) that is supreme (*shang*). Possessed of courage (*yong*) but devoid of morality (*yi*), a gentleman will make trouble while a small man will be a brigand."[34]

I do not think that the English word "supreme" is a satisfactory rendition of the Chinese word *shang* 上. To be sure, occasionally it may be proper to render *shang* as "supreme." But in many cases, the word *shang* simply means "up" or "high" as opposed to "down" or "low." So, we must pay close attention to context. In the above-cited text, *yi* appears to be a special quality that one can possess, just as courage is a quality that one can have. Since "courage" (*yong* 勇) is a virtue, it is only natural to think that *yi* in this context also refers to a virtue.[35] If so, it is a character trait rather than the fitting relationship between an act and the circumstances. Given that the contrast made in the dialogue involves only two qualities, namely *yi* and *yong*, it seems more appropriate to say that *yi* is superior to *yong* in the hierarchy of values. Alternatively, *yi* is a superior quality in comparison with *yong*. Thus, it is apropos to translate *shang* in the passage as "superior" or "more important." Kongzi thinks that *yi* is more important than *yong* because when an aristocrat is possessed of *yong* but devoid of *yi*, he tends to cause political disturbance, while when a commoner is possessed of *yong* but devoid of *yi*, he is prone to commit crimes. In both cases, it is quite natural for Kongzi to insist on the importance of *yi* as a regulatory and balancing character trait that restrains, informs, and tempers *yong*, which many of his young disciples tended to indulge.

Whether to translate *shang* as "supreme" or "superior" is pivotal, because if *yi* were supreme, it would be superior to *ren*. However, if *yi* is only superior to *yong*, its relation to *ren* cannot be determined by implication because in the dialogue there is no mention of *ren*. In passage 14.4, Kongzi teaches that if one possesses *ren*, he must possess *yong*, while what he says here in 17.23 implies that one can have courage without having *yi*. Thus, nothing concerning the relation between *ren* and *yi* seems to follow from either passage or the conjunction of the two. Nevertheless, from what has been said thus far we can draw the following conclusions. First, what Lau quotes as a textual support for his claim that *yi* is the ultimate moral standard becomes immaterial when the translation of *shang* is changed from "supreme" to what it should be, "superior." Second, even if we were to grant that *yi* means "supreme" in this passage, Lau's assertion about *yi* cannot be substantiated, because *yi* in the context clearly refers to a virtue rather than a relationship, and according to Lau no moral virtue can be the ultimate standard.

Although Kongzi did not spell out the true relationship between *ren* and *yi*, we can infer a great deal about the relationship between these two by carefully examining what he says elsewhere. In passage 2.24, he observed, "Faced with what is right, to leave it undone shows a lack of courage." If one perceives what is right but does not do it because it is risky, one lacks courage. Here "courage" (*yong*) is understood as a disposition to do what is perceived or known to be right; it therefore does not mean courage in a broad sense but in a narrow sense, namely *moral* courage. Doing the right thing sometimes requires great moral courage. For instance, it takes courage to rescue a baby in a burning building. There are many circumstances under which moral courage is called for. But what does moral courage have to do with *ren*? As we may recall, Kongzi's dictum about the relationship between *ren* and *yong* is this: while he who has *yong* does not necessarily have *ren*, he who has *ren* must possess *yong* (14.4). What needs to be pointed out is that in this context *yong* is used to refer to moral courage. We are justified to infer from passages 14.4 and 2.24 that a *ren* person must be a person having *yi*. Why? Because the *ren* person must possess moral courage; a morally courageous person does not leave what is right undone; a *ren* person therefore is one who consistently does what is right; according to Lau, a person who consistently does what is right is a righteous person.[36] Hence, a *ren* person must be a righteous (*yi*) person. If this reasoning is correct, the relationship between *ren* and *yi* has to be that *ren* determines both *yi* as the rightness of an action and *yi* as the righteousness of the agent. It follows that *ren* is more basic than *yi*, rather than the other way around as Lau claims.

But, Lau might respond along the following lines. The *ren* person must possess *yong*, but *yong* possessed by a *ren* person is not necessarily moral courage. Remember that moral courage is understood as a disposition not to leave undone what is perceived or known to be right.[37] How do we know that a *ren* person is capable of perceiving or knowing what is right? If he cannot perceive or know what is right, he cannot do it even if he possesses courage. I believe that this response can be dealt with by drawing on the interchangeability of the two honorifics "the benevolent person" (*renren* 仁人) and "the gentleman" (*junzi* 君子).[38] According to Lau, the epithets "the benevolent person" and "the gentleman" are interchangeable.[39] This observation of his is indeed borne out directly or indirectly by many of Kongzi's remarks. On one occasion Kongzi says that the gentleman is free from worries and fears, and elsewhere he says that the benevolent man has no worries.[40] To be sure, whether they are interchangeable or not may vary with context. For example, Kongzi in 17.23 uses *junzi* and *xiaoren* to refer to people of different social standings. However, when Kongzi contrasts "the gentleman" who is conversant with "rightness" (*yi* 義) with "the petty man" who is conversant with "profit" (*li* 利),[41] it is obvious that by those epithets he is referring to different character traits rather than social statuses. It follows from 4.16 and the interchangeability of "the gentleman" and "the benevolent person" that the benevolent person must be conversant with rightness. Since the benevolent person is conversant with what is right, and morally courageous, he will not leave what is right undone. Thus, the "benevolent" (*ren*) person must be a "righteous" (*yi*) person. If this is correct, then ultimately it is *ren* that determines consistently right conduct, which in turn determines the righteous character. To Lau's claim that "a man is righteous only in so far as he consistently does what is right," it should be added that he consistently does what is right because he is conversant with what is right; what makes him conversant with what is right is the very fact that he is a *ren* person.[42] Since *ren* is the overarching virtue and motive, Lau's assertion that "the rightness of acts has little to do with the disposition or motive of the agent"[43] is refuted.

Lau might say that my argument only touches on the relation between the virtue *ren* and the virtue of *yi*. However, he might argue that, in addition to "rightness" or "righteousness," *yi* also pertains to morality. It is *yi* construed as morality that confers moral value to character traits, conduct, or rules. It is *yi* as morality that carries the moral guarantee not only of itself but also of every virtue, every act, and every rule. That is what he means when he says that *yi* is the ultimate ethical norm.

> When used in a general sense, sometimes the only possible rendering is "moral" or "morality." . . . Rightness is basically a character of acts and its application to agents is derivative. A man is righteous in so far as he consistently does what is right. The rightness of acts depends on their being morally fitting in the circumstances and has little to do with the disposition or motive of the agent.[44]

So, it appears that *yi* refers to the correct relationship between an action and the circumstances under which it is performed or omitted. But how do we know whether an action is morally fitting or not? How do we know whether such a relationship obtains? Lau does not seem to have provided an answer. All moral theories have to explicate the nature and the foundation of morality. Lau's *yi*-based reading of early Confucian ethics leaves such crucial questions largely unanswered.

One might question the necessity of a single moral standard. Why can't there be two moral standards—*yi* for action, *ren* for character? The answer to the question is twofold. Theoretical simplicity is one of the considerations because a bifurcated standard of morality tends to complicate moral appraisals. But the main reason has to do with how early Confucians see the relationship between the agent and her actions. It is the motive of the agent that determines what she does. As the cliché goes, "Good people do good deeds." Confucian ethics is preoccupied with moral self-cultivation, which for the most part is what distinguishes it from many forms of Western ethics.[45] We have reason to believe that Confucians' preoccupation with character cultivation rests on their belief that one's character determines her actions. The disciple Youzi drives this point home when he says in 1.2, "It is rare for a man whose character is such that he is good as a son and obedient as a young man to have the inclination to transgress against his superiors; it is unheard of for one who has no such inclination to be inclined to start a rebellion."[46] He then goes on to say that the Confucian gentleman devotes his efforts to the root (*ben* 本).[47] One's moral character is a root that determines the value or the disvalue of her actions.

By way of conclusion, I shall venture an answer to the question of where the ultimate moral standard is to be found in early Confucian ethics. In *Analects* 17.21, there is an interesting exchange between Kongzi and his disciple Zai Wo.

> Zai Wo asked: "Three years mourning for one's parents—this is quite long. If a gentleman stops all ritual practices for three years, the practices will decay; if he stops all musical performances for three years, music will be lost. As the old crop is consumed, a new crop grows up, and for lighting the fire, a new lighter is used with each season. One year of mourning should be enough." The Master said: "If after only one year, you were again to eat white rice and to wear silk, would you feel at ease?"—"Absolutely."—"In that case, go ahead! The reason a gentleman prolongs his mourning is simply that, since fine food seems tasteless to him, and music offers him no enjoyment, and the comfort of his house makes him uneasy, he

prefers to do without all these pleasures. But now, if you can enjoy them, go ahead!" Zai Wo left. The Master said: "Zai Wo is devoid of humanity. After a child is born, for the first three years of his life, he does not leave his parents' bosom. Three years mourning is a custom that is observed everywhere in the world. Did Zai Wo never enjoy the love of his parents, even for three years?"[48]

In this passage, Kongzi made the moral judgment that Zai Wo was inhumane (*buren* 不仁) on the grounds that the latter was emotionally callous toward his parents. This seems to demonstrate that for Kongzi, one's emotional attitude rather than external action is the basis of moral assessment. He reached that conclusion by comparing the coldness of heart manifested by the disciple Zai Wo against the ideal moral psychology that the gentleman should exhibit under such circumstances. It seems clear that for Kongzi, an infraction of the *li* is not the true basis for calling someone *buren*; a lack of warmth or compassion is. Emotional callousness may manifest itself in a variety of ways. In Zai Wo's case, it is his being able to enjoy fine food and clothing during the period of mourning that exposes his deficient emotional attitude.

On many occasions, Kongzi characterizes the gentleman in affective terms. For example, "The gentleman feels neither fear nor worry."[49] The gentleman's feeling neither fear nor worry is attributed to his feeling no guilt (*jiu* 疚) in the course of his introspection.[50] It seems that Kongzi is more concerned with the gentleman's emotional attitudes than with any other aspect of his life: the gentleman *loves* others; he feels neither *fear* nor *worry*; he feels no guilt; he would feel *ashamed* (*chi* 恥) if he were to prosper as a result of participating in a corrupt regime.[51] Not only does Kongzi characterize the gentleman in emotive terms such as calmness and serenity, he also portrays the petty person in contrasting emotional colors (7.37). It should be noted that the emotional attributes mentioned by Kongzi are characteristic of the ideal Confucian gentleman. In addition, we must realize that Kongzi is not saying that one should not worry or fear at all. It is a specific type of worry or fear that he thinks the gentleman should not feel: the type engendered by a guilty conscience. It is perhaps in this connection that Kongzi taught his disciples to set their hearts on *ren* in a steadfast fashion, so they will be free from immorality (4.4), which is the key to maintaining a guilt-free consciousness.

Thus, we conclude that for Kongzi certain emotional attitudes constitute the gentleman's moral psychology, and ultimately it is *ren* that motivates the gentleman's actions toward his fellow human beings and determines the kind of emotive makeup that he possesses. Hence, *ren* is rightfully the basis of Confucian moral evaluation.

The dialogue between Kongzi's principal successor Mengzi and his interlocutor provides yet another clue that may help us locate the foundation of early Confucian ethics.

> Chunyu Kun [the then well-known debater] asks: "Is it the rule that males and females shall not allow their hands to touch in giving or receiving anything?" Mengzi replies: "It is the rule." Chunyu asks: "If a man's sister-in-law be drowning, shall he rescue her with his hand?" Mengzi says: "He who would not so rescue the drowning woman is a wolf."[52]

Perhaps most of us would agree with Mengzi that the morally fitting thing for the man to do in this scenario is pull his sister-in-law out of peril with his hand even though that would be a violation of the relevant *li*. If, in this exigent situation, the man were overly concerned about whether his action is morally fitting (*yi*) or whether it is in accordance with the *li*, he would be guilty of having "one thought too many," as Bernard Williams would say.[53] But Mengzi does not reach the verdict that failing to save her would be wrong or that the *li* should be overridden under the circumstances by measuring the man's behavior against some ultimate standard *yi*. For Mengzi, a failure to act in this case is wrong because it is contrary to the psychological makeup of a decent person; it deviates from what Mengzi sees as a basic human quality, which he calls "a heart that cannot bear to see the suffering of others" (*ceyinzhixin* 惻隱之心). According to Lau's reasoning, the scenario that Mengzi and his interlocutor were discussing offers a perfect opportunity to illustrate the ultimate standard of *yi*. But, Mengzi made no mention of *yi*. Instead, he applied a standard that is so simple, so intuitive, and so natural that decent human beings regularly use it in their everyday ethical encounters. If the man refused to save his drowning sister-in-law with his hand because he did not want to offend against the *li*, he would be a "wolf," which exemplifies *buren* (the absence of humanity or compassion). This shows, in a clear and decisive manner, that *ren* or *buren* is the basis of moral evaluation in early Confucian ethics.

If the virtue of *ren* is the cornerstone of Confucian morality, a question of what is the best way to acquire it arises immediately. Not surprisingly, Confucian ethics is in a position to offer a time-tested answer to the question. So, resting early Confucian ethics squarely on the basis of *ren* will lead in the direction where its rich resources for moral self-cultivation can be tapped into, and as a result contemporary Western virtue theory can be complemented by what early Confucian ethical thinkers have to offer.

Notes

1. For a survey of recent literature on virtue ethics, see Michael Slote, *Morals from Motives* (New York: Oxford University Press, 2001); Christine Swanton, *Virtue Ethics: A Pluralistic View* (New York: Oxford University Press, 2003); Rosalind Hursthouse, *On Virtue Ethics* (New York: Oxford University Press, 1999).

2. Slote, *Morals from Motives*, 5–7.

3. *Pinyin* is the official Romanization system of the People's Republic of China (PRC) and has been gradually replacing the traditional Wade-Giles system. It is now in popular use outside the PRC not only for scholarship but also for journalism. The *pinyin* form of "Confucius" is "Kongzi"; "Mencius," "Mengzi"; "Hsun Tzu," "Xunzi." In this chapter, however, I use "Confucian" rather than "Kongzian."

4. Andrew Plaks, trans., *Ta Hsüeh and Chung Yung* (New York: Penguin, 2003), 5.

5. See Kwong-loi Shun, "*Ren* and *Li* in the *Analects*," in Bryan W. Van Norden, ed., *Confucius and the Analects: New Essays*, (New York: Oxford University Press, 2002), 57. An influential proponent of the priority of *li* is Herbert Fingarette. See his *Confucius: the Secular as Sacred*, (Prospect Heights, IL: Waveland Press, 1972).

6. Paul R. Goldin argues that Xunzi relies on a notion of the *dao* as the basis of his ethical philosophy. See his *Rituals of the Way: The Philosophy of Xunzi*, (Chicago: Open Court, 1999).

7. Here *yi* is understood as the fitting relationship between an action and the circumstances under which the action is performed.

8. That *ren* is the most fundamental means that it is the "ground floor" of moral evaluation. For example, the value of an action is judged, in the final analysis, on the basis of whether it is motivated by *ren* (humanness, benevolence, compassion, warmth of heart) or the opposite of *ren*, namely *buren* (inhumanness, malevolence, callousness, coldness). Confucians see *ren* as the ethical ideal or the highest moral perfection. So, there can hardly be anyone possessing *ren* in the full sense of the word. But it does not follow that one cannot attain *ren* to a substantial degree.

9. See James Rachels, *The Elements of Moral Philosophy* (Boston: McGraw-Hill, 1999), 191. Other objections include Gilbert Harman's dismissal of character or personality. See Gilbert Harman, "Moral Philosophy Meets Social Psychology: Virtue Ethics and the Fundamental Attribution Error," in *Proceedings of the Aristotelian Society* (1998–1999): 315–31; "No Character or Personality," in *Business Ethics Quarterly* 13 (2003) 87–94.

10. Lau, *The Analects*, 88.

11. *Analects* 8.13; ibid., 94. *Youdao* and *wudao* may be understood in the same way in some other places, such as 5.2, 5.21, 15.7.

12. Lau, *The Analects*, 59. One might be tempted to think that *xiao* rather than *ren* is the foundation of early Confucian ethics because it is regarded as the precursor of *ren*. I agree that *xiao* precedes *ren* with respect to moral cultivation, but it seems too

narrow in scope to qualify as the basis of ethical assessment. In some passages, however, early Confucians talk of *ren* in terms of *xiao*. For example, "Loving one's parents (*xiao*) is benevolence (*ren*)." Lau, *Mencius*, 184.

13. Lau, *The Analects*, 137.
14. Shun, "*Ren* and *Li* in the *Analects*," 57.
15. See Tu Wei-ming, *Humanity and Self-Cultivation: Essays in Confucian Thought* (Berkeley, CA: Asian Humanities Press, 1979), 5–16; D. T. Suzuki, *A Brief History of Early Chinese Philosophy* (London: Arthur Probsthain, 1914); Homer H. Dubs, *Hsuntze: The Moulder of Ancient Confucianism* (London: Arthur Probsthain, 1927).
16. Simon Leys, trans., *The Analects of Confucius* (New York: W.W. Norton, 1997), 39.
17. See Philip J. Ivanhoe, *Confucian Moral Self Cultivation*, second edition, (Indianapolis, IN: Hackett, 2000), 4.
18. See Raymond Dawson, trans., *The Analects* (New York: Oxford University Press, 1993), 12, 24. See also Lau, *The Analects*, 104–105.
19. The Chinese character 仁 consists of two parts: "human being" 人 and "two" 二.
20. Lau, *The Analects*, 61.
21. See Ivanhoe, *Confucian Moral Self Cultivation*, 5. One objection that has been leveled against virtue ethics is that it places too much emphasis on the goodness of the agent's own life and character. A good response to this sort of complaint is perhaps to point out, as Ivanhoe does, that "the ultimate aim of and justification for moral self-cultivation is harmonious relationships between people." The cultivation of virtue is not a self-indulgent game; some virtues such as caring or *ren* are inherently relational and other-regarding.
22. Lau, *The Analects*, 14.
23. Ibid., 27.
24. Ibid.
25. Ibid.
26. Rachels, *The Elements of Moral Philosophy*, 191. For a brief survey of the full range of objections to virtue ethics and responses, see Rebecca Walker and Philip J. Ivanhoe, eds., *Working Virtue: Virtue Ethics and Contemporary Moral Problems* (Oxford: Oxford University Press, 2006).
27. Lau, *The Analects*, 144.
28. See Immanuel Kant, *Groundwork of the Metaphysics of Morals*, trans. Mary Gregor (New York: Cambridge University Press, 1997), 10.
29. Slote, *Morals from Motives*, 17–18.
30. James Legge, trans., *Confucian Analects, The Great Learning, and The Doctrine of the Mean* (New York: Dover Publications, 1971), 192–193.
31. John Knoblock, trans., *Xunzi: A Translation and Study of the Complete Works*, vol. 2 (Stanford, CA: Stanford University Press, 1990), 202–203.
32. It should be noted that in the *Analects* the term *yi* primarily describes

behavior rather than a person. This can be seen in 2.24, 16.1, and 18.7. However, in some places, such as 4.16 and 5.16, the word appears to be used to describe a certain quality associated with a person. The juxtaposition of *yi* and *yong* in 17.23 also seems to suggest that *yi* is a character trait. The use of *yi* as a describer of character became more frequent and explicit in the *Mengzi*.

33. Lau, *The Analects*, 27.
34. Ibid., 147–148.
35. Some scholars have written on the role of courage in early Confucian morality. See Lee H. Yearly, *Mencius and Aquinas: Theories of Virtue and Conceptions of Courage* (Albany: State University of New York Press, 1990); Xinyan Jiang, "Mencius on Human Nature and Courage," *The Journal of Chinese Philosophy* 24 (1997): 265–289.
36. Lau, *The Analects*, 27.
37. Ibid., 66.
38. According to some commentators, Kongzi consciously revalues the sense of *junzi* and transforms it from a word used to designate hereditary rank to a notion of a morally excellent person, a paradigmatic individual who sets the tone and quality of life for ordinary moral agents. See Philip J. Ivanhoe, *Ethics in the Confucian Tradition*, second edition (Indianapolis, IN: Hackett, 2002).
39. Lau, *The Analects*, 15.
40. Ibid., 100, 113, 128.
41. Ibid., 74.
42. Ibid., 27.
43. Ibid.
44. Ibid.
45. Ivanhoe, *Confucian Moral Self Cultivation*, ix.
46. Lau, *The Analects*, 59.
47. Ibid.
48. Leys, *The Analects of Confucius*, 88–89.
49. Lau, *The Analects*, 100, 113, 128.
50. Ibid., 113.
51. Ibid., 124.
52. James Legge, trans., *The Works of Mencius* (Reprint, New York: Dover Publications, 1970), 307.
53. Bernard Williams, *Moral Luck* (New York: Cambridge University Press, 1981), 18.

Chapter 7

Is Sympathy Naive?

Dai Zhen on the Use of *Shu* to Track Well-Being

Justin Tiwald

The mid-Qing philosopher Dai Zhen 戴震 (1724–1777) is famous for his criticisms of orthodox Neo-Confucianism, especially of the Cheng-Zhu 程朱 School that had, by his time, prevailed over intellectual life and state institutions for several centuries.[1] The heart of his critique rests on a controversial series of claims about the Confucian emotional attitude of sympathetic understanding (*shu* 恕) that he found to be essential for moral virtue.[2] As Dai sees his Neo-Confucian adversaries, their account of moral agency puts a stranglehold on sympathetic understanding, for their strictures against the use of desire in moral reasoning prevents someone from sympathetically appreciating other human beings in the requisite ways. Without having healthy desires of one's own, and a sufficient understanding of what those desires should be, we fail to discern the standards of good order (*li* 理) inherent in our condition.

This much is routinely observed. What is less appreciated, however, is that Dai's claims about the importance of sympathy and the desires in moral reasoning are parasitic on a claim about the importance of sympathy and the desires in reasoning about human welfare or well-being. We depend on them to know the standards of good order because, in large part, we depend on them to know what is *good for* people. The importance of this to Dai's critique is attested by his tendency to portray it as an insight he recovered from the ancients, after it was lost on the Song-Ming Neo-Confucians and their adherents.[3] It is also attested by some of his most plaintive statements, repeated like a refrain, describing the state of blindness brought about by his Neo-Confucian predecessors' impoverished picture of moral deliberation. Without the desires and *shu*, he laments again and again, we preclude ourselves from appreciating the ways in which our general moral guidelines or ideals can become detached from real-world avenues of benefit and harm and thus find ourselves *unknowingly* "bringing irreparable harm (*huo* 禍) to all under Heaven."[4] It is this particular function of sympathetic understanding, where it serves as a way of tracking benefits and harms that I focus on here.

Most of us believe that sympathy figures prominently in helping us to better appreciate benefits and harms, and I find the same unspoken assumption in much discussion of *shu*. However, I also find that the mechanism we usually imagine sympathy to rely on for tracking well-being tends to greatly oversimplify and thereby underestimate its importance.

Consider, for example, a case in which a powerful mayor wants to raze an entire neighborhood to make room for airport expansion but, on realizing some sympathetic appreciation for the residents of that neighborhood, is led to look elsewhere for real estate. How, in particular, has sympathy brought about this change of heart? Normally we assume that it is the mayor's act of imagining himself in the place of the residents (an act I shall call "perspective-taking") that enables him to sympathetically appreciate the extent of the harm he might do.[5] Through sympathy, he imagines what it would be like to lose the home in which multiple generations of one's family were raised, and he focuses on the profound psychic injury it does to deprive someone of a lifelong community. The problem with this picture, however, is that for purposes of appraising benefits and harms, the affects and interests we imaginatively attribute to others are not always the right ones. For example, we might attribute to others desires they do not have, or they might well have desires that are self-destructive. The response, then, is usually to correct for the desires that we imaginatively simulate, and to do so by specifying that they should be rational or *informed* desires—those that we would have with working faculties and under full information.

This is the move I find to be, at one and the same time, missing from Dai's account and profoundly unfair to sympathy's robust role in moral deliberation. It is unfair to sympathy because it tends to slough off the hard work of determining which desires are the right ones onto something else, when in fact it is sympathy itself that does a great deal of this work. This move is missing from Dai's account because it tends to portray the final arbiter of benefits and harms as a kind of idealized first person, deliberating (rationally and with full information) about what she wants. For Dai Zhen, as I illustrate, wanting something alone is not enough to make it good for us. It must also be something others would want *for* us, insofar as they sympathetically understand us. I find in Dai

Zhen a more robust and plausible account of *shu* than mere perspective-taking allows, and this chapter is devoted to the explication of this account.

A word about terminology. In making this argument, I refer to the ability to track benefits and harms as an ability to track "welfare" or "well-being." I use these latter terms in a thin sense, as describing whatever it is that is increased or decreased when one does well or does poorly. The advantage of using it in this way is that it helps to unify Dai Zhen's many statements to the effect that the more orthodox picture of moral agency prevents its adherents from taking account of various forms of harm in their moral deliberations. Whether a particular iteration of this refrain invokes the "harming of others" (*huo ren* 禍人),[6] or more dramatically the "injury" (*shang* 傷) done to "the people" (*min* 民),[7] the point is the same: without making use of our own desires and *shu*, we have no way to guarantee that our moral judgments will take account of the well-being of the affected parties.

To be sure, there is no single word in Dai Zhen's philosophical lexicon that corresponds to "welfare" or "well-being." However, it would be a mistake to conclude from this that there is nothing systematic to say about human well-being and its function in Dai's moral thought. Indeed, if we look almost anywhere in the history of philosophy, well-being tends to be the one normative concept most conspicuous in its absence, for moral thinkers of all ages have rarely written about well-being as such and have instead assumed (much like an ordinary speaker today) that their audiences will understand implicitly that references to such things as "happiness" or "prosperity" all have some bearing on a common thing—well-being—and furthermore that this common thing is important for ethics.[8] Indeed, we should be worried if it were not.

How does a sympathetic understanding of others bring their well-being to bear on our moral evaluations? Here I suspect most of us have a ready answer: by allowing us to reconstruct the *point of view* of others, allowing us to experience it (or some simulation of it) for ourselves. Such is the nature of this sort of exercise, however, that it cannot possibly be a dependable indicator of well-being on its own. Consider the particular kind of perspective-taking advocated by Dai Zhen, where we track the good of others, in part, by asking what we would "desire" (*yu* 欲) if we were them.[9] This might work well enough in certain paradigmatic cases, when weighing the important and nearly universal desires for companionship, nourishment, a stable source of income, and so forth. But surely there are times when the moral agent's desires are simply the wrong ones to use in the synthesis of the other's point of view. I mean this in at least two senses. First, they might be "wrong" in the sense that the other may not have them, thus making the object of desire less beneficial for the other than it is for the moral agent. I should always bear in mind, for example, that not everyone is fond of keeping cats as pets, as I am.[10] Second, they might simply be "wrong" in the sense that they have little relationship to well-being, whether or not they inform our reconstruction of the other's point of view. I might legitimately share with Wang a powerful yearning to see our home team win. But it would be strange to say that achieving the object of our desire (the triumph of our home team) contributes to Wang's well-being in the same way that having a constant source of nourishment does, even if she desires it with the same intensity. Just because Wang has the desire, in other words, it does not follow that satisfying it will contribute to her welfare.

If we want to preserve the perspective-taking contributions of sympathy, then we will have to prop them up with further insights and specifications. We will have to find some way of making those desires that have an intimate relationship to the other's well-being, and only those desires, normative for our sympathetic reconstruction of her point of view, so that we do not mistakenly project a strong desire for house cats on an ailurophobe, or an unhealthy obsession with winning on anyone. Something must aid our exercise in perspective-taking so as to guarantee that we extend the right sorts of desires to others, and the key test of those desires, surely, will be whether they do an adequate job of tracking the ways in which the other can be benefited or harmed—that is, ways in which circumstances will affect the other's welfare.

This is surely in the spirit of Dai Zhen's project. Dai does not think that just *any* desire we happen to have should contribute to our sympathetic reconstructions of another's point of view. When Dai refers to the use of "desires" in moral deliberation, he means specifically those desires that belong to the "ordinary feelings of human beings" (*ren zhi changqing* 人之常情).[11] These include the desires that belong to us by nature and have a universal or near-universal status in ordinary human beings.[12] They are also explanatorily basic desires—that is, desires in terms of which we can legitimately explain why one wants something more specific or idiosyncratic. Thus, a longing to share a plate of fettuccini with one's beloved is explained in terms of hunger for food (*shi* 食) and a desire for romantic love (*nannü* 男女).[13]

Most of us believe that our desires provide us with crucial insight into well-being, and that they do so in part because our good is importantly related to desire satisfaction. Part of what makes lifelong companionship a good for me, it seems, is that (at least under certain idealized circumstances) I want it. Dai Zhen shares these views deeply and emphatically, but it is not clear that he shares it for the reasons we might expect. Generally speaking, we could give two sorts of accounts of how desire satisfaction is related to well-being. One would be to see desire satisfaction as beneficial by virtue of some independent value, such as the pleasure or happiness that results from attaining one's desired ends. We cannot take much joy in life, we might think, unless we sometimes meet our felt goals and ambitions; thus, desire satisfaction is useful instrumentally, to facilitate joy. If there is an obvious alternative to the view that desire satisfaction is good by virtue of some independent value, it is that desire satisfaction *simply is* the good. That is, to satisfy someone's desires is just what it means to benefit that person.

Of these two general strategies, certainly one of the prevailing temptations is to read Dai as advocating the second. Dai Zhen identifies the sage-kings' concern about their subjects' states of well-being (identified in classical sources by such terms as "hardship" [*kun* 困] and "poverty" [*qiong* 窮]) with their attendance to their subjects' desires. Furthermore, desire fulfillment (*sui yu* 遂欲) forms an important leitmotif in Dai's moral philosophy, being invoked again and again as having a much-neglected explanatory power in proper moral judgment.[14]

There is considerable evidence to suggest, however, that if anything Dai prefers a variant of the first of the two ways of relating desire to well-being, where the fulfillment of desires gets its worth from some other more fundamental and independent value. In Dai's case, however, the likely candidate for the latter value would not be happiness or pleasure as such, but would almost certainly be "life fulfillment" (*sui sheng* 遂生). "In human existence," Dai declares, "there is no greater affliction than to lack the means to fulfill one's life (*sui qi sheng*)."[15] Life, for Dai, brings with it its own set of demands.[16] That is, just by virtue of being living creatures, we all have needs for certain goods, such as sustenance and development. The needs that attach to life as such then take different forms according to the inborn "nature" (*xing* 性) of the living thing in question.[17] And it is to the particular desires that arise from the structural requirements of living (and, we might add, "growing") that the truly virtuous or "humane" (*ren* 仁) person is supposed to attend: "If in desiring to fulfill one's own life, one thereby fulfills the lives of others, this is humanity."[18]

Conceiving welfare as "life fulfillment," in turn, allows Dai to link it more directly with the supreme good (*shan* 善) of sustaining the universe's generative or life-producing processes (*sheng sheng* 生生).[19] "Life" (*sheng*) becomes a good when put into harmonious action with the productive forces of Heaven and Earth. This is not to say that it is intrinsically good: to be valuable it must cohere with natural forces, as a working part of the whole.[20] But life also has demands of its own, being inherently dynamic and productive, and in these demands we find our grounds for pursuing our own well-being. In other words, life fulfillment has value prior to and partially independent of our desiring it, and it is the high price we put on the life in ourselves that inspires us to act in our own interest: "Because all creatures of blood and breath know the love of life and fear of death, *therefore* they pursue benefit and avoid harm."[21]

The question we must ask then is how someone like Dai Zhen can maintain both that *shu* (or "sympathetic understanding") helps us to track the well-being of others by projecting certain desires onto them and at the same time that it does not commit us to endorsing the judgments informed by whatever desires we happen to have. How can we be more selective about the sorts of desires we imagine the other having, so as to give the life-fulfilling ones more normative weight? Here I think we can mention two general answers. First, we might imagine that independent constraints are imposed on the desires selected by *shu*. Second, we might imagine that *shu itself* is selective about the desires that it causes us to synthesize. As I argue, Dai thinks the first sort of answer is helpful to a degree, but he is unusual in stressing the second answer as well.

In the spirit of the first answer, one might point out that we are not always obliged to endorse the picture of the other's psychological landscape that our sympathetic imaginations are inclined to create.[22] We might imagine a fellow fanatical fan being willing to sacrifice his career to see the home team win, but on reflection allow that this preference is simply too strong or irrational. Another appealing strategy is to regulate the sorts of desires that go into our deliberations in the first place. I would be less inclined to attribute wild or self-destructive desires to Wang if I myself am a person of moderate temperament, or at least if I can recognize which of my desires would be inappropriate. Dai's philosophical antagonist Zhu Xi 朱熹 (1130–1200) tackles a perceived problem in mistaken desires in just this way, suggesting that we first see to it that we clearly understand the standards of moral order (*ming li* 明理) and rectify our hearts and minds (*zheng xin* 正心) and only then proceed to use ourselves as the standards by which we measure others.[23]

Dai Zhen certainly believes we should avail ourselves of these sorts of correctives. A crucial component of being a good judge of others' inclinations, for example, is having at least reasonably well-ordered inclinations oneself. And Dai allows that we can develop a knack for second-guessing our sympathetic judgments over time.[24] But it is much less certain that Dai would share the intuitive grounds for adopting these strategies as I have described them above. To motivate these strategies, after all, I simply assumed that some check against mistaken desires had to be introduced either before the exercise of *shu* (in the corrective inspired by Zhu Xi) or after it (in pointing out that we could refuse to endorse our *shu*-based judgments). But this omits another possibility that, when compared with our everyday processes of moral deliberation, should strike us as the far more natural one: namely, that *shu* itself plays some critical role in determining which sorts of desires are true indicators of our well-being and which are not.

We can appreciate the importance of this latter alternative by comparing it with the model inspired by Zhu Xi.[25] By Zhu Xi's account we begin either with refined desires in ourselves, or at least by specifying which desires would qualify as refined, and once we have done that we go on to practice *shu*. But this fits awkwardly with our everyday experience of sympathy-based moral reasoning (which *shu* may well not be, by Zhu's reading). If some exigency tempts me to miss a lunch with George, and I want to imagine how George might feel about this before committing to it, it would be strange to say that I should have perfectly "rectified" desires in advance of putting myself in his shoes. A major motivation for Dai's turn to *shu* is his supposition that it can help less-than-ideal moral thinkers muddle through their daily lives,[26] and for these purposes Zhu's prerequisites seem too rigorous to put into practice. It makes much more sense to say that my attempt to sympathetically reconstruct his point of view itself plays some selective role, helping me to determine which sorts of desires I should take into account as I proceed. Much as grief for the passing of a loved one, for example, lays bare the ways in which the deceased contributed to our personal fulfillment—ways of which we often had little or no awareness prior to grieving—so, too, does sympathy help to focus and make more vivid the facts that are salient for determinations of well-being.

If we can accept this as a psychological possibility, then this presents us with two distinct models of sympathetic understanding. Under the first model, *shu*'s real work in tracking well-being is accomplished through perspective-taking. Its primary contribution to my attempt to understand George, and know what is good for him, lies in my imagining myself as him, feeling as he would feel and wanting as he would want. *Shu* is "naive" in the sense that it adopts a set of desires uncritically. This is not to say that *we* adopt them uncritically—as we saw, this naive model is perfectly compatible with the view that we should exercise discretion either before or after our sympathetic reconstruction of the other's point of view. But it does imply that *shu* exercises no discretion itself, and this is precisely what the second model rejects. For the latter, which I shall ultimately attribute to Dai Zhen, *shu* plays a crucial part in helping us to determine which sorts of desires are true indicators of well-being, because *shu* is not just an exercise in perspective-taking, but also a way of valuing a person.

To explicate this more robust account of *shu*, let me begin by offering a diagnosis of the motivations for the naive model of *shu*, where its contribution to estimations of welfare lie exclusively in perspective-taking. One of the chief reasons that this model is so alluring is that we moderns (especially those of us who are steeped in modern philosophy and social science) are predisposed to lend a certain explanatory authority to first-person deliberations about one's own desires.[27] If I want to say why a particular apple is good for Mary, I will be inclined to tell a story that ends in claims about what Mary wants. I will most likely explain that she has a hunger for this particular kind of apple, and that the sustenance it offers will help her to get other things that she desires. If I cite benefits that do not immediately invoke her desires—for example, if I mention that having an apple will help to sustain her concentration through the next few hours of work—I am likely to explain the goodness of these other things in terms of more fundamental desires (such as the desire to do good work, to win a promotion, etc.). To be sure, it will not always be the case that Mary wants the apple, for it is not always the case that people want what is best for themselves. But we tend to correct for this problem by saying that the apple is something she *would* want if only she were apprised of all of the relevant information and capable of making sound inferences from that information. If only she knew that eating it would improve her concentration, and if only she knew how it tasted, she would then desire it.

So understood, this deference to informed judgments about one's own desires helps to explain why we tend to believe perspective-taking does all of the relevant work. After all, to determine what constitutes Mary's well-being, it is sufficient to know what she would (under epistemically ideal circumstances) want. If I err in determining what she would want, this is because I make bad inferences, or I do not have access to all of the relevant facts (for example, that she has an allergy to apples). But these are mistakes in reasoning or information gathering, not mistakes in sympathizing itself. Thus, the explanatory power attributed to Mary's informed desires has an important epistemic implication as well. My inquiry into the constituents of her well-being may safely stop at the point that I am able to determine what Mary would ideally want. Sympathizing with Mary may require more than this kind of perspective-taking, but insofar as we rely on sympathy to know what's good for her, this perspective-taking exhausts its epistemic contribution.

For Dai Zhen, both the naive account and its motivating assumptions would be highly dubious. The first and perhaps most notable problem is that it commits us to a peculiar doctrine about altruistic or disinterested desires: namely, that they are always mistaken desires, and that it would be impossible to rationally want something self-sacrificial (or at least not beneficial) in light of full information. Since the informed desire theory holds that my good is whatever I would rationally want given full knowledge of a certain kind, it is committed to the view that I could never under those circumstances want something bad for myself. This is a major criticism of "informed desire" or "full information" theories of welfare in contemporary philosophy and social science, a criticism that Amartya Sen has captured succinctly in accusing informed desire theorists of "definitional egoism."[28] And it is not difficult to see how it would run against the grain of Dai Zhen's deeply Confucian understanding of human moral psychology.

Consider, for example, the desire of parents for their children's future health and prosperity. It is reasonable to assume, surely, that many mothers and fathers would in light of full information quite rationally want things for their children that come at great cost to themselves. Many are willing to give up a great deal of their freedom and leisure to see to it that their children have the kind of lives that, long after their parental benefactors are gone, the children will continue to find meaningful and satisfying.[29] And this sacrificial urge to provide for the long-term well-being of one's children tends to be both deeply felt and something of which its possessors are intimately aware. If this sort of thing does not qualify as a desire, it is difficult to imagine what would.

Defenders of the informed desire approach might try to explain this phenomenon away by suggesting that in fulfilling the interests of one's children, the benevolent parent also fulfills her own interests—that the utility function of the parent reflects the utility function of the child, as economists sometimes put it. But this is too facile an explanation. The very language of this sort of sacrifice requires that we allow for trade-offs between parent and child welfare. One might even feel a powerful drive to give up her life in order to spare her child from pain, and while it might give her some comfort to know the benefits of her sacrifice as she goes to her grave, it would be both wrong and unfair to describe such comfort as a good for her that is proportional to the strength of her desire for it.

Given the place of prominence of filial piety in the Confucian moral order, Dai tends to stress the particular subset of desires where the sacrificial relationship is reversed, so as to highlight the filial disposition to want the well-being of one's parents over and above one's own. This disposition exists not just in human beings, but (Dai claims) in any living creature that has an awareness of its parents and thus can be seen even in the way birds feed their mothers in old age.[30] But despite this emphasis, Dai is clear that many kinds of self-sacrificial inclinations exist, not only for one's parents, but also for one's progeny, one's mate, and even in some minimal sense for members of one's own species.[31]

These sorts of phenomena are ones that any reasonable picture of human psychology must accommodate, and they point to an entire sphere of informed desires that do not fall neatly within the purview of self-beneficial ones. More to the point, however, is that they point to a more nuanced account of self-interest (*si* 私). Consider what sense (or nonsense) we would have to make of the claim that Martin, who is fully informed about the choices before him, "wants his own good." For an informed desire thinker this sort of statement would be redundant: the fact that Martin wants *anything* under these epistemically ideal circumstances is sufficient reason to take it to be good for him. But I suspect that most of us will find that this goes against our considered judgments, for we tend to understand self-interest not just as wanting whatever we would want under full information, as having a certain self-directed pro-attitude. To be self-interested is to consider one's own well-being valuable and thus to desire it as an end.[32] This, surely, is a noticeable feature of Dai Zhen's understanding of self-interestedness:

> Whether one cares self-interestedly only for oneself (私於身), or whether one extends [this care] to those near and dear to oneself, these are both kinds of humane love. To care for oneself is to be humane toward oneself (仁其身), and to extend it to those near and dear to oneself is to be humane toward one's intimates.[33]

There are a few things to note about this passage. First, if Dai thought that informed desires were definitionally egoistic, it would be strange to add that self-interest (*si*) requires the attitude of "being humane toward" (or "loving humanely" [*ren* 仁]) oneself. This sort of attitude, understood by most Confucian thinkers as requiring a substantial mechanism of psychological habits and attitudes, would appear to be the epiphenomenal icing on the motivational cake. Having accurate desires would already be enough.

Second, Dai's point here is that self-interest and generous feelings toward one's intimates are not really different in kind. Both share a fundamental feature in common. What is it? If we look at the way Dai sets up this proclamation about self-interest, we can begin to see the contours of an answer:

> All creatures of blood and *qi* know the love of life and fear of death, and therefore pursue benefit and avoid harm. Although they differ in understanding, they are nevertheless the same in not going beyond this love of life and fear of death.... The love of that which has given one life [one's parents], the love of that to which one has

given life [one's children] . . . all of this proceeds from the love of life and fear of death.[34]

Earlier I suggested that Dai Zhen's account of well-being is best understood as what he calls "life fulfillment" (*sui sheng*), a phrase that evokes Dai's highest good, "producing and sustaining life" (*sheng sheng*). Here again Dai makes the connection between life and well-being explicit: insofar as we love life and fear death, he says, we seek benefits and try to avoid harms. The question, however, is whose benefits we seek and whose harms we avoid, and Dai's answer is that it depends on whose life we love. Whether we want our parents to fare well or whether we want ourselves to prosper, both sorts of want share a common attitude: namely, a love of the life that belongs to the person in question. This suggests, *pace* the informed desire view, that knowledgeable desiring is not, ultimately, a sufficient condition for self-interest. To be self-interested we must also have the right sort of feeling—"love" (*huai* 懷)—toward our own life, with all of the structural demands of which that life is constituted.

To be sure, it is much easier to elicit a love of one's own life than it is to love another's. Dai seems to assume that for most of us the latter will never come so effortlessly as the former, which is one reason why the imaginative exercise of putting oneself in another's place is so important.[35] But Dai reminds us that just because our self-love comes relatively effortlessly we should not assume that this feeling, so crucial to wanting the good of someone else, is somehow missing in cases where the life in question is one's own. To care deeply about one's own well-being requires the same robust feeling of attachment as caring deeply about the well-being of anyone else.[36]

The final point to make about the passage on *si* is that it has implications not just for the motivational requirements of self-interest, but for the epistemic requirements as well. That is, we depend on a self-directed sense of humanity even to understand what is in our own self-interest. To be humanely disposed toward someone is more than a matter of being inclined to act on a series of prespecified ends, as though it could be our humanity that drives us to help a child, but something else that specifies the particular ways in which the child needs help. Humanity is also the virtue by which we come to recognize which ends are worthwhile in the first place.[37]

This helps to fill out the more robust, nonnaive account of *shu* that we need. It suggests that this felt attachment to someone's life and life fulfillment, over and above the attachment to someone's desire fulfillment, is doing some of the necessary work in helping us to distinguish the truly self-interested desires from the rest, even in the cases where the desires in question are our own. There is remarkably strong prima facie evidence for this more nuanced phenomenology of self-interest. Surely we can distinguish between "what we want" and "what we want for our own sake," at least much of the time. I know that having my home team win would not benefit me in proportion to the strength of my desire for it, and it seems likely that my ability to adopt some caring or loving stance toward myself has something to do with this insight.[38] Needless to say it is not *sufficient* for this insight—and Dai Zhen is eager to supplement our deliberations with the refinement in judgment and knowledge of the world that comes with successful self-cultivation—but it is *necessary* all the same. Most of our attempts to take the well-being of others into account requires this "love of life and fear of death" at a minimum. It is an intellectualist's fantasy that we will appreciate the relevant demands of life with sufficient depth, that we will be able to see them vividly, without this love.[39]

In the fundamental matter of taking proper account of a person's welfare, this "love of life"—so often invoked by Dai—is absolutely vital. However, there is a second contribution made by "being humane toward oneself" that I want to offer in a slightly more tentative way, and that contribution is a shift in point of view. For Dai Zhen, the feeling of humanity or benevolence toward someone, which he understands as a feeling aimed at "fulfilling one's life,"[40] almost always contains within it some sympathetic understanding of the people whose lives are to be fulfilled. To be sure, not all close followers of Kongzi (Confucius) see humanity as constituted by some exercise of *shu*, and many of Dai Zhen's Neo-Confucian predecessors insist that *shu* should eventually drop out of our deliberative repertoire as we strive to become humane people.[41] But for Dai Zhen *shu* figures centrally in being humane, and generally speaking one cannot be the latter without at the same time exercising the former.[42] It is quite likely, therefore, that self-interest requires "humanity" because the latter includes within it a kind of sympathetic understanding. The act of considering myself from a sympathetic stance—as a concerned observer might consider me, comparing her case to my own—plays an important part in helping me to highlight the desires whose ends are important for my own life fulfillment.

A revealing detail in this respect is Dai's tendency to describe *shu* not just as a way of studying the feelings of others, but also as manner of "returning to oneself" (*fan gong* 反躬),[43] an expression he takes from the "Record of Music" ("Yueji" 樂記).[44] For Dai Zhen, "returning to oneself" is essentially the form of self-examination that we undertake in order to introspectively evaluate our behavior before we commit to it. So quite naturally, Dai typically presents it as something we should do before imposing ourselves on others. "Whenever one does something to another," he offers, "one should return to oneself and calmly reflect: If another were to do this to me, would I be able to bear it?"[45] This may seem to suggest that we use it primarily to gain insight into the would-be psychological landscape of others, but if we examine Dai's analysis of the expression more carefully, we see that it does more work than this. Additionally, it also helps us to distinguish between *our own* desires, telling us which ones are superfluous or meddlesome and which ones really count. And those that really count are the core of basic desires that we share in common with other human beings. This is a notion that Dai takes once again from the "Record of Music," noting how it attributes to all of us a common set of essential dispositions or true feelings (*qing* 情) to which belong the desires that are most essentially our own.[46] Thus, the process of "returning to oneself" accomplishes at least two things: it helps us to understand how we would feel were we in another's shoes, but importantly it also helps to clarify which desires we are rightly expected to take into account. Surely the latter accomplishment sheds as much light on ourselves as it does on others.

"When certain doctrines enter deeply into the hearts of human beings," Dai declares, "their harm is great, and yet no one is able to awaken to them."[47] Dai is clear that he sees both a healthy use of one's own desires, as well as a proper reliance on *shu*, as the remedy for the prudential blindness that he finds in the moral ideals of his age. What I have tried to do here is show that, in an important sense, the latter is more fundamental than the former. It is our success at understanding ourselves as objects of sympathy that informs our evaluations of well-being, and not the other way around. *Shu* brings with it the right emotional attachment and sufficient distance from internal point of view to shed light on the sorts of interests and inclinations that truly matter, and so it becomes less the flimsy exercise of perspective-taking and more the familiar emotional attitude of sympathetic understanding as we characteristically see it in our everyday deliberations. As such, it is better suited to serve as the more fundamental source of insight into the human good.

Notes

Acknowledgments: My thanks to P. J. Ivanhoe, Julia Tao, and Yu Kam-por for comments on an earlier draft of this essay. I am also indebted to Chris Fraser, Koji Tanaka, and the many other scholars who participated in the Fourteenth Conference of the International Society for Chinese Philosophy, where I first presented a version of the argument I make here.

1. The chief philosophical works I cite here are Dai's *On the Good* (*Yuanshan* 原善), *Remnants of Words* (*Xuyan* 緒言), and especially *An Evidential Study of the Meaning of Terms of the Mengzi* (*Mengzi ziyi shuzheng* 孟子字義疏證), hereafter *Evidential Study*. A reliable and widely available edition of the two most important of these works, *On the Good* and *Evidential Study*, is attached as a lengthy "appendix" to Hu Shi's 胡適 *The Philosophy of Dai Dongyuan* (*Dai Dongyuan de zhexue* 戴東原的哲學) (Reprint, Taipei: Taiwan shangwu, 1996), 201–239, 240–337. *Remnants of Words* appears in the *Complete Collection of Dai Zhen* (*Dai Zhen quanji* 戴震全集), vol. 1, ed. Dai Zhen Research Group (Beijing: Qinghua daxue chubanshe, 1991), 64–116. Other primary texts of Dai's will be cited as needed. My somewhat controversial translation of *Xuyan* as *Remnants of Words* (referring to the remnants of *the sages'* words) follows Yu Yingshi, *Lun Dai Zhen yu Zhang Xuecheng*, (Hong Kong: Longmen shudian, 1976), 100–101.

2. *Shu* has been variously understood as the Confucian Golden Rule, the practice of moral reciprocity, and (more often than not) as a distinctively Confucian form of sympathy. Dai himself describes it as "taking oneself and extending it to others" (*Evidential Study*, chap. 15 [*li*/15]), and I have argued elsewhere that this is best understood as encompassing a form of sympathetic understanding, where we imagine ourselves by analogy to be in another's place, and so for a time value them like we value ourselves (*Acquiring "Feelings That Do Not Err": Moral Deliberation and the Sympathetic Point of View in the Ethics of Dai Zhen* [Ph.D. diss., University of Chicago, 2006]).

3. To quote from Dai's closing indictment of the Neo-Confucians in his *Evidential Study*: "When Yao and Shun worried about the 'hardship and poverty within the four seas,' or when King Wen 'looked upon the people as if they were injured,' was there even a single affair in which they were not planning on behalf of the desires of these people?" The wisdom of Wen and the sage-kings, here, lies in the recognition of two facts. First, one cannot know the substantive moral standards of good order (*li*) without also knowing what is good or bad for the would-be beneficiaries of those standards in the first place. To attend to the good, as these ideal figures demonstrate, is to attend to what is identified in classical sources by the terms "hardship" (*kun* 困), "poverty" (*qiong* 窮), and "injury" (*shang* 傷). Later in the same closing statement, Dai says that those who insist on ignoring the desires in their deliberations will bring misfortune or calamity (*huo* 禍) on others (*Evidential Study*, chap. 43 [afterword]). Second, the way we attend to the well-being of others, and so attempt to overcome hardship, poverty, and other afflictions, is just by "planning on behalf of their desires."

4. *Evidential Study*, chap. 40 (*quan*/1). See also chaps. 5 (*li*/5), 10 (*li*/10), 41–42 (*quan*/2–3), 43 (afterword), and *passim*.

5. See, for example, Nancy Sherman, "Empathy and Imagination," in *Midwest Studies in Philosophy* 22 (1998): 82–119, especially her remarks on sympathy (p. 110).

6. See the end of the final chapter of *Evidential Study*, chap. 43 (afterword).

7. *Evidential Study*, chap. 43 (afterword).

8. To understand the basic argument in J. S. Mill's *Utilitarianism*, for example, it is crucial that we be able to identify such turns of phrase as "in the interest of the

agent himself," "for the benefit of the individual," or "having full worth" as bearing on the same kind of good (viz. human well-being), and that there are things we can say about this good as a kind—for example, that it should be cashed out in terms of happiness. See Alan Ryan, ed., *Utilitarianism and Other Essays* (New York: Penguin Books, 1987), 272–338, especially 290–298.

9. Dai's favored account of *shu* comes from its locus classicus in *Analects* 15.24: "What you would not desire yourself, do not inflict upon others" (*Evidential Study*, chap. 5 [*li*/5]).

10. This sort of problem has been aptly described as a "paternalism" of desire attribution. See, for example, Herbert Fingarette's "Following the 'One Thread' of the *Analects*," *Journal of the American Academy of Religion: Thematic Issue* 47s (September 1979): 373–405, especially 384–385, 388–395; P. J. Ivanhoe's "The 'Golden Rule' in the *Analects*," in *Confucius Now: Contemporary Encounters with the Analects*, ed. David Jones (LaSalle, IL: Open Court, 2007), 81–108.

11. See Dai's *Evidential Study*, chap. 5 (*li*/5), and his remarks on chapter 13 of the *Doctrine of the Mean*, in the "Supplemental Commentary on the *Doctrine of the Mean*," in *The Complete Writings of Dai Zhen*, vol. 2, ed. Zhang Dainian (Hefei: Huangshan she, 1994), 47–83, especially 61.

12. *Evidential Study*, chap. 2 (*li*/2).

13. Ibid., chap. 21 (*xing*/2).

14. For example, notice an important passage in chap. 10 (*li*/10) of the *Evidential Study*, where Dai says the sage "governs the empire by embodying the feelings of the people and fulfilling the desires of the people, and so the kingly way is complete." See also chaps. 30 (*cai*/2), 40 (*quan*/1), 43 (afterword), and *passim*.

15. *Evidential Study*, chap. 10 (*li*/10). See also chap. 40 (*quan*/1).

16. See Dai's analysis of the Mengzi-Gaozi debates, in which Gaozi maintains that "nature" (*xing* 性) means "life" (*sheng* 生) (*Mengzi* 6A1–6; *Evidential Study*, chap. 21 [*xing*/2]). Following the parameters of this debate, Dai's discussion of "life" is notably confined to things with "consciousness" or "awareness" (*jue* 覺) and therefore omits plant life. On this point see also the "question" section of chap. 27 (*xing*/8).

17. *Evidential Study*, chap. 31 (*cai*/3).

18. Ibid., chap. 10 (*li*/10).

19. More literally, the process of "growing life," a reference to the "Appended Remarks" section of the *Book of Changes* (*Yijing* 易經, part 1, chap. 5).

20. *On the Good*, 1.1 (other discussions of *sheng sheng* and its moral significance appear in 1.3, 1.4, 2.1, 3.1, and 3.16). Dai, we should note, is not a welfarist. That is, he does not think that the only thing that counts as good, ultimately, is welfare or well-being. He also builds in the requirement that human life maintain a kind of continuity with natural generative processes, and it is actually from this latter sort of good that human welfare derives its moral value (*Evidential Study*, chap. 36 [*ren, yi, li, zhi*, 1]). In this respect, as in many others, Dai's moral thought resonates deeply with Xunzi's. See P. J. Ivanhoe's "A Happy Symmetry: Xunzi's Ethical Thought," in T. C.

Kline III, ed., *Ritual and Religion in the* Xunzi, (Albany: State University of New York Press, 2008), 63–87.

21. 凡血氣之屬皆知懷生畏死, 因而趨利避害. Here the Chinese for "therefore" (*yiner* 因而) subordinates the second clause to the first, so that the second (seeking after profit and avoiding harm) happens under the condition of the first being true (knowing the love of life and fear of death) (*Evidential Study*, chap. 21 [*xing*/2]). In other words, "therefore" should *not* be read in the merely evidentiary sense of "there is smoke therefore there is fire." Rather, it is *because* we love life that we pursue profit, and thus Dai clearly implies that loving one's life is a prerequisite for seeking after one's own good. Dai Zhen makes strikingly similar statements in *On the Good*, 2.2, and *Remnants of Words*, 1.16.

22. A point made by Nancy Sherman, "Empathy and Imagination," 110–111.

23. If we do not take these precautions, he says, "then that which we desire will not necessarily be that which we should desire, and that which we detest will not necessarily be that which we should detest. If, without examining these things, one hastily uses his own desires as the standard for that which he imposes on others, then even if his intentions are impartial (*gong* 公) his deeds will be self-serving (*si* 私)" (*Concordance to Master Zhu's "Questions and Answers on the Four Books,"* ed. Toshimizu Goto [Hiroshima: Hiroshima Daigaku Bungakubu, 1955], 487).

24. *Evidential Study*, chap. 41 (*quan*/2).

25. I say this model is "inspired by" Zhu Xi, rather than directly attributable to him, because it is uncertain that Zhu is particularly concerned that the right desires be directed toward one's own good. It might be, after all, that he sees it primarily as a matter of making them line up with the moral good. As Zhu is generally a eudaemonistic thinker, I suspect he believes they should line up with both, but his analysis in the *Questions and Answers* (quoted above) is ambiguous.

26. In chapter 10 of the *Evidential Study*, Dai notes that a great deal of speculation about moral wisdom focuses on the sage figure, and yet that the rest of us still need to call on our own less-than-sagely faculties in order to resolve our everyday affairs: "All people have business that concerns the household, the affairs of state, and the world. Can it really be that we must await the wisdom of the sage before we can act?" I have argued elsewhere that Dai offers *shu* as the preferred form of moral deliberation for imperfect adjudicators like ourselves (*Acquiring "Feelings that Do Not Err,"* chap. 1).

27. For example, we find this tendency in such luminaries as John Rawls (*Theory of Justice* [Cambridge, MA: Harvard University Press, 1971], chap. 7), R. M. Hare (*Moral Thinking: Its Levels, Method, and Point* [Oxford: Clarendon Press, 1981], chap. 5), and Joseph Raz (*The Morality of Freedom* [Oxford: Clarendon Press, 1986], chap. 12).

28. Amartya Sen, *Choice, Welfare, and Measurement* (Oxford: Basil Blackwell, 1982), chap. 4.

29. Mark Overvold has made effective use of a case much like this one in "Self-Interest and the Concept of Self-Sacrifice," *Canadian Journal of Philosophy* 10 (1980): 105–118, especially 108.

30. Not all animals show the same sort of filial piety, nor do they tend to make the same sorts of sacrifices for their fathers. But Dai says this is because they are unaware of their parentage, not because they lack the relevant dispositions. See *Evidential Study*, chap. 21 (*xing*/2).

31. All living creatures show some basic willingness to sacrifice for members of their own species, Dai says, insofar as they demonstrate a great reluctance to eat their own kind (*Evidential Study*, chap. 21 [*xing*/2]).

32. As the ethicist Stephen Darwall points out, a depressive or self-loathing person might not want her own good, and while we might tell her that she is misinformed about what she wants, there is nothing *conceptually* incoherent in her saying "I know what I really want, and what I really want is bad for me." She may simply fail to value herself (and thus what is good for her) in the way that we would expect (*Welfare and Rational Care* [Princeton: Princeton University Press, 2002], 5–6).

33. *Evidential Study*, chap. 21 (*xing*/2).

34. Ibid.

35. Except, perhaps, in the problematic case of the sage, who is able to extend such love to others. I discuss this likely exception in *Acquiring "Feelings that Do Not Err,"* chap. 2, section 6.

36. It sounds awkward to use language normally reserved for moral praise to describe the essentially self-serving accomplishment of wanting one's own good. And Dai's handling of the phraseology reflects this awkwardness, specifying that the love of one's self and intimates are mere "kinds of humanity" (that is, they are in the territory of humanity or humane love [*ren zhi shu* 仁之屬]). But even if we can only speak in terms of *quasi*-humanity (or *quasi*-humane love) the basic point remains the same: the core attitude that motivates the love of others (a kind of care or concern for a particular person that Dai cashes out as a "love" of that person's "life") is essentially the same attitude that motivates the love of oneself.

37. *Evidential Study*, chaps. 21 (*xing*/2), 36 (*ren, yi, li, zhi*/1), 41 (*quan*/2), and *passim*.

38. I owe this crucial observation (and much else in this essay) to Darwall's *Welfare and Rational Care*. I describe some fundamental differences between Dai and Darwall in *Acquiring "Feelings that Do Not Err,"* chap. 5, section 3.

39. To hark back to an earlier analogy, this is as unlikely as it is that we can fully appreciate someone's everyday, often invisible contributions without some powerful emotion like grief to highlight them. Grief helps to focus our attention on the little things that the deceased has done for the griever, making the absence of these things more palpable to the griever, and thus enabling her to recognize and appreciate the deceased's contributions in a way that would never be available to her without her grief.

40. See the opening lines of *Evidential Study*, chap. 36 (*ren, yi, li, zhi*/1).

41. Cheng Yi 程頤 (1033–1107), Zhu Xi, and Wang Yangming 王陽明 (1472–1529) all regard *ren* as a virtue not unlike *shu* in its results, in that it makes one do things that harmonize with the desires of others, but as a means they regard *shu* as being too

deliberative and affectively laden for truly humane thoughts and behavior. On this point, see David Nivison's "Golden Rule Arguments in Chinese Moral Philosophy," in *The Ways of Confucianism*, ed. Bryan Van Norden (Chicago: Open Court, 1996), 69–70.

42. Most commentators agree that one can be *shu* (sympathetically understanding) without exhibiting the fuller virtue of *ren*. But they appear to differ on the question of whether one can be *ren* without also at the same time being *shu*. Dai Zhen is clear that at least the nonsages among us cannot and cites Mengzi to make his case: "To act out of robust sympathetic understanding—in seeking humanity, there is nothing closer than this" (強恕而行, 求仁莫近焉; *Mengzi* 7A4, discussed in Dai's *Evidential Study*, chap. 41 [*quan*/2]). See also the last two steps of the three-step ascent to humane virtue, as Dai describes it: "To take one's self and extend it [to others] is 'sympathetic understanding' (*shu*), and to share in the sorrows and joys of others is 'humanity' (*ren*)" (*Evidential Study*, chap. 15 [*li*/15]).

43. Ibid., chaps. 2 (*li*/2), 11 (*li*/11).

44. "When one's loves and aversions are not regulated internally, and one's understanding is led astray by external things, one cannot *return to oneself* and the heavenly patterns of good order are extinguished" ("Record of Music," chap. 19 of *Record of Rituals*, *Sibu congkan* edition, 11.7b5–8); emphasis is mine.

45. *Evidential Study*, chap. 2 (*li*/2).

46. Here, Dai uses the term *qing* not in the descriptive sense of affective dispositions that we all tend to have, but in the more selective sense of essential traits of character that all of us will have if nurtured in the right way, under conditions of sufficient discipline and self-restraint. I use "*true* feelings" as a shorthand for this latter, more normative sense of the term.

47. *Evidential Study*, chap. 43 (afterword).

Chapter 8

The Nature of the Virtues in Light of the Early Confucian Tradition

Eirik Lang Harris

In this chapter, I take a prominent and plausible conception of virtues from the Western philosophical tradition, apply it to some early Confucian texts, and see where it succeeds and fails. In this way, I show how this conception of virtues needs to be revised.[1] To some, it may seem strange to take Western concepts of virtue and see how they hold up in light of the early Confucian tradition. However, if Western virtue ethicists take themselves to be prescribing for everyone, as opposed to simply for those within their own cultural background, then they must be willing to take into account challenges that may arise from outside their own tradition. And, insofar as the early Confucians were developing a virtue ethic of their own,[2] insights gleaned from their thought may well advance contemporary Western virtue ethics, pointing out some of its shortcomings and highlighting possible solutions.

The particular conception of virtues I am starting with is one of virtues as correctives, which was made prominent by Philippa Foot in her paper "Virtues and Vices"[3] and further developed by Robert C. Roberts in his article "Will Power and the Virtues."[4] On Foot's account, "the virtues are *corrective*, each one standing at a point at which there is some temptation to be resisted or deficiency of motivation to be made good."[5] This conception captures certain aspects of the virtues. However, I wish to demonstrate that virtues that are often thought of as correctives are not *best* characterized in this way, at least on the general understanding of correctives. I will do this in two ways. First, I show that being a corrective is only a contingent feature of these virtues. Second, I demonstrate that "self-love," which carries many similarities to other so-called corrective virtues, is a plausible candidate for the status of virtue while not being a corrective, even in a contingent way. In addition, I want to show that there is another class of virtues that the idea of virtues as correctives completely misses. I will call this class of virtues "inclinational virtues." Finally, I explain why expecting the notion of a corrective to accommodate the idea of inclinational virtues is unwise.

There are at least two distinct ways one could use the early Confucian tradition to elucidate a contemporary discussion of the virtues. The first would be to try to reconstruct and put forward a comprehensive early Confucian account of the virtues. Such a project would necessitate a much longer treatment than I can give here. In addition, while it makes sense to discuss an early Confucian virtue ethic tradition, it would be a mistake to assume that the underlying structure of the virtues did not differ between texts such as the *Lunyu* 論語 (*Analects*) and the *Mengzi* 孟子. The second approach is to selectively choose passages from these early Chinese texts and apply the conception of virtues as correctives to them to see where they force us to rethink our ideas about the nature of virtues and prompt us to recast the discussion of the nature of virtues in a different light.[6]

In this discussion of the virtues I draw heavily from ideas found in the *Lunyu* and the *Mengzi*, two early and important Confucian texts. It is important to note that in my discussion of the virtues I am not relying on any particular Chinese term but am rather discussing things that the early Confucians would think of as good character traits that contribute to the flourishing of individuals and their society. As such, I am simply using a "thin" account of the virtues, a description that has little in the way of theoretical content, but which could be agreed on by both the early Confucian thinkers and more contemporary Western thinkers.[7] I am not, as might be assumed, relying on an equation of the Chinese character *de* 德 as an equivalent of the English "virtue." This character, while often translated into English as "virtue," has aspects that are not normally associated with our Western concept of virtue. It is, we might say, a "thick" concept, and what I am interested in here is simply the underlying "thin" concept.[8] I wish to take as a starting point for this discussion a thin account of virtues as dispositions of character that contribute in direct and substantial ways to the flourishing of individuals and their communities.[9] Given such a thin account, we can analyze thicker accounts of the virtues, such as the ones given by Foot and Roberts and those given in the *Lunyu* and *Mengzi* and see the extent to which they can be supported.

A Contribution from the *Lunyu*

Several passages from the *Lunyu*, attributed to the early Chinese thinker Kongzi 孔子 (Confucius), are quite useful for thinking about our intuitions about virtue and are equally useful in helping us draw out some of the implications of these virtues.[10] As such, I begin my inquiry into the nature of the virtues by taking a look at some of the passages from this text that may be helpful in leading us toward a fuller conception of the virtues. The first passage I look at is an autobiographical sketch of Kongzi in *Lunyu* 2.4:

> The Master said:
> At fifteen, my aim was on learning;
> At thirty, I took my stand;
> At forty, I had no doubts;
> At fifty, I knew Heaven's Mandate;
> At sixty, my ears were attuned;
> At seventy, in following my heart's desires I did not transgress the boundaries.[11]

Here, Kongzi describes his learning about and implementing Heaven's Mandate in his life. Although neither virtue nor the Way (*dao* 道) are mentioned here, in following Heaven's Mandate, Kongzi would be following the Way, and this would ensure that he was acting in a virtuous manner.[12]

What is interesting about this passage for our purposes is the idea that acting virtuously is a gradual and learned process. Kongzi at fifteen was focused on understanding the virtues and how to act so as to become virtuous. We can understand the process here as consisting of a back and forth, with an understanding of the virtues informing Kongzi's actions and his actions aiding in filling out his understanding of virtue.[13] Even given his understanding of virtue, there was still a tension between what Kongzi knew to be the right thing to do and where his desires led him. That is to say, while knowledge of the Way is part of successfully following it, there is some sense in which knowing the virtuous path and following the virtuous path are two distinct things.

There are at least two possible ways to understand this potential problem. One might fail to follow the Way because of *akrasia*. That is, it could be that an individual has moral knowledge but does not act on this moral knowledge because she is overcome by some other temptation. But failing to follow through and act on knowledge might also be because of *acedia*. This arises when, even though there is no overriding temptation, the individual cannot motivate herself sufficiently to act in accordance with her moral knowledge.[14]

The problem that Kongzi had seems to have been one of *akrasia* rather than *acedia*. The whole autobiography indicates that he desires to become virtuous and works toward this end. He was not an individual who simply came across this knowledge but could not motivate himself to act. Furthermore, the fact that he was seventy before he could follow his desires and still act virtuously indicates that, before this time, there were tensions between his desires and what he saw as morally correct action. These tensions, then, presumably led him, in at least some circumstances, to act in ways he took to not be virtuous. If someone like Kongzi, who had an active desire to act virtuously from the time he was young, had the problem of his desires leading him away from virtue, this would certainly imply that there are in general strong tendencies within humans to act against the virtues.

Although Kongzi is not explicit about this, it seems quite plausible to say that the reason acting in a virtuous manner is so difficult is because our desires often pull in the direction of vice. And, if this is correct, then a picture begins to emerge of a relationship between virtues and vices. Indeed, it may look like Kongzi has in mind an idea of virtues as correctives. Kongzi certainly does not develop such a picture in detail, but as it coincides with certain trends in contemporary virtue ethics, it is a theory that is worthy of more consideration.

Virtues as Correctives

As mentioned earlier, one prominent and influential contemporary account of the virtues as correctives comes from Foot. Foot begins with a conception of virtues as being general beneficial characteristics that humans need to possess both for their own sake and for the sake of others. This, though, is not sufficient to determine what a virtue is, she argues, because there are many other things that humans need to possess, such as physical strength, memory, and good health, none of which she wishes to call virtues. Rather, she argues that virtues belong to the will,[15] and that they must actively engage the will. With this in mind, Foot goes on to argue that "man's virtue may be judged by his innermost desires as well as by his intentions."[16] From this point, she continues to argue that the virtues are corrective, that each one stands "at a point at which there is some temptation to be resisted or deficiency of motivation to be made good."[17] So, in order for something to be a virtue for Foot, it must relate to a vice that serves as a temptation. In elucidating this idea she gives us an example, arguing that it is "*only* because fear and desire for pleasure often operate as temptations that courage and temperance exist as virtues at all."[18]

Foot's argument is the following. In order for an action to be virtuous: (1) the action must be deliberate, and (2) the action must be corrective of a *general* temptation that should be resisted or a *general* deficiency of motivation that should be made good.

With this understanding of virtues as correctives, an immediate objection comes to mind. Certainly Kongzi at seventy was virtuous, but by this time he no longer had the vices for which the virtues are thought to serve as correctives. Foot makes claims that lead one to think that there is a necessary connection between the virtues and their corresponding vices. She claims, for example, that "if people were as much attached to the good of others as they are to their own good there would no more be a general virtue of benevolence than there is a general virtue of self-love."[19] However, she is not making the strong claim that in order for something to be a virtue, it must act as a corrective in all individuals. Nor is she even claiming that it must serve as a corrective for the individual whose dispositions are being analyzed. Rather, she is making a weaker claim that in order for something, such as courage, to be a virtue, the vice to which it is related, cowardice in this case, must be a general temptation.

This more nuanced elucidation of what it means for virtues to be correctives means that Foot is immune to a charge from Kongzi that she cannot account for the virtue possessed by someone who delighted in the Way, whose desires accorded with the Way to such an extent that this person did not feel the pull of any vices. Given this understanding of virtue, a person may possess the virtue of courage even if she is not herself tempted by fear into cowardice, so long as in general people are tempted by fear to act in a cowardly fashion. As such, Foot would be perfectly happy to accept that Kongzi's dispositions upon reaching seventy years of age were virtuous even though these dispositions were not accompanied by any temptations toward vices.

Indeed, she would likely argue that part of what is virtuous about Kongzi is that he has completely internalized[20] virtue and thus his actions reflect not only his intentions but also his innermost desires. Quoting from John Hershey's book, *A Single Pebble*, Foot makes reference to a guide who saves an injured child: "His action, which could not have been mulled over in his mind, showed a deep, instinctive love of life, a compassion, an optimism, which made me feel very good."[21] This would seem to lead Foot to the conclusion that there is something more virtuous about someone who has internalized the virtues to the extent that expressing them is simply an outpouring of his natural emotions, feelings, and tendencies.

We see a similar sentiment in the *Lunyu*:

The Master said:
Knowing it is not as good as liking it;
Liking it is not as good as delighting in it. (6.20)

Kongzi said:
To be born knowing it is the highest.
To study and know it is next.
To have difficulties and learn it follows next.
To have difficulties and to not learn, the people consider this to be the lowest. (16.9)

These passages raise several very interesting questions. First, if we take the "it" (*zhi* 之) in 6.20 and 16.9 to refer to the Way (*dao* 道),[22] which is a plausible reading,[23] then we can understand Kongzi as promoting an appealing sort of thought. He is saying that simply knowing (*zhi* 知) the Way is not as good as liking (*hao* 好) it, and simply liking the Way is not as good as delighting (*le* 樂) in it. Liking and delighting in the Way are subsequently higher planes of virtue for Kongzi, planes for which one should strive once one has come to know the Way.

In addition to this claim, Kongzi is also saying that the highest sort of man is one who is born already understanding what the Way requires of him. This may initially seem like an absurd claim, but it can be taken in a way that actually seems quite palatable. It may not be that such a person is born already understanding all the implications of the demands of the Way, but rather that such a person is born with a strong inclination and aptitude for understanding and following the Way. These sorts of people are then the moral equivalent of what in sports we call "a natural."[24] Indeed, this seems to be how Kongzi views his favorite disciple, Yan Hui. We may plausibly read Kongzi as thinking that Yan Hui was one born knowing the Way as described in the previously quoted *Lunyu* 16.9.[25] The implication here seems to be that Yan Hui is a natural, someone who was born with a strong inclination to understand and follow the Way. As such, on hearing what Kongzi has to say, he immediately apprehends the truth of it and does not need to go through a process of arguing with Kongzi to come to understand why Kongzi is correct. It is in this way, then, that he is one who is "born knowing it."

However, if we accept that there is something more admirable about a natural, or even if we only want to say that Kongzi at age seventy is more virtuous than someone who has to consciously repress his own desires in order to follow virtue, then we start to see some problems with the idea of the "virtues as correctives" model.

It does not seem too strange to say that people who have not yet inculcated the virtues to such an extent that these virtues become what they desire in every situation are not as virtuous as those who can follow their heart's desires in acting virtuously.[26] Those who still have to struggle and who think of themselves as being in some way forced to make difficult choices in order to act virtuously are not as virtuous as those who, like Kongzi at seventy, are able to follow their heart's desires and still act correctly.

This is not to take anything away from such people. There is certainly something admirable about going through such a struggle in which virtue wins, and these people can be thought of as being in the category of people who know the Way but have not yet come to like it or delight in it. As such, we can think of them as being in the same category as Kongzi put himself between the ages of fifty and seventy in *Lunyu* 2.4. It is quite estimable to be in this category. However, it is certainly a more admirable achievement if virtues are inculcated to the extent that one's personal desires track them consistently.

If this is a plausible way of thinking about what it means to be virtuous, then thinking about virtues as correctives runs into the following difficulty. It seems strange to say that virtues cannot exist without corresponding vices but at the same time think that the hallmark of the most virtuous of people is that they do not have these vices.[27] Indeed, it seems that if we do think that there is something more admirable about people who lack the vices for which the virtues act as correctives, then there is a real sense in which a world inhabited by Kongzi's highest class of human being can be thought of as a better world than one inhabited by people who are always tempted by, and sometimes succumb to, various vices.[28] And, if we wish to say that the people inhabiting such a world are virtuous, as I think we would be inclined to do, then virtues are not necessarily dependent on vices, even in a more general sense. This argument, then, is similar to the one that Roberts makes in his article "Will Power and the Virtues," when he argues that the virtues of will power are "corrective in the significant sense that, in our present psychological condition but not in every imaginable one, they are needed to keep us on the path of virtue and our higher self interest."[29]

But, once we make this concession, then it is natural to question why we cannot, to borrow Roberts's terminology, regard as virtues traits that, in certain psychological conditions, although not in our current one, would be necessary to orient and motivate us to feel and act in appropriate ways in the sense of keeping us on the path of goodness. If we can conceive of such traits as virtues, as I will argue that we indeed can, then, in the end, it will seem that being a corrective is not in general necessary to make something a virtue. At most, Foot and Roberts can claim only that it may be the case that in our world, being a corrective is a sufficient condition for a trait's being a virtue.[30] This, though, is a much weaker claim.

To recap, thinking through these passages from the *Lunyu* reinforces our intuitions that the virtues are correctives. However, we are also shown that there are other things that we wish to say about the virtues that cannot be said if we take the corrective model too seriously. In the end, it seems that the most that can be said of virtues of this nature is that they have the *potential* to serve as correctives, and whether they do so in a particular world is simply a contingency of that world.

Self-Love as a Virtue?

In an attempt to show that there are traits that we would want to call virtues, but which could not be so thought of unless we adopt my claim that virtues need be no more than potential correctives, I would like to turn the discussion to "self-love" in an attempt to show both why it is best thought of as a virtue and how it cannot fit into either Foot's or Roberts's account of virtues as correctives.[31]

In thinking about the potential of self-love to be virtuous, it may be useful to take a look at the next important thinker to pick up on strands of Kongzi's thought, namely Mengzi 孟子 (Mencius). In the section 4A10 of the work that bears his name: "Mengzi said: One cannot talk with those who do violence to themselves and cannot do anything with those who discard themselves. Disparaging ritual and rightness is what is called doing violence to oneself; saying 'I cannot dwell in benevolence or start from rightness' is what is called discarding oneself."[32] Although this passage nowhere mentions the word "love" or discusses "self-love," it does make the claim that one must have a certain conception of the self as having ethical potential if one is to be able to even engage in a moral life. This is what I am getting at when I speak of "self-love." It is not the Kantian "dear self" nor is it something leading to a narcissistic conception of the self. Rather, it is a necessary regard for the self, without which it would be impossible to engage the world in a moral manner.

We see a direct linking of self-love to the motivation for ethical improvement a few chapters later in the *Mengzi*. In 6A12, Mengzi tells us:

> Now, if one has a ring finger that is bent and cannot be straightened, even if it is neither painful nor impairs one's actions, if there is someone who could straighten it, then one would not think the road between Qin and Chu is too far to travel, because one's finger is not as good as other people's. If one's finger is not as good as other

people's, then one knows to dislike it, but if one's heart is not as good as other people's, then one does not know to hate it. This is called an inability to understand the relative importance of things.

And, immediately following, in 6A13, we see him argue:

As for a *tong* or *zi* tree of one or two hand widths in circumference, anyone who wants it to live will understand the means by which to nourish it. But when it comes to one's self, one does not understand the means by which to nourish it. Certainly it could not be that one's love for one's self is less than that for the *tong* or *zi* tree! This is the height of not reflecting!

Taken together, these three passages indicate that Mengzi is extremely aware of the relationship between self-love and the motivation for ethical improvement.[33]

Indeed, the importance of self-love is not new, and it is recognized even in nonvirtue-based accounts of morality. For example, Christine Korsgaard takes Kant to conclude that we must take ourselves as important if we are to take anything to be important,[34] and a utilitarian must have as much regard for himself as for others. As such, it seems that a moral obligation toward the self is fairly easy to tease out of these theories.

It appears that Mengzi is correct to say that in order to develop other things that he thinks of as virtues (benevolence, rightness, etc.), it is first necessary to have a certain regard for the self. If this is the case, then self-love appears to fit in with my original bare-bones description of virtues as dispositions of character that contribute in direct and substantial ways to the flourishing of individuals and their communities.

Now, the passage just cited does seem to show that Mengzi regards the vice of "moral helplessness" (i.e., the lack of self-love) to be a genuine and possibly even common problem in his time. However, the simple fact that moral helplessness is genuine and possibly common does not mean that the reason self-love is important is *because* of the prevalence of this moral helplessness. We can easily make sense of someone who argued that actually the lack of self-love is not a prevalent vice while still arguing that possessing self-love is an important virtue. The reason why self-love is important is not grounded in the fact that it serves as a corrective. Rather, it is grounded in the fact that it is a necessary component of a flourishing life.

If this is the case, then the link between virtues and vices becomes even more tenuous, and the way in which we can think of virtues as correctives becomes much weaker than either Foot or Roberts desires. If we still wished to retain the vocabulary of correctives, then it would have to go somewhat along the lines that I originally mentioned, namely that we could conceive of a world in which particular virtues served as correctives to general tendencies people had. So, self-love may be a corrective insofar as we can conceive of a world in which people are generally susceptible to self-denigration or a lack of self-respect. However, the fact that this is not the normal state of our world does not preclude self-love (properly conceived) from being a virtue. Furthermore, it is highly desirable for people who suffer from low self-esteem to cultivate self-love, for such a regard for the self is thought to be a virtue necessary for the return to health.

Inclinational Virtues—A Different Type?

I now turn my attention to another sort of virtue whose relation to the idea of correctives is even more tenuous than anything we have seen so far, namely "inclinational virtues." As I use this term, inclinational virtues are virtues because of their being good inclinations, traits that incline one toward the direction of what is good.

One of the best introductions to this topic is *Mengzi* 2A6, which goes:

> Mengzi said: People all have hearts that cannot bear the suffering of others. The former kings had hearts that could not bear the suffering of others, and [as a matter of course] they had governments that could not bear the suffering of others. If one uses this heart that cannot bear the suffering of others to implement a government that cannot bear the suffering of others, then ruling all under Heaven is [as easy as] rolling something around in the palm of one's hand. As for why I have said that all people have hearts that cannot bear the suffering of others, suppose that someone was to suddenly see a child about to fall into a well. All would have hearts that were frightened, alarmed, distressed, and pained, and these feelings arise not to gain favor from the parents of the child, nor to seek praise from grieved friends, nor from hating the child's cry.
>
> From this, we can see that one who lacks a heart that feels others' pain is not a human being, one who lacks a heart able to feel shame and disgust is not a human being, one who lacks a heart that can decline and yield is not a human being, and one who lacks a heart able to distinguish between right and wrong is not a human

being. A heart that feels compassion is the sprout of benevolence, a heart able to feel shame and disgust is the sprout of rightness, a heart able to decline and yield is the sprout of ritual propriety, and a heart that knows right and wrong is the sprout of wisdom.

People have these four sprouts just as they have their four limbs. Having these four sprouts and yet saying of oneself that one is incapable [of virtuous action] is to injure oneself, and saying of one's lord that he is incapable [of virtuous action] is to injure one's lord. All people have these four sprouts within themselves, and once they discover that all they must do is broaden and fill them out, then it is like the first light of a fire or the breaking through of a spring. If one can fill them out, then they will be sufficient to protect the four seas. If one does not fill them out, then they will not be sufficient even to serve one's own parents.

In this justly famous passage, Mengzi gives us much to think about in relation to virtue ethics. He uses this thought experiment to argue for the existence of inclinational virtues by giving us an example of how people would instinctively react to a particular situation, namely the sight of a child about to fall into a well. The feelings of fright, alarm, distress, and pain that would inundate anyone's heart who was to see such a sight indicates that human beings are naturally inclined to have certain tendencies that we would want to label as virtuous. Farther on in this passage, he identifies the four "sprouts" (*duan* 端) of virtue that he believes every normal human possesses, just as they possess their four limbs. Everyone, he says, feels compassion, as well as shame and disgust. Further, everyone truly has the capacity for knowing right from wrong and has a heart able to understand when to decline and yield. These, then, correspond to the four cardinal virtues of the *Mengzi*: benevolence (*ren* 仁), rightness (*yi* 義), wisdom (*zhi* 智), and ritual propriety (*li* 禮).

Mengzi wishes us to start with the natural feelings we have in certain situations and attempt to come to understand why we should have these same feelings in other instances. Mengzi does not believe that on understanding his thought experiment about the child about to fall into the well, the reader will thereupon feel motivated to act virtuously in every situation. He is simply saying that such feelings as arise from thinking about watching a child about to fall into a well can assist one in finding and expressing the correct feelings and actions in other situations.[35]

There are two ideas that seem to arise out of Mengzi's analysis. First, there are things that we can appropriately think of as virtues that are not corrective in the sense that there is any deficiency of motivation to be made good.[36] Rather, it is the motivation itself that contains within it the beginnings of virtue. The circumstances that bring out a virtuous response in a person have nothing to do with any corrective that the person has applied to himself. Rather, it is a situation in the world itself, something over which the person has no control, which leads to the virtuous response. The second idea that arises out of Mengzi is more problematic, namely that these inclinational virtues are natural.

While the first claim seems right, the second may seem more dubious (especially to those who have read Xunzi 荀子). It is thus important to note that it may be possible to have inclinational virtues that are not natural. For example, it seems plausible that habituation can lead one to being inclined to act in certain virtuous ways, even if there is nothing natural about these inclinations. Indeed, returning to the autobiographical sketch of Kongzi in *Lunyu* 2.4, it is not implausible to postulate that part of what Kongzi was doing in following his heart's desires at age seventy was acting in accordance with inclinational virtues that he regarded as learned rather than natural.

Now, one might say that what I have been calling inclinational virtues are nothing more than correctives to excessive self-interest. As Mengzi argues, the instinctive feelings of fright, alarm, distress, and pain that everyone would feel on witnessing a child about to fall into a well not only tells us that people all have the sprouts of virtue within themselves, but also that these inclinations do not arise as a counterbalance to excessive self-interest. However, there is a passage in the *Mengzi* that may lead us to return to thinking of virtues as correctives, namely 6A15. In this passage,

> Gongduzi asked: All are equal in being human, but some are great people while others are petty people; why is this?
> Mengzi said: Those who follow their greater part become great people while those who follow their lesser part become petty people.
> Gongduzi said: All are equal in being human, yet some follow their greater part while others follow their petty part; why is this?
> Mengzi said: The position of the ears and eyes is not to reflect, and thus they are misled by things. When things interact with other things, then they simply lead them along. The position of the heart is to reflect. If it reflects, then it attains; if it does not reflect, then it will not attain. This is that which Heaven has given to us. If one first takes a stand in reference to what is greater, then what is lesser cannot contend with it. This is how one becomes a great person.

This passage certainly makes it clear that we will not necessarily be swayed by our moral intuitions. And, as A. C. Graham interprets this passage, we can only develop our full moral potentialities if the mind "is continually active, judging the relative importance of our various appetites and moral impulses." Indeed, as Graham understands Mengzi, following one's nature is not "a matter of surrendering to natural inclination."[37]

However, this passage must be read in light of 6A17, which follows close on its heels: "Mengzi said: The desire to be worthy of esteem is the way in which our hearts are the same. All humans have within themselves that which is worthy of esteem. It is simply that they have not reflected upon this." Here, as Bryan W. Van Norden notes, Mengzi is pointing out that "humans are, intrinsically, evaluative animals," that we "are creatures who desire to feel worthy, to be esteemed, to lead lives which have moral value."[38] So, while it is the case that we have to concentrate on the impulses that we have in order to strengthen them, the fact that we *do* have them is the central point. Certainly, as one develops virtues, filling out these inclinations so that they spread into all areas of one's life, there will be instances where they do act as correctives to certain actions that violate them. However, at the most fundamental level, they are inclinational and not corrective. It is simply that under certain circumstances, they may be expressed in a corrective fashion.[39]

In the preceding passages, Mengzi gives us reason to think that there is an additional type of virtues, namely inclinational virtues. These virtues are ones that ensure we act on certain good inclinations we naturally have. Furthermore, we can make sense of the idea of inclinational virtues that arise out of something like habituation, even if natural inclinations are not present. And, importantly, it does not seem that these virtues can be boiled down to correctives to excessive self-interest.

Conclusion

Throughout this chapter, I have attempted to apply the concept of virtues as correctives to both the *Lunyu* and the *Mengzi* in an attempt to see where it succeeds and fails, and I believe that I have shown where and how this conception of virtues is in need of revision. The idea of virtues solely as correctives does give us an important insight into how certain virtues manifest themselves in our societies. Certainly, few if any of us are born in Kongzi's highest state, and the vast majority of people (or maybe even all) belong to his lowest two states. This being the case, many virtues will actually manifest themselves in the ways described by Foot. However, it is still simply a contingent fact that they act as correctives. My example of "self-love" was meant to point out that there are traits that we wish to think of as virtues that do not seem to counteract general vices, though they do seem to have the other characteristics of the virtues Foot labels as corrective. Furthermore, analysis of virtues as correctives does not seem to be able to allow for the possibility of inclinational virtues, virtues that at the most fundamental level do not and cannot act as correctives to deficiencies in motivation because they express the natural desires of human beings in general.

Now, it may be the case that if we broaden our notion of what it is to be a corrective, all these virtues could be made to fit under its umbrella. Such a sense would be far different from anything proposed by either Foot or Roberts. The inclinational virtues have nothing to do with faults in human beings. So, why do we tend to think that these inclinational virtues are actually virtues? One could postulate that it is because in at least certain instances, they correct for problems in the world. The world such as it is allows for the possibility of children falling into wells and getting hurt, and at least some inclinational virtues might be thought of as correcting for these problems in the world. This sense of virtues as correctives may be tenable, but it is certainly vastly different from Foot's or Roberts's accounts.

I would like to close, then, with a couple of reasons to think that simply expanding our concept of correctives is not the most appealing way to go. First off, by broadening the conception of what it means to be a corrective to include the possibility of being a corrective in some possible world and to include being a corrective to problems in the world as well as being correctives to motivational deficiencies, we seem to lose some of the usefulness of the concept. It started out as a way of allowing us to look at certain character traits and tell if they were virtues by looking for associated vices that acted as general temptations. Now, however, its usefulness as a guide to the virtues has been lessened, and its content has become much more vacuous.

However, this is not the only reason to be wary of taking such an approach. Returning to our bare-bones concept of the virtues as dispositions of character that contribute in direct and substantial ways to the flourishing of individuals and their communities, we see nothing that leads us to conclude that there must be a tension, either within the will of the individual or between humans and nature. It does not seem at all implausible to postulate that there are dispositions of character that contribute to human flourishing but that do not do so by correcting for problems in the world. Certainly, some virtues may compensate for tendencies we have to engage in actions that are not good. The corrective model may explain these virtues well. However, there also seem to be virtues that simply make something that would otherwise be acceptable, better. Such virtues do not seem to fit into the corrective model.

Indeed, it is problematic to say that the feelings of fright, alarm, distress, and pain that arise when one sees a child about to fall into the well are *corrective*. It may well be that the action that results from these feelings is a corrective to problems in the world. However, to the extent that we wish to claim that simply being inclined toward these feelings is a virtuous disposition, then no matter how far we try to expand the scope of "corrective," it will never be sufficient to encompass what we think of as virtues.

The concept of virtues as correctives has been extremely useful in forming a framework within which to think of the passages from the *Lunyu* and the *Mengzi*. However, analyzing these passages also demonstrates that this conception of virtue ethics runs into problems. Given that these two texts develop a virtue ethic of their own, the insights gleaned from their thought can be extremely useful in advancing contemporary virtue ethics. The idea that the virtues we may otherwise think of as correctives are not properly thought of in this way is one of these advances; the idea of a set of virtues appropriately labeled inclinational virtues is another. And there may well be additional advances that we can make by thinking more deeply about these and other early Confucian texts.[40]

Notes

1. Within the realm of virtue ethics, some of the most important questions revolve around the problem of the nature of the virtues, for if one cannot explicate the nature of the virtues, then it becomes impossible to determine with any confidence, clarity, or precision what things are virtues. If we are unable to carry out this task, then no matter how appealing the idea of a virtue ethic might be, it simply could not be constructed on anything resembling a firm philosophical foundation. This does not mean that virtue ethics fails if there is no property common to all the virtues. It would be possible to argue, as some scholars have, that there are different sorts of virtues, and each of these different sorts have their own unique characteristics. However, regardless of whether we say that there is one category of virtue or multiple categories of virtues, unless we are able to make a determination about what is *essential*, then it seems virtue ethics will lack a solid foundation.

2. Although it is not universally accepted that the early Confucians are best thought of as virtue ethicists, there are numerous scholars arguing for this view. See, for example, Nicholas Gier, "The Dancing *Ru*: A Confucian Aesthetics of Virtue," *Philosophy East and West* 51, no. 2 (2001): 280–305; Eric L. Hutton, *Virtue and Reason in* Xunzi

(Ph.D. diss., Stanford, 2001); Edward Slingerland, "Virtue Ethics, the *Analects*, and the Problem of Commensurability," *Journal of Religious Ethics* 29, no. 1 (2001): 97–125; Bryan W. Van Norden, *Virtue Ethics and Consequentialism in Early Chinese Thought* (Cambridge: Cambridge University Press, 2007); Jiyuan Yu, "Virtue: Confucius and Aristotle," *Philosophy East and West* 48, no. 2 (1998): 323–347. For a dissenting view, see Yuli Liu, *The Unity of Rule and Virtue: A Critique of a Supposed Parallel between Confucian Ethics and Virtue Ethics* (Singapore: Eastern Universities Press, 2004). For my purposes, it is sufficient that a virtue ethics reading of early Confucianism is widely supported and plausible.

3. Philippa Foot, "Virtues and Vices," in her *Virtues and Vices and Other Essays in Moral Philosophy* (Oxford: Basil Blackwell, 1978), 1–18.

4. Robert C. Roberts, "Will Power and the Virtues," in *Virtue and Vice in Everyday Life*, eds. Christina Sommers and Fred Sommers (New York: Harcourt Brace, 1993), 266–288.

5. Foot, "Virtues and Vices," 8. Emphasis in original. I lay out Foot's position more fully further on.

6. In choosing to look at the *Lunyu* and the *Mengzi*, I do not wish to imply that these are the only early Chinese texts that can help inform contemporary virtue ethics. The *Xunzi* 荀子 certainly provides a virtue-based account of morality. In addition, early Daoist texts such as the *Laozi* 老子 and the *Zhuangzi* 莊子 also have the potential to help clarify our understanding of the nature of virtue. For an illuminating article on the concept of virtue in the *Laozi*, see Philip J. Ivanhoe, "The Concept of *de* ('Virtue') in the *Laozi*," in *Religious and Philosophical Aspects of the Laozi*, eds. Mark Csikszentmihalyi and Philip J. Ivanhoe (Albany: State University of New York Press, 1999), 239–257.

7. For an extended discussion of "thick" and "thin" accounts as they apply to doing comparative philosophy, see Bryan W. Van Norden, "Virtue Ethics and Confucianism," in *Comparative Approaches to Chinese Philosophy*, ed. Bo Mou (London: Ashgate, 2003), 99–121. In this paper, Van Norden also provides a solid counterargument to the claim that we cannot say that a thinker held a particular concept ("virtue" in this case) unless there is a term in his vocabulary for expressing this concept. See also his *Virtue Ethics and Consequentialism in Early Chinese Thought*.

8. For a discussion of the relationship between virtue (or, more specifically, *virtus* as used by Aquinas) and Mengzi's use of *de*, see Lee H. Yearley, *Mencius and Aquinas: Theories of Virtue and Conceptions of Courage* (Albany: State University of New York Press, 1990). See also David S. Nivison, *The Ways of Confucianism* (Chicago: Open Court, 1996), especially " 'Virtue' in Bone and Bronze," 17–30, and "The Paradox of 'Virtue,' " 31–43. In these articles, Nivison lays out the early Chinese concept of *de*, pointing out the ways in which *de* encompasses aspects of the contemporary notion of virtue while also noting characteristics of *de* that are quite distinct and have no correlative place in our own notion of virtue.

9. Different Western theorists describe such a thin account of the virtues in various ways. Philippa Foot says, "virtues are in general beneficial characteristics, and indeed ones that a human being needs to have, for his own sake and that of his fellows" ("Virtues and Vices," 3).

10. There is considerable controversy over the extent to which the *Lunyu* is an accurate reflection of the views of Kongzi himself. However, most scholars are in agreement that the majority of the *Lunyu* was compiled by later followers of Kongzi, so we can see these ideas as coming from a particular tradition of thought. None of my argument depends on the passages I cite actually coming from Kongzi's mouth. Rather, what is important for my argument are the ideas expressed in this text. A similar point can be made about the *Mengzi*.

11. All translations are my own.

12. Note that this does not mean that he was acting *from* virtue, as opposed to simply acting *in accordance with* virtue.

13. The key point here is that understanding what virtue is and how to be virtuous is a *process*.

14. For a detailed discussion of the distinction between *akrasia* and *acedia*, see Bryan W. Van Norden's introduction to David S. Nivison, *The Ways of Confucianism*, 2–3.

15. What Foot seems to be trying to get at by arguing that the virtues belong to the will is that what is good about an individual of virtue is that this individual's will is good and that virtues must engage the will. In order to determine what a virtue is we must look at what is wished for, as well as what is actually sought. Foot acknowledges that the connection between the will and virtue is not as simple as this and needs to be modified by a recognition that wisdom is a virtue, albeit one connected to the will in a different fashion. See Foot, "Virtues and Vices," 4–8.

16. Ibid., 5. However, unfortunately, Foot does not go into detail here as to how desires fit into her account of the virtues, other than to note that this supposition captures certain intuitions we have about what it mean to be virtuous.

17. Ibid., 8.

18. Ibid., 9. Italics mine.

19. Ibid.

20. Now, some may object to my use of the word "internalize" here because it may suggest an outside-in conception of self-cultivation. That is, it may imply a "reformation" rather than a "developmental" model of self-cultivation. (For more on this difference, see Philip J. Ivanhoe, *Confucian Moral Self Cultivation*, 2nd ed. [Indianapolis, IN: Hackett, 2000].) There are two replies to this. First, I am attempting to give an account of what Foot's reaction to Kongzi might be, and I believe that this may well be how she would see him. Second, although Mengzi specifically advocated a developmental model of self-cultivation (as we shall see later in this chapter), there is nothing in the *Lunyu* that should lead us to think that it advocates such a model. Indeed, while Xunzi

was the first Confucian writer to explicitly advocate a re-formation model of self-cultivation, what little we see in the *Lunyu* can lead us to this model just as easily as it can to the developmental model.

21. Foot, "Virtues and Vices," 4–5.

22. It is important to understand here that the Way (*dao* 道) is closely related to virtue. If one follows the Way, then one acts in a virtuous manner.

23. Many translators translate this passage without commenting on the meaning of *zhi* 之, but it is clear that we cannot simply substitute any term into its place. It would be absurd to believe that Kongzi would say, for example, "To know murder is not as good as liking murder; to like murder is not as good as delighting in murder." Therefore, we have to draw our understanding of *zhi* from our understanding of Kongzi's overall message, and this leads us back to the Way and virtue. Arthur Waley notes in *The Analects of Confucius* (New York: Macmillan, 1938), 119, that the *zhi* in 6.20 (numbered 6.18 in his translation) should be taken as the Way, as does Edward Slingerland in *Confucius Analects: With Selections from Traditional Commentaries* (Indianapolis, IN: Hackett, 2003), 59. James Legge, in his translation of the *Lunyu* in volume 1 of *The Chinese Classics* (Hong Kong: Hong Kong University Press, 1960), says in a note on page 191 that the *zhi* has a referent that must be *dao* 道 (the Way) or *li* 理 (the pattern of the universe). In doing this, he appears to be following Zhu Xi's 朱熹 commentary to the *Lunyu* found in his *Sishu zhangju jizhu* 四書章句集注. There, Zhu Xi notes that Yin Tun 尹焞 takes the *zhi* to refer to the Way. And, as Cheng Shude 程樹德 notes, Zhu Xi's *Zhuzi yulei* 朱子語類, appears to explain this passage with reference to *li* 理 (pattern). See Cheng Shude, *Lunyu jishi*, 4 vols. (Beijing: Zhonghua shuju, 1997).

Another possibility would be that this *zhi* refers to *li* 禮, the rituals that govern actions and ensure that they accord with the Way. This interpretation, while not one that is found within the early commentaries, is certainly possible. Indeed, we can see some textual evidence for such an account if we look at *Lunyu* 8.8, where we see the following: "The Master said: be stimulated by the *Odes*, take your stand on ritual, and be perfected by music." From this passage, we can see a relation with the autobiographical sketch in *Lunyu* 2.4. It is quite possible that at thirty, when Kongzi took his stand, he was doing so in reference to ritual. This then allows us to draw a close connection between following ritual and according with the Way. However, even if the *zhi* refers to ritual rather than directly to the Way, this does not weaken my argument, because this would leave Kongzi saying that simply knowing rituals is not as good as liking them, and simply liking rituals is not as good as delighting in them. The reason one would want to come to know rituals, like rituals, and even delight in them is because by acting in accordance with them, one is acting in accordance with the Way. I thank Eric L. Hutton for bring this to my attention.

24. Many thanks to P. J. Ivanhoe for suggesting this analogy.

25. Yan Hui appears numerous times in the *Lunyu*. In *Lunyu* 2.9, we see the following: "The Master said: I talked with Yan Hui for an entire day without him disagreeing with me, and so he seems stupid. However, when we retire and I observe him in private, I see that his actions are indeed sufficient to illustrate what I have taught. Yan

Hui is actually not stupid." In addition to this passage that praises Yan Hui's abilities, we see the following in *Lunyu* 5.9:

> The Master said to Zigong: Who is better, you or Yan Hui?
>
> Zigong replied: How dare I compare myself to Yan Hui? Yan Hui hears one thing and understands ten. I hear one thing and understand two.
>
> The Master said: You are not as good as Yan Hui. You and I, we are not as good as Yan Hui.

On the face of it, this passage seems to indicate that Yan Hui had a special talent for understanding things he is being taught, a talent that exceeds even Kongzi's. We also see in *Lunyu* 7.20 that "the Master said: I was not born knowing it, but since I like antiquity, I hasten to seek it." So, if we take Kongzi at face value, Yan Hui is better than Kongzi himself, and thus on a higher rung than Kongzi, who was not born knowing the Way. Of course, such a reading of these passages goes against the great neo-Confucian synthesizer, Zhu Xi, who takes great pains to explain away these passages by arguing, among other things, that this was just a demonstration of Kongzi's humility that he would disclaim what he actually possessed. In a similar attempt, the early Chinese commentator He Yan 何晏 argues that in 5.9 Kongzi's claim that neither he nor Zigong is as good as Yan Hui is simply exaggeration meant to comfort Zigong.

26. Indeed we see a parallel in Aristotle's discussion of the *enkratic* (continent) person in Book VII of his *Nicomachean Ethics*.

27. On strict grounds, what would be most strange to say would be that virtue cannot exist without the corresponding temptations toward vice existing within a person, but at the same time think that the hallmark of the most virtuous people is that they lack temptations toward vice. Certainly this is not what Foot wants to say. But, as I hope to demonstrate, the strangeness that we do see in Foot's account, coupled with the alternative explanation I give, gives us strong reason to suspect such an account.

28. It seems that there are, in general, three possible worlds. There is the world in which individuals are not tempted, and thus there is no wrongdoing. There is also the world in which individuals are tempted but do not give in to temptation, and thus there is no wrongdoing. We can think of such a world as being populated by Aristotle's *enkratic*, or continent, individuals. Finally, there is the world in which individuals are tempted and occasionally give in to this temptation, engaging in wrongdoing. This, then, would be a world composed of those whom Aristotle would call *akratic*. The contrast that is pertinent here is the one between the first and the second of these possibilities—the difference between a world populated by virtuous individuals and one populated by *enkratic* individuals.

29. Roberts, "Will Power and the Virtues," 233.

30. This point about virtues necessarily being correctives is one that Foot would insist on. See Foot, "Virtues and Vices," 8.

31. It may be questioned whether the term "self-love" is appropriate in this case. Certainly arguments could be made for using "self-confidence" or "self-respect" to

convey this idea. I retain the term primarily because it is used by Foot. Also note that Foot is adamant that self-love cannot be a virtue, precisely because it is not a corrective. See ibid., 9.

32. All translations are my own.

33. I thank Bryan W. Van Norden for bringing the latter two passages to my attention. In 5A9 as well, the sage Boli Xi's decision to flee when his life was at stake is taken as evidence of his wisdom, further pointing to the fact that self-love is an important virtue for Mengzi. (However, this does not mean that love for one's life should always trump. See, for example, 6A10, where it is clear that there are values above that of life. There are times when virtue dictates self-preservation, and times when it does not.)

34. Christine M. Korsgaard, *The Sources of Normativity* (Cambridge: Cambridge University Press, 1996), 122. Jean Hampton also discusses a proper sense of self-respect based on "a sense of your own intrinsic and equal value as a human being" in her article "Selflessness and the Loss of Self," *Social Philosophy and Policy* 10 (1993): 135–165. For someone who deals with self-love from the point of view of virtue ethics, see Christine Swanton, *Virtue Ethics: A Pluralistic View* (Oxford: Oxford University Press, 2003), esp. 133–145.

35. Mengzi is not saying that the virtues themselves are innate. Rather, it is that the sprouts of virtue are innate. We act virtuously once we learn to extend these sprouts.

36. There are two different ways we might look at a deficiency of motivation. It could mean that there is simply a lack of motivation. However, it could also mean that we have the motivation, but it is not sufficiently strong to ensure action. If the former is the case, then the virtues would give an individual a motive for action that she would otherwise not have. If the latter is the case, then virtue would simply ensure that the inclinations that one has will be acted on, not that the virtue will make up for a complete lack of motivation. Foot does not clarify how she takes this deficiency in motivation. For Mengzi, it seems clear that the virtues ensure we act on certain inclinations that we innately possess. And, as I note further on, we can make sense of having inclinations even if they are not innate in the Mengzian sense.

37. A. C. Graham, "The Background of the Mencian [Mengzian] Theory of Human Nature," in *Essays on the Moral Philosophy of Mengzi*, eds. Xiusheng Liu and Philip J. Ivanhoe (Indianapolis, IN: Hackett, 2002), 1–63.

38. Bryan W. Van Norden, "Mengzi and Xunzi: Two Views of Human Agency," in *Virtue, Nature, and Moral Agency in the* Xunzi (Indianapolis, IN: Hackett, 2000), 102–134.

39. Notice, too, that if one were to take a theological view and say that these inclinations are good because they are what Heaven has endowed us with, then their role as correctives will also be contingent.

40. In addition to Philip J. Ivanhoe and Eric L. Hutton, who have both read through numerous drafts of this chapter, I would like to thank Benjamin Crowe, Elijah Millgram, Anya Plutynski, Cynthia Stark, Julia Tao, Bryan W. Van Norden, J. Daniel Ward, David Wong, and Kam-por Yu for their comments, though I have not been able to incorporate all their excellent suggestions.

Chapter 9

The Values of Spontaneity

Philip J. Ivanhoe

Introduction

There is a widespread intuition that acts displaying "spontaneity" possess value at least in part by having this quality. Spontaneity may be taken as the sole or primary source of an action's value or it may be thought to be a reason to further value an action that is considered good for other reasons as well, for example, because it realizes some independent worthwhile end. Spontaneous actions may be valued for a variety of reasons: these actions may be thought to be more aesthetically appealing for agents or observers, they may be valued for the joy that they engender or because they help one to relax or live longer, and so forth. Although I do not discount the importance of these kinds of values, my primary interest in this chapter is with views that accord some kind of ethical value to spontaneous actions.

Many people share a belief in the value of spontaneity, but there is less of a consensus concerning what spontaneity is. We find two primary senses of the word "spontaneity" in Western writings. The first takes spontaneity to be that quality of actions that arise or proceed "entirely from natural impulse" or that come "freely and without premeditation or effort."[1]

Spontaneity in this sense is most often used to describe the activity of plants, nonhuman animals, or poets.

The second sense of spontaneity takes it to be "voluntary and unconstrained action on the part of persons."[2] That is, spontaneous actions are those that arise or proceed freely from an autonomous agent. Versions of this second sense of spontaneity are prominent in philosophical writings. For example, Thomas Hobbes describes voluntary actions, by which he means roughly actions that are not motivated by fear, as "spontaneous."³ One of the most elegant and influential expressions of this second sense of spontaneity is found in the writings of Immanuel Kant. For Kant, spontaneity is the ability to think and act in the world independently of the determinations of desire. Reason can provide an order distinct from and independent of what Nature offers, and rational agents can perceive and act in the world according to the norms and principles of such an order. Moreover, they have the ability to *know* that they are seeing and acting in this way.⁴ On such a view, spontaneous actions demonstrate the characteristic quality of Kant's distinctive notion of free will. They are expressions of an autonomous agent's unique ability to transcend the natural order and produce genuine actions as opposed to mere events.

The two senses described above share the idea that spontaneous actions are characterized by the absence of constraint or external coercion, but apart from this they are different and to some degree incompatible. On the first, spontaneity describes a state from which Kant's free and autonomous rational agents purportedly must break free. And yet, this sense of spontaneity is thought to provide a firm—though not moral—standard for plants, animals, and poets. In general, it is *good* when plants, animals, and poets operate without obstruction or constraint and express "natural impulse(s)" that come "freely and without premeditation or effort." According to the Kantian version of the second definition, spontaneous actions express the ability of rational, free, and autonomous agents to transcend the natural order. This ability serves as the ground of human dignity and when properly employed provides the basis for normative moral claims.⁵

In the discussion above I have followed the convention that seeks to distinguish the normative component of our two senses of spontaneity by maintaining that in the former cases we are concerned with describing the proper natural functions of plants and animals, or certain aesthetic values of poetry, while in the latter, Kantian case we are talking about *moral* normativity. Perhaps this distinction can be made to work, but it is not as neat as it might first appear to be. For example, many people endorse the view that an ethical action that arises or proceeds with ease and "without premeditation or effort" can be *morally better* than one that is carried out only after prolonged consideration and with difficulty.⁶ Sorting out such issues and the various aspects of these two senses of spontaneity are beyond the scope of this chapter, though I return to these two Western senses of spontaneity in the conclusion. My remarks are intended only to set the stage for my primary concern, which is to describe and analyze two early Chinese views of spontaneity.⁷ I take as my primary sources Confucian and Daoist texts from the pre-Qin period (i.e., before 221 BCE).⁸ My goals are first to describe two related yet distinct types of spontaneity, which I shall refer to as "untutored" and "cultivated" spontaneity, and show that they share deep and important similarities. Next, I argue that the similarities they share are the primary source of the feelings of satisfaction and joy that such actions are thought to arouse in both those who perform and those who observe them. Finally, I argue that these two early Chinese conceptions of spontaneity can help us to understand some of our own intuitions about the ethical value of spontaneity.[9]

Untutored Spontaneity

In order for "untutored spontaneity" to occur, an action must arise more from basic instincts and inclinations than from any sort of training or reflection. Such spontaneity is not something that needs to be learned or can be substantially improved through practice. In these respects it is not an acquired ability.[10] Actions that display this quality often are said to occur with little or no prior reflection or effort and instead are thought to be motivated by deep, standing, innate dispositions to perceive, evaluate, and respond to events and situations in certain ways. If one is lacking in this form of spontaneity, the cause is thought to lie in the loss of abilities and inclinations that one earlier possessed. Those with such diminished capabilities somehow have taken on a mode of being in the world that interferes with certain native abilities and blocks the flow of authentic human sensibilities and responses. The idea that a person loses something important when they leave behind the ability to appreciate and engage in the unself-conscious playfulness of a child is one example of this kind of intuition.[11] Another example is the belief that one who has grown excessively callous to suffering has "lost touch" with an innate and spontaneous capacity for sympathetic care that is critical for both one's own and other people's well-being. Such people might "think too much" and allow their thinking to derail their natural, spontaneous reaction or they may have become habituated to callousness by unreflectively and repeatedly committing callous acts. In either case, something foreign to their true nature imposes itself on and covers up a spontaneous spring of compassion.[12] These examples of the loss of playfulness or sympathetic care suggest how a certain conception of spontaneity can be seen in ethical terms. For if the innate ability or tendency that is obstructed is in fact an important constituent for personal and social well-being, its loss can be seen as harm to oneself and others.

The discussion above points to another characteristic feature of untutored spontaneity: how one who lacks it can come to have or regain it. Since untutored spontaneity is thought to be part of one's inherent nature—something not acquired or substantially improved through learning, reflection, or practice but something that one can lose the use or awareness of—the only way to achieve it is somehow to "go back" to it. According to early Daoists, one regains untutored spontaneity by eliminating whatever it is—for example, wrongheaded beliefs and practices, debilitating habituation, or the general ill effects of socialization—that is blocking or interfering with the smooth functioning of one's nature.[13] The only way to "develop," or more accurately to free up and deploy, untutored spontaneity is by paring away or eliminating the "unnatural" impediments blocking its operation. Once these impediments are eliminated, untutored spontaneity will begin to function on its own and inform one's attitudes, perceptions, and actions. This is a defining feature of untutored spontaneity, captured in the notions of *wuwei* 無為 (nonaction) and *ziran* 自然 ("so of itself" or "so on its own").[14] The former offers an ideal for actions according to which what one does simply flows out of one without self-conscious reflection, striving, or effort. The latter describes the ideal for states of affairs according to which each thing or event maintains its natural, unadulturated condition.[15] Anything that occurs in accordance with these ideals will happen "spontaneously" and in harmony with the Way, which is the goal within the Daoist scheme of things.

Early Daoists believed that our spontaneous abilities and tendencies represent a variety of values and are critical for leading a good and satisfying life. What we naturally and spontaneously tend to do promotes our true best interests by helping us to avoid direct harm and excess and to track and pursue what is really good for us. Shielding one's face from an object thrown at one or retracting one's hand from something too hot are two examples of untutored spontaneity that illustrate one reason why it is thought to be a good way to be. In both cases, the spontaneous response has good results, helping the agent to avoid direct harm. Early Daoists believed that human beings in their natural state in general are much more aware of and responsive to the world around them, more prepared to ward off the dangers that human beings inevitably must confront in the course of their lives. The way in which native hunters are more aware of and responsive to the forest around them than are more sophisticated city slickers captures this idea well.[16] Early Daoists also believed that our spontaneous desires reliably guide us toward basic, sound, and fulfilling lives and away from the unhealthy excesses and unnatural ideals that lead most people to grief. Daoists think that in the absence of false ideals and artificial stimulation, our natural desires tend to settle on and find contentment in modest and healthy sources of satisfaction.

Untutored spontaneity is valuable because it helps us to avoid dangers and excesses and orients us toward healthy life goals. In these ways it helps us to "keep ourselves whole" and "live out our years."[17] Seen in this light, untutored spontaneity is an essential feature of a healthy and flourishing life. It also is valuable because the desires it keeps individuals from developing often prove harmful to other people as well as to the person who has them. The unhealthy tendencies that result from excessive desires overflow and spread harm beyond individual agents. They are thought to be the chief cause of mischief and wickedness to both self and others and the primary source of social and political disorder and unrest. Since untutored spontaneity purportedly enables one to steer clear of such errant dispositions, it has clear claim to ethical value as an important means toward a range of desirable ends.

In addition to serving as a means to such goods, untutored spontaneity is valued as the only way to experience certain profoundly satisfying states of ease, peace, and comfort. When one acts "spontaneously" or "naturally," one's actions "flow" out of unpremeditated dispositions. One is as much a conduit for as the source of one's actions, and so one is not plagued or vexed by worries about whether one has chosen wisely or is doing the right thing. One is practicing *wuwei* (nonaction) and feels that what one does is the fitting, appropriate, and called-for response to the situation at hand. As Nature acts through one, one feels a profound sense of ease, security, confidence, and peace. Rather than feeling alienated from the world or from one's own desires, actions, and projects, one feels perfectly at home among them, and the movements and attitude of such a performer have at least some power to generate similar feelings in those who observe the person. Untutored spontaneity offers a way to transcend one's individual perspective, to join and move in harmony with the greater patterns, processes, and purposes of Nature. These different, highly desirable psychological goods, which collectively I refer to as a sense of "metaphysical comfort," are important constituents of untutored spontaneity and point to a sense in which it is not merely instrumentally but also intrinsically valuable.[18] I argue that they are also a part of our second form of spontaneity.

Cultivated Spontaneity

Cultivated spontaneity does not "just happen" in the sense that it cannot occur without first engaging in concerted and sustained efforts at learning, reflection, and practice. And yet, such efforts only make cultivated spontaneity possible, they are not the sufficient causes for its occurrence. For example, one needs such training in order to play the piano in a spontaneous manner, but such training does not guarantee that one's playing will exhibit the quality of spontaneity, nor does it compel one to play whenever one encounters a piano. There is a sense in which genuine cases of cultivated spontaneity do in fact "just happen." These cases seem to flow or erupt up out of the agent in the same way and with all the ease, confidence, peace, and comfort that is claimed for cases of untutored spontaneity. As in the former case, such actions are expressions of deep, standing dispositions within a person. However, with cultivated spontaneity, these dispositions reflect a "second nature" that is at least partially, often to a significant degree, and perhaps always largely acquired.[19]

The way an accomplished pianist plays her instrument—interpreting what appears on the score and investing it with her personal sense, feelings, and experience—or the free and fluid exchanges shared by members of an ensemble, as they contribute their individual riffs to a performance, display cultivated spontaneity. Their music is flowing out of them with the joyful freedom and elegance that are characteristic signs of such spontaneous behavior, and yet no one imagines that they are playing their instruments for the first time. The ability to engage in such spontaneous play presupposes an extended period of learning, practice, and innovation and is based on an acquired skill or set of skills. It is an ability that arises out of a sustained course of training, but the ease, flexibility, and critical presence of the agent distinguish it from simple programming.

Given that cultivated spontaneity requires special effort and prior experience, the method to develop it is dramatically different from what we described as the ideal means toward untutored spontaneity. In the former case, one sought ways to identify and eliminate artificial impediments that had been imposed and were working to block the free flow of one's standing natural tendencies. In the case of cultivated spontaneity, there are no such tendencies to free up and let loose. Although it is true that one begins life with certain capacities and abilities, these need to be shaped, directed, and informed in order to function well in activities that display cultivated spontaneity. One of the primary goals of someone seeking to develop any form of cultivated spontaneity is to *acquire* the right kind of standing dispositions. In order to do this, some type of explicit training—a kind of socialization or enculturation—is necessary for establishing even the possibility of spontaneity. Instead of a paring away of obstructions, one aims at building up the right constellation of abilities, habits, sensibilities, and judgment.

One of the clearest and most engaging descriptions of the process leading to this ideal is found in Kongzi's own spiritual autobiography: "The Master said, 'At fifteen, I committed myself to learning. At thirty, I took my place in the world. At forty, I no longer harbored doubts. At fifty, I understood the Mandate of Heaven. At sixty, my ears were attuned. At seventy, I followed my heart's desires without transgressing propriety.' "[20] Musical performance offers rich and productive examples of cultivated spontaneity and is a primary example in Confucian discourse, but any activity that involves skillfulness, broadly construed, will do as well. Every game or sport involves the range of features described above, and one of the clearest qualities recognized in accomplished players of such games or sports is the spontaneity of their performances. Even the most accomplished "technician" is deemed inferior to someone whose play exhibits the flexible, free flow of spontaneity. Given the purposes of this chapter, I focus on a type of activity that in the modern West is not often thought of or explored as an example of spontaneity but which was regarded by early Confucians as an important illustration of the most important and valuable type of spontaneous behavior. The activity I have in mind is an example of what we call "social behavior" or what in many Confucian contexts is commonly described in terms of the performance of "rituals" or "rites."

No one would deny that, for the most part, ritual or social behavior in general is something that one acquires through learning and practice and that one can improve through additional reflection and experience. Bowing to those you meet or shaking their hands are learned behaviors not reflexes or natural tendencies. Nevertheless, once one is properly acculturated into a given society, these behaviors usually happen immediately, unreflectively, and with various levels of comfort and ease. In the right context and absent anything unusual, such behaviors reliably and regularly flow out of people. Indeed, under normal conditions, if such behaviors are not forthcoming or are performed in a stiff, odd, or indifferent manner, it is taken as a sign that something is amiss.

Confucians have argued that even a regular and competent ritual performance often falls short of their ideal. What is not yet clear, even in such cases, is whether the performer has truly internalized the full and proper sense of ritual and its overall aims and whether these are present in each performance. The proof that this higher standard has been met is that rituals are performed regularly in a free, fluid, and flexible manner, that the agent regularly succeeds in achieving the proper ends of rituals, and that the performer takes satisfaction and delight in so acting. These are taken as signs that the agent indeed has internalized the letter and the spirit of the rites. Such people are able to carry out elegant and moving ritual action even in the most unusual and demanding circumstances. Their ritual performances always display the quality of spontaneity.

In other words, in order for a ritual performance to exhibit the ideal of spontaneity, it must not only be well rehearsed and competently performed, it must also be an expression of personal commitment and concern and display appropriate sensibility and judgment. Only someone who has the right attitudes, concerns, and good sense, as well as the right training, is going to be able to perform with the ease, elegance, and creativity of ritual at its best. Such a person will be able to amend, bend, and at times suspend the norms of ritual action in light of a greater understanding of what ritual aims to achieve.[21] And only such people find profound satisfaction and delight in the performance of ritual, for they appreciate the deep and distinctive reasons behind such forms of behavior. For such people, ritual is not a mindless habit but an extremely mindful and fulfilling expression of deeply held values through finely honed skills. As Mengzi said, rather than simply acting righteously or benevolently, such people *act out of* benevolence and righteousness.[22] Accomplished ritualists are not just technicians but artists, the social equivalent of musical virtuosi.

If we accept something like this as a plausible account of cultivated spontaneity in ritual performance, we must now turn to the task of finding within it sources for ethical value. In the case of untutored spontaneity, we explored several candidates for ascribing ethical value. One purported virtue of untutored spontaneity was that it leads people away from courses of action and ways of life that inevitably harm them and toward flourishing and more satisfying lives. Untutored spontaneity also is thought good because the excessive desires and tendencies that it helps one to avoid often prove harmful to others as well as to one's self. A final and distinctive source of value in untutored spontaneous action is the freedom from anxiety and the sense of belonging, peace, and harmony—what I called "metaphysical comfort"—that such actions generate in those who perform them and in those who observe such performances as well. Are there correlates to these values in the case of cultivated spontaneity? I believe the answer is "yes."

One might try to make the case that the discipline involved in becoming a great artist or skilled craftsperson itself is of value both to the artists and to those around them. It could be that one of the most important experiences human beings can have is found in the course of taking up and mastering such a discipline—roughly what traditional Indian thinkers called "yoga." I don't think that it is difficult to defend a properly qualified version of this claim, and this idea is related to some of what I argue below. However, I am not going to defend this more general claim here. Instead, I focus on the more limited case of social ritual, for there we find several clear correlates to the values claimed for untutored spontaneity.[23]

Those who are accomplished in social norms and practices are widely regarded as living lives that keep them and those around them from a variety of harms and excesses and that further lead them toward goods that are critical for a flourishing and satisfying life. And so, it seems as though cultivated spontaneity offers versions of the first two values we discussed in the case of untutored spontaneity. As a matter of fact, shared norms and practices are needed to make any recognizably social life possible. If well chosen and carefully constructed, they also have the potential to make lives decent and satisfying as well.[24] When individuals have internalized the norms and practices of a given society, they are able to interact with others in a free and fluid manner that on the one hand enables everyone to get at least more things done, and that on the other offers individuals a sense of community, common purpose, and comfort. If we did not have norms and rituals governing how to meet and greet one another, how to share in and express grief for the deceased, appreciation to the deserving, or the joy of marriage or birth, our lives would be much less fulfilling and humane. Bereft of such shared norms and practices, we would cease to live distinctively human lives. Members of a human society share a common cultural language that not only enables them to coordinate their work and cooperate freely, but that also affords them a sense of shared history and common cause. It also provides them with a wealth of widely recognized and freely traded stories, expressions, images, and ideals. This points toward the third source of value discussed earlier: metaphysical comfort.

In the case of untutored spontaneity, our prereflective sensibilities, tendencies, and actions were said to connect us with a deeper, more authentic nature that had become lost in the process of socialization. Those who engage and act in accordance with this deeper nature feel a profound sense of ease, comfort, peace, and joy. They are able to see beyond and cut through the hypocrisy, posturing, and falsehoods of the everyday social world and draw freely from the uncontaminated fount of Nature. This was the view of early Chinese Daoists who expressed a profound skepticism concerning the value of society along with a remarkable faith in the benign character of human nature. They believed that the violence, prejudice, callousness, and so forth, that describes so much human action is not an expression of what we really are. Rather, such tendencies, habits, and attitudes are corruptions of our true nature and distortions of our most basic inclinations.

One need not accept every aspect of this rosy picture of human nature in order to find insight in such a view. Our nature is much more of a mixed bag than the early Daoists claimed it is, but there is still great wisdom in recognizing that at least *some* of our basic attitudes and most fundamental needs and desires are for the most part benign and that these remain with us, even in the midst of our bewilderingly complex technology.[25] As noted above, there is a convincing case, made by Joel Kupperman, that an open, curious, and playful attitude—often found in young children—is one such tendency that Zhuangzi urged us to guard and nurture throughout life. Failing to preserve, heed, and appreciate these aspects of ourselves may well lead us to less satisfying and even miserable lives. Ignoring or suppressing these basic needs and desires might indeed be part of what drives us to do some of the worst things we do.

E. O. Wilson has made a compelling case that human beings have a profound and enduring need for Nature, what he calls *biophilia*.[26] In an earlier essay, I argued that an important aspect of this human need for Nature is a desire to feel at home in the larger natural world, to find our place within this much greater and complex scheme of things.[27] This desire is one important expression of our need for "metaphysical comfort." Early Daoists claimed that those fully in touch and engaged with the natural and authentic self enjoy such a sense of comfort. They feel at home in Nature and respond to it with ease, efficacy, and delight—no matter what might come their way. As we have seen, this is one of the central values claimed on behalf of untutored spontaneity. At first glance, it may seem as if there is no correlate to this kind of value for Confucians or for cultivated spontaneity in general, but a second look reveals that such is not the case.

As a prelude to exploring this issue, it is important to recall that even among early Confucians there is a range of different views about the degree to which ritual or social action is an expression of untutored, nascent tendencies. At one extreme, Mengzi held that our moral sensibilities are the developed expressions of natural "sprouts" of virtue. Human social behavior is cultivated, but, on the model of agricultural cultivation, it is not something wholly invented or artificial. At the other extreme, Xunzi argued against Mengzi's view and claimed that ritual and human culture are inventions, perfected through an extended course of trial and error, and inculcated in human beings as the only way to reform their basically bad and destructive nature. For Xunzi, social norms and practices are artifacts—like vases or wheels—products of human ingenuity.

Both of these early Confucians believed that their teachings were true to Kongzi's original vision, and one can find evidence for either side in the *Analects* and other early teachings attributed to Kongzi. I am not going to enter into the various issues and debates regarding these different interpretations of the tradition. For the purposes of this chapter, Xunzi's view offers the more useful account, for he explicitly denies that the spontaneity displayed in ideal ritual performances is in any direct way an expression of natural inclinations or tendencies.[28] His philosophy offers a stark contrast with what we find among early Daoists, and there are good reasons to think that this is at least in part the result of his conscious attempt to distinguish Confucianism from this early rival.

There are two ways in which Xunzi's view offers the promise of metaphysical comfort. The first derives from Xunzi's claim that by following the Confucian Way one will be led to a life that not only satisfies one's basic desires and opens up new, more sophisticated forms of satisfaction, but that also leads one to live in harmony with the greater patterns and processes of Nature. I have referred to this latter virtue of the Confucian Way as its ability to establish a "happy symmetry" between human needs and desires and the rest of Nature.[29] People who cultivate themselves to the point where they spontaneously act in ways that harmonize their needs and desires with those of the rest of the Natural world will feel a sense of comfort and peace and take satisfaction and joy in living this sort of life. This is one of the most powerful reasons one can have for living a life that is informed and animated by a lively concern for what we today call "the environment." However, according to Xunzi, this satisfying sense comes only to those who have made a self-conscious choice to live a life that establishes this happy symmetry with Nature. It is not something one can enjoy simply by following prereflective intuitions and tendencies. The latter will lead only to a life of personal, social, and environmental chaos and disaster.

In addition to the possibility of establishing a happy symmetry with Nature, Xunzi offers a parallel and wholly human form of metaphysical comfort. He argues that by taking on the right kind of second nature—specifically a reverent and caring social nature—we open up a way of life that connects us in deep, complex, and satisfying ways with a vast network of other human beings—both living and deceased. There is an immediate parallel here with the way that untutored spontaneity claims to open us up to the possibility of harmonizing with Nature. In both cases, there is an expansion of the self and a joining with something remarkably greater and more complex than oneself. Whenever one is socialized or enculturated into some form of human activity, one participates in a living tradition of individuals who recognize and appreciate what one does.[30] This is true whether one is practicing the rituals and norms of a given religion or society or engaging in some particular craft or skill.

If one takes up the practice of a musical instrument, one takes on a tradition of playing that inevitably influences and to a large extent informs how one proceeds. If one masters the instrument, one uses it and the tradition is a means to express one's individual creativity. However, the possibility of enjoying the satisfaction of playing creatively and spontaneously is established and sustained by the tradition. Were there no tradition, there would be nothing with which to play. In the case of cultivated spontaneity, which involves humanly created traditions of ritual, skill, and craft, tradition—understood broadly—plays the role of Nature. In this respect, when we take on a "second nature," we join in and engage a "Second Nature"—a humanly constructed, cultural life world.[31] Xunzi's ideal nests the second Nature within the first. The sense of ease, comfort, belonging, and joy that are the marks of spontaneous play require a traditional reservoir of accumulated past activity. This is what creates the possibility and provides the power of what flows out of one in the course of spontaneous performance.

It is the background of tradition that generates the special feeling, characteristic of spontaneity in all its forms, that one's actions are in tune with and flow out of something much larger, more complex, and valuable than oneself. One of the most distinctive features of both untutored and cultivated spontaneous action is a sense of giving oneself up to or "losing oneself" in what one is doing. In the midst of spontaneous activity, one feels as if one is being guided and carried along the proper path by forces greater than oneself.[32] Abandoning oneself to these powers and following the path they lay open to one is an important constituent of the sense of spontaneity. It is why one feels spontaneous actions are not purely or even primarily a result of one's personal decision, why one feels they are fitting and proper, and why they give rise to what I call metaphysical comfort, which often brings with it a profound and special sense of joy. In the case of untutored spontaneity, Nature purportedly provides this larger context, guiding pattern, and energizing force; in the case of cultivated spontaneity, tradition of one sort or another plays this critical role.

Comparing the Two Types

The two types of spontaneity described above not only share a similar formal structure, but to some extent they also always partake of each other. The rhetoric of those who advocate the respective types at times present them as two radically different models, but in practice they often represent more a difference in emphasis than wholly distinct types. This does not dissolve the important differences between these two ideals, but it does help us to see how they actually function to inform human lives. The mutual interaction and exchange between them can be discerned when we look more carefully at the two traditions chosen to represent them.

Confucian thinkers always rely explicitly or implicitly on a picture of human nature being developed, channeled, or released to achieve the ideal of a spontaneous, ethical agent.[33] As noted earlier, the case of Mengzi presents a clear hybrid of the two types that I have described. Mengzi insisted that while our moral inclinations require care, nourishment, training, attention, and growth, they exist in nascent form and must arise out of innate inclinations, tendencies, and tastes. Even Xunzi, who argued against this aspect of Mengzi's view, relies on there being proto-moral aspects of our nature—such as our love of kin and our enjoyment of harmony—that can be "conscripted" into the cause of the ethically good life.[34]

Although early Daoists are known for their general rejection of culture and so-called civilization, the people they describe as offering paradigms for how to live often are involved in distinctively human activities that require some level of training and cultural context in order to take place at all. This is especially clear in the case of Zhuangzi, whose skillful paragons of the Way engage in activities like carving up sacrificial oxen, shaping wheels, or crafting musical bell stands—all skills that require training and tradition in order to learn and do well.[35] Zhuangzi's way is not so much a rejection of civilization as a way to live uncorrupted within it. This is one reason why his philosophy offers no program of social or political reform. In this last respect, the *Zhuangzi* differs from the *Daodejing*, which does insist on radical social and political reform. Nevertheless, the primitive agrarian utopia described by this latter classic also implies a distinctively human type of life. People are to find satisfaction in the lives of small rural communities. They are to return to the use of "knotted cords" as a means of accounting for their possessions, but they still have possessions, count them, and seek to keep track of what they own.[36]

The point of noticing the ways in which the two ideals of spontaneity often are intermixed with each other allows us to distinguish between what we might call the "rhetoric" versus the "reality" of spontaneity.[37] This difference can be seen by examining a particularly insightful example drawn by Kupperman in his description of Kongzi's conception of "naturalness."[38] Kupperman points out that Daoists on the one hand regard socialization as an impediment to naturalness or spontaneity; on the other hand, they do not advocate "giving general vent to feelings."[39] Excessive emotions of all kinds are regarded as bad by the Daoists, for example, feelings of anxiety and distress about things like death, disease, or other forms of bodily harm. Kupperman revealingly suggests that Beatniks share these two features of the Daoist ideal. They, too, regard society as an impediment to an authentic and fulfilling life. Normal society represents the life of "squares," who are phonies to themselves and others. Beatniks seek to be "cool," and this requires a rejection of the square life. However, it also requires one to curb certain natural or spontaneous enthusiasms. One is not simply to give vent to one's emotions, to "let it all hang out."[40] *That* would not be cool.

I accept Kupperman's description and, as should be clear by now, I have learned a great deal from and been inspired by his analysis here and elsewhere. However, we don't agree about the proper description of one aspect of early Daoism that is important for the issue currently under consideration. Kupperman does not believe that the Daoist ideal was conceived of *by them* as "a return to one's original nature."[41] Instead, he thinks that they believed we all need to work at eliminating our natural tendency for feelings like anxiety. My view is that early Daoists thought "we" only feel such distress because most of us have been corrupted by socialization. I think the same is true about Beatniks—if there are any still around—though I am not committed to this latter claim.

Having stated this difference, I also believe that there is a way for our views to be drawn closer together. Kupperman is correct to claim that in both the case of early Daoists and modern Beatniks, the ideal that they represent *in fact* requires them to transform their basic natures in various ways. This would be an expression of what I am calling the *reality* of their form of spontaneity. What I am claiming is that their *rhetoric* tends to present the more radical view that their way of life represents the original, uncorrupted expression of human nature. At least in the case of the Daoists, this is what gives their ideal much of its power. They claim to offer us a way back to what we *really are* in the depths of our being.

Nature and nurture are notoriously difficult to separate and for the good reason that in the case of human beings, creating culture is a core feature of what we by nature do.[42] The creation of culture and the formation and allegiance to various traditions of belief and practice are expressions of our need to belong to something greater than ourselves. What once we did by instinct (Nature) we now attempt to do through innovation and imagination (Second Nature). Such efforts reflect and support larger religious and cultural systems of belief and practice, though, as Xunzi argued, there is a range of possibilities regarding how one might see the relationship between Nature and culture.[43] In any event, the important point for the present study concerns the sense of satisfaction and ease and also of fittingness, peace, comfort, and joy that accompanies spontaneous action. Even in cases where our approval is not warranted, we tend, at least initially, to approve of actions that are done with spontaneity. Most people dismiss such cases as expressions of a "merely aesthetic" appreciation of spontaneity. Aside from the issue of how "mere" the value of aesthetic appreciation is—I believe it is a fundamental and essential aspect of human life—my claim is that there may well be a deeper sense behind our appreciation of even foul things that are done in a skillful and spontaneous manner. For even as we consciously reject such actions, we are drawn to the fluid ease and comfort with which they are performed. They offer us a tempting counterfeit of the metaphysical comfort we all seek.

Conclusion

I would like to offer a brief assessment of some of the ethical claims made or implied by our two forms of spontaneity and suggest some ways in which an understanding of these early Chinese views might help us to understand some of our own intuitions concerning the value of spontaneity.

Untutored spontaneity presupposes that Nature offers us a valid normative standard and reliable guide. In the case of early Daoism this gets expressed as a kind of faith in the benign and in some respects benevolent operation of Nature.[44] There are familiar problems with such a view though there is also a convincing case to be made that contemporary accounts of Nature as voraciously competitive and fundamentally savage are no less myth than more romantic accounts of Nature as nurturing and benevolent.[45] In between such extremes lies the more complex terrain of reality, and on this ground one can find resources to engage in a project of philosophical retrieval. I have noted Kupperman's argument on behalf of childlike playfulness—to which one could easily add curiosity and wonder—and Wilson's and my arguments for the critical importance of our natural fascination with and deep need for Nature. Other natural human tendencies such as our innate inclination for sympathetic concern and our need for and appreciation of recognition are important features of a full and satisfying life. These different aspects of human nature need to be set within a larger conception of the human good, which will shape and direct these innate human inclinations, but they remain important and arguably critical features of this more mature and comprehensive constellation.

In one way or another, tutored spontaneity presupposes that social practices and norms provide a valid normative standard and reliable guide, and there are familiar problems here as well. While traditional forms of life may well offer a variety of genuine goods, including a kind of metaphysical comfort, these may be gained at a cost that informed and reflective people may not be willing to pay. Just as early Daoists tended to express an excessive faith in Nature, Confucians have tended to embrace tradition too closely and uncritically. However, in responding to the errors of excessive traditionalism, we should not err in the opposite direction. We should not fail to consider whether in fact some traditional practices are well founded and defensible nor ignore or undervalue the important goods that come only through having a shared tradition.

This study of early Chinese conceptions of spontaneity can aid our understanding in at least three distinct ways. First, an appreciation of Confucian and Daoist conceptions of spontaneity helps us to appreciate why it is valued in the particular ways that it is by people influenced by these two traditions. Second, because several early Chinese claims about the nature and value of spontaneity find close correlates in other cultures, including our own, a better understanding of these early Confucian and Daoist views can help us sort out, get clear about, and properly evaluate our own intuitions concerning the nature and value of spontaneity. Third, there are good reasons to engage in a project of philosophical retrieval that seeks to preserve the defensible aspects of these broadly held intuitions about the nature and value of spontaneity.

For example, I have argued that one of the values of both Confucian and Daoist forms of spontaneity is that they offer a sense of metaphysical comfort. There are recognizable correlates to this search for metaphysical comfort among reflective individuals in the modern West as well. We, too, are seeking to find a home within our own communities and larger society as well as an appropriate and satisfying relationship with the greater Natural world. These deeper desires are expressed in terms of a search for such things as "recognition," "meaning," "authenticity," or "environmental concern" and reflected in the widespread approval of "natural" or "spontaneous" actions or states of affairs. There is nothing inherently irrational in having or following such intuitions. On the contrary, not to recognize that one is part of a larger society and greater natural processes and patterns is contrary to reason and ultimately delusional.[46] The project of retrieval that I am advocating simply seeks a rationally defensible and overall satisfying sense of such fundamental intuitions and desires.

Human beings are creatures that by nature alter their nature, or at least profoundly affect the way their nature is expressed, by transforming their environment and mediating and modifying their interactions with the world through technology. And so, if human beings are to find a "home" in the world, there will have to be at least in some respects a house: something they design and build. Humans have as deep a need to innovate and construct as they do to settle into the natural landscape. This is one of the great tensions to be found in human existence, but a tension is not a contradiction and need not lead to conflict. One way of living within, easing, and even drawing strength from this tension is to find a way to see the constructed parts of our existence as offering us the kind of home that normally is associated only with Nature. As mentioned earlier, this is one of the defining features of Xunzi's philosophical project. Contrary to thinkers like Freud, Xunzi argues that human beings can only find complete satisfaction within a constructed social order, but he insists that it must be an order that takes account of and fits them comfortably within Nature.

And so, untutored and cultivated spontaneity face similar challenges. They rely too much on expressions of faith in the wisdom of Nature and culture, respectively. Many of our "spontaneous" responses to the situations we face are poor guides for how to act, and many traditional beliefs, attitudes, and practices cannot withstand reflective scrutiny. If we succumb to our deep need to feel at home in the world and uncritically accept and follow either Nature or culture we may well experience a kind of metaphysical comfort, but it is not a comfort we should feel comfortable enjoying. However, both Nature and culture provide resources with which to fashion a good and fulfilling life. What we need to do is examine the various beliefs, attitudes, practices, and norms that each advocates and decide which are reasonable and good to pursue. This would give us a way to retain the best, both in our untutored nature and in the accumulated wisdom of the traditions that have brought us to where we are today. As unreasonable as it is uncritically to advocate the authority of Nature or culture, it is equally unreasonable to insist on transcending either. Indeed, it is impossible to live wholly outside of these twin constituents of human life. The initial intuition noted at the beginning of this chapter, that certain spontaneous actions express a special sense of ethical value, is not misguided. The challenge is to appreciate which ones can sustain such value under the light of reverent but rigorous scrutiny and criticism.

In my introductory remarks, I noted two senses of "spontaneity" commonly encountered in the Western tradition. The first takes spontaneity as what arises or proceeds "entirely from natural impulse" or "coming freely and without premeditation or effort." Versions of such a view can be found in a variety of influential Western thinkers and movements, most clearly Romanticism, and a sense for the value of such unpremeditated and natural action is still widely held by contemporary people throughout Western societies. The second sense of spontaneity takes it to be "voluntary and unconstrained action on the part of persons." As noted earlier, this sense of actions that arise or proceed freely from an autonomous agent finds distinct and influential expressions in the writings of thinkers like Hobbes and Kant. The former understands spontaneity as occurring when we have the freedom to choose and pursue what we desire; the latter understands it as arising through the freedom to exercise and follow our will.

It is easy to see how our discussion of early Chinese views of spontaneity, especially untutored spontaneity, can help in understanding expressions of the first "Western" sense of spontaneity. Our analysis shows that underlying the sense of the value of such action lies a set of beliefs about the character of human nature and how it can be corrupted by unreflective participation in society. Although one should not elide the significant differences between Daoism and Western Romanticism, these schools of thought share a remarkable similarity in valuing untutored human nature and worrying about the deleterious effects of "socialization."[47] In light of our exploration of early Daoist views, we can see more clearly why Western Romantics were such strong advocates of spontaneity and Nature. It also should be clear that if one ignores or eliminates from either Daoism or Romanticism their background assumptions concerning the character of human nature or the Natural realm, their advocacy of spontaneity becomes difficult to understand.[48]

Our study of early Chinese views of spontaneity can help in other ways as well. As we have seen, the goal of both untutored and cultivated spontaneity is to discover or develop a sensibility that can guide us through the world in an effective and satisfying manner. Either way, the normative standards for how one should act are for the most part outside the agent—in the book of Nature itself or in cultural institutions, norms, and practices that transform human beings and locate them in a greater natural order. If one rejects the idea that one can in some sense discover normative standards outside the self and instead looks exclusively to the individual's desires or will, one will tend toward more formal conceptions of the standards needed to guide one through the world.[49] If one places a greater emphasis on individual desires, one is led to views like contractarianism. If one chooses to emphasize a certain conception of the will, one is led to views like Kant's.

In either case, one will tend to understand spontaneity primarily in terms of our second "Western" sense: as a mark of "voluntary and unconstrained action on the part of persons." Such thinkers agree in valuing spontaneous actions because they are characterized by the absence of constraint or external coercion. However, the nature and value of what one ought to do with such freedom describes different and distinctive ethical ideals. For contractarians, spontaneity is a sign of the freedom to pursue the things that we desire. It may itself be valued in part as a desirable experience to have, but its primary value lies in what it implies about our ability to pursue the things we want. For Kant, spontaneity is an expression of a rational, free, and autonomous will. Its value is not unlike or unrelated to the value of the beautiful or the sublime.

As different as thinkers such as Shelley, Hobbes, and Kant are from the early Chinese thinkers that we have examined—as well as from one another—there still are some important similarities among their conceptions of spontaneity. All of them hold that spontaneity involves the absence of constraint or coercion and that it represents an important human good. I will suggest though not here argue for the further claim that their views about the value of spontaneity are grounded ultimately on their different conceptions of what it is to be a human being and related pictures of human nature. I believe it is also true that they all hold that a life characterized by spontaneous action is fulfilling in a special way because only such action allows one to both realize one's nature and locate oneself in some greater and more complex scheme of things. Whether this scheme is conceived as pristine and unadulterated Nature, a free and lawful society of equals, a kingdom of ends, or some conception of the Way, spontaneous action enables us to participate in something deeper, grander, and more important than just ourselves and offers us some sense of metaphysical comfort and perhaps even joy.

Notes

Acknowledgments: My views on the issue of spontaneity in early Chinese thought have been profoundly influenced by the work of Joel Kupperman. In particular, two remarkably insightful essays have taught me much and stimulated my thinking: "Confucius and the Problem of Naturalness" and "Spontaneity and Education of the Emotions in the *Zhuangzi*," both in *Learning from Asian Philosophy* (Oxford: Oxford University Press, 1999), 26–35, 79–89. This chapter is dedicated to Kupperman with the hope that there is something in it worthy of his legacy. Thanks to Eric L. Hutton, T. C. Kline III, Li Chenyang, Donald J. Munro, and Justin Tiwald for comments and suggestions on earlier drafts.

1. *The Compact Edition of the Oxford English Dictionary*, vol. 2 (Reprint, Oxford: Oxford University Press, 1979), 2977.

2. Ibid.

3. In *Of Liberty and Necessity*, Hobbes describes both of our two "Western" senses of spontaneity. He begins by noting that the first sense pertains to the natural actions of animals, "the *bee* when it maketh honey, does it *spontaneously*; and when the *spider* makes his web, he does it *spontaneously*." However, because such actions are not based on prior deliberation, they are not done by "election" and hence are not "voluntary." Voluntary actions of the right sort are also "spontaneous." Hobbes goes on to say, "all *voluntary* actions, where the thing that induceth the *will* is not *fear*, are called also *spontaneous*, and said to be done by a man's *own* accord." From Richard S. Peters, ed., *Body Man, and Citizen: Selections from Thomas Hobbes* (New York: Collier Books, 1962), 247–48.

4. Henry Allison refers to this quality as a "taking as" or "self-determination," which is something conceived but not experienced—that is, merely intelligible. See his lucid and revealing study, *Kant's Theory of Freedom* (Cambridge: Cambridge University Press, 1990), 36–41.

5. For a thorough discussion of the problem of moral normativity and a defense of a Kantian version, see Christine M. Korsgaard, *The Sources of Normativity* (New York: Cambridge University Press, 1996), 7–166.

6. Without using the word "spontaneity," Philippa Foot defends this kind of idea in her essay "Virtues and Vices" in regard to different levels of ethical ideal. See *Virtues and Vices* (Berkeley: University of California Press, 1978), 1–18. See especially the example of the "head tracker" from the novel *A Single Pebble*, 4–5.

7. The quality of being spontaneous or natural is expressed by a variety of terms and in a range of different ways in the Chinese philosophical tradition. The word most often translated as "spontaneity" is *ziran*, which literally means "so of itself," or "so on its own." Like most Western versions of spontaneity, this Chinese notion implies a lack of outside constraint or coercion. Actions or states of affairs that manifest the quality of being *ziran* are normative for the early Chinese and, as I will argue below, they are so because in one way or another they manifest an objective natural order. This marks them as significantly different from the Kantian sense of spontaneity.

8. I will draw my examples and evidence from three Confucian texts—the *Lunyu*, *Mengzi*, and *Xunzi*—and two Daoist texts—the *Daodejing* and *Zhuangzi*.

9. I won't argue for this point here, but the similarities between these senses of spontaneity and what Mihalyi Csikszentmihalyi calls "flow" offer at least prima facie evidence for the claim that the quality of spontaneity describes a state or quality of action that is valued across a broad range of cultures. See Mihalyi Csikszentmihalyi, *Flow: The Psychology of Optimal Experience* (New York: Harper & Row, 1990).

10. As we shall see, this is one of the clearest ways in which untutored is distinguished from cultivated spontaneity. The Confucian Xunzi, an advocate of cultivated spontaneity, goes out of his way to distinguish his ethical ideal from what I am calling untutored spontaneity by insisting on the kind of contrast—between things that cannot be learned and perfected and those that can—that I am drawing here. For anthologies that provide an introduction to the philosophical study of Xunzi, see T. C. Kline III and Philip J. Ivanhoe, eds., *Virtue, Nature, and Agency in the* Xunzi (Indianapolis, IN: Hackett, 2000); T. C. Kline III, ed., *Ritual and Religion in the* Xunzi, (Albany: State University of New York Press, 2008). For comprehensive studies of Xunzi's ethical philosophy, see T. C. Kline III, *Ethics and Tradition in the* Xunzi (Ph.D. diss., Stanford University, 1998); Eric L. Hutton, *Virtue and Reason in* Xunzi (Ph.D. diss., Stanford University, 2001). Although I claim that the ideal of untutored spontaneity is shared by early "Daoists" such as Laozi and Zhuangzi, it should be clear that I am referring primarily to texts and in the latter case the most representative portions of texts (the "Inner Chapters"). Also, as I have argued in several essays and books, I believe that these two classics offer related but distinctive visions. Laozi's view offers a less ambiguous example of the ideal type of untutored spontaneity, while Zhuangzi's view is more developed and complex. Zhuangzi believes that at least for many people, they cannot attain this ideal state without a sustained course of practice. However, as I have argued at length, such practice is always guided and informed by prereflective intuitions and tendencies. See

the discussion in *The Sense of Antirationalism: The Religious Thought of Zhuangzi and Kierkegaard* (Carr, Karen L. and Philip J. Ivanhoe, 2010. Hong Kong, SAR and Appleton, WI. Copyright Karen L. Carr and Philip J. Ivanhoe): 103–109. Thanks to Carine Defoort for pointing out the need to address such issues.

11. Joel Kupperman makes a good case that one of the primary goals of Zhuangzi's philosophy is to cultivate a sense for and appreciation of such childlike playfulness. See his "Spontaneity and Education of the Emotions in the *Zhuangzi*."

12. Although I use examples from early Daoist texts as my primary illustrations of untutored spontaneity, in the course of this chapter, it becomes clear that the two models I present are ideal types. In actual practice, both Daoists and Confucians tend to present hybrid pictures in which the two models are combined. This is especially true of the Confucian thinker Mengzi. Mengzi argues that those who display the kind of callousness that I describe here have "lost" an original compassionate inclination. He explicitly denies that such sensibilities are "welded onto us from outside." For his use of the metaphor of "losing" an innate endowment, see *Mengzi* 6A8, 6A11, and so forth. For his denial that moral sensibilities are welded onto or infused into us from outside, see 6A6. Nevertheless, Mengzi insists that no one can display virtuous dispositions accurately and reliably without a great deal of reflection and practice. This aspect of his thought tends to distinguish him as an advocate of cultivated spontaneity.

13. For a brief discussion of these ideas, see Philip J. Ivanhoe, trans., *The Daodejing of Laozi* (Indianapolis, IN: Hackett, 2002), xv–xxx. It is worth noting that many Buddhist thinkers and most Neo-Confucians advocate a view that is much closer to "untutored spontaneity," though the specific content of what "comes naturally" distinguishes these traditions both from the Daoists and from each other.

14. The notion of *wuwei* is often described as characteristically Daoist. However, without denying the importance of *wuwei* for early Daoists, it is important to appreciate that the term and different expressions of the ideal are found throughout the early Chinese tradition. For a helpful study of *wuwei* in the early Chinese tradition, see Edward Gilman Slingerland III, *Effortless Action: Wu-wei as Conceptual Metaphor and Spiritual Ideal in Early China* (New York: Oxford University Press, 2003). Compare, though, my comments in "The Paradox of *Wuwei*?" *The Journal of Chinese Philosophy.* 34.2 (June, 2007): 277–287.

15. For a revealing analysis of these concepts in the ethical philosophy of the *Daodejing*, see Liu Xiaogan, "An Inquiry into the Core Value of Laozi's Philosophy," in *Religious and Philosophical Aspects of the Laozi*, eds. Mark Csikszentmihalyi and Philip J. Ivanhoe (Albany: State University of New York Press, 1999), 211–238.

16. This example also is in keeping with the Daoist tendency to privilege the beliefs, attitudes, sensibilities, and actions of nonelite members of society—farmers, artisans, and craftsmen—over elite members—educated scholars, officials, and the like. Compare Foot's example of the "head tracker" mentioned in note 6.

17. These as well as the psychological goods described below are some of the benefits that Daoist texts like the *Daodejing* and *Zhuangzi* claim accrue to those who

follow the Way. For a discussion of this issue, see Carr and Ivanhoe, *The Sense of Antirationalism*, 86–90.

18. The idea here is that in the earlier cases, at least some of the values associated with spontaneity—for example, avoiding certain physical harms—appear to be less directly tied to the state of spontaneous action itself. In the case of metaphysical comfort, spontaneity appears to be constitutive of the particular sense of confidence, ease, comfort, peace, and so forth, that is valued. For a discussion of the idea of "metaphysical comfort," see my "Nature, Awe, and the Sublime," in *The Philosophy of Religion*, Peter A. French, Theodore E. Uehling Jr., and Howard K. Wettstein, eds., *Midwest Studies in Philosophy*, vol. 21 (Notre Dame, IN: University of Notre Dame Press, 1998), 98–117.

19. The standing dispositions that are the basis of this type of spontaneity can make it difficult to perform certain actions in the self-conscious and often awkward manner characteristic of the period before one acquired the disposition. For example, it takes special effort and skill for an accomplished pianist to play the piano in the halting and uncertain manner of a beginner. Such play simply is not "natural" for the accomplished pianist. I owe this point to comments made by Eric L. Hutton.

20. *Analects* 2.4.

21. This ability is an important aspect of Kongzi's teachings about the "golden rule." For my understanding of this issue, see "The 'Golden Rule' in the *Analects*," in *Confucius Now: Contemporary Encounters with the Analects*, ed. David Jones (LaSalle, IL: Open Court, 2007), 81–108.

22. This line paraphrases Mengzi's description of the remarkable ethical achievement of the sagely Emperor Shun. See *Mengzi* 4B19. Mengzi as well as other early Confucians often used musical performance as an example and metaphor for harmonious social interaction. It could serve both of these functions because musical performances were often an important component of ritual activity. For one of the most memorable examples in the *Mengzi*, see 5B1, where Mengzi compares Kongzi to a "complete symphony."

23. Csikszentmihalyi's work, cited in note 9, offers some evidence for the more general claim.

24. Allan Gibbard has argued that one of the primary virtues of shared norms is their power to facilitate social cooperation. See his *Wise Choices, Apt Feelings: A Theory of Normative Judgment* (Cambridge, MA: Harvard University Press, 1990), 64–80. In addition, those who have argued for the importance of "recognition" and the value of shared forms of life insist that shared norms and practices provide a necessary constituent of a decent and fulfilling life. See Charles Taylor, "The Politics of Recognition," in *Multiculturalism*, ed. Amy Guttman (Princeton, NJ: Princeton University Press, 1994), 25–73. Such claims are closely related to the arguments I shall make below concerning the "metaphysical comfort" that a shared form of life can offer.

25. Note, too, that there are plausible and compelling ways of incorporating innate tendencies and inclinations into a mature understanding and attitude that sees the self as connected in deep and pervasive ways with the rest of the world. We should avoid committing what Ken Wilbur calls "the pre/trans fallacy": conflating prepersonal

with transpersonal states of mind. Wilber argues that Freud commits one version of this mistake by taking all religious states as expressions of regression, while Jung at times errs in the opposite direction by valorizing infantile forms of thought. Although I am not convinced that this is the way early Daoists conceived of their ideal states, it offers a powerful way to retrieve and enhance many of their insights. See Ken Wilber, "The Pre/Trans Fallacy," in *Paths beyond Ego: The Transpersonal Vision*, eds. Roger Walsh and Frances Vaughan (Los Angeles: Jeremy Tarcher, 1993), 124–130.

26. See Edward O. Wilson, *Biophilia* (Cambridge, MA: Harvard University Press, 1984); Stephen R. Kellert and Edward O. Wilson, eds., *The Biophilia Hypothesis* (Washington, DC: Island Press, 1993).

27. See my "Nature, Awe, and the Sublime."

28. Though I think it wrong to paper over or attempt to explain away the differences between these two early Confucians, it is important to note that Mengzi's use of agricultural metaphors to describe the process of self-cultivation makes clear that he does not endorse uncultivated spontaneity as his ideal. He is not advocating a life in which we allow our untutored nature to find its own way. That would make him more a Daoist. For a discussion of this aspect of Mengzi's philosophy, see my *Confucian Moral Self Cultivation* (Indianapolis, IN: Hackett, 2000), 18–22; *Ethics in the Confucian Tradition: The Thought of Mengzi and Wang Yangming* (Indianapolis, IN: Hackett, 2002), 88–93.

29. See Philip J. Ivanhoe, "A Happy Symmetry: Xunzi's Ethical Thought," in *Ritual and Religion in the* Xunzi, 63–87.

30. For a discussion of the roles that tradition plays in Xunzi's ethical philosophy, see chapter 5 of Kline, *Ethics and Tradition in the* Xunzi, 205–241. A similar conception of the value of tradition is an unstated implication of Alasdair MacIntyre's notion of "goods internal to practices." See his *After Virtue* (Notre Dame, IN: University of Notre Dame Press, 1984), 187–191. One of the most remarkable things about Xunzi's view is his claim that an appreciation of this fact *deepens* one's sense of satisfaction. Xunzi argues that only those who recognize that most of the activities in which they engage and which they enjoy are part of ongoing tradition find full satisfaction in what they do. Only such people see themselves and what they do as part of a long and majestic lineage. And so, while it is not in any way necessary for a contemporary musician to know and appreciate the tradition of which she is a part, Xunzi insists not only that she in fact *is* a member of such a tradition, but also that she will know and appreciate both her art and herself more fully when she comes to realize and embrace this fact. Wynton Marsalis offers a contemporary example of someone who shares this particular sensibility in regard to his profession.

31. The "Second Nature" that we take on is distinct from original Nature in many ways. One clear example is the independent "life" of literary creations. A literary work is always in some sense a response to the world. However, it can define a novel way of living within the world. Moreover, it can inspire later works that are as much responses to *it* as to the world. For example, *Apocalypse Now* is as much a response to *Heart of Darkness* as to the Vietnam War.

32. Though Daoists and Confucians offer different and incompatible descriptions of the Dao, or "the Way," and express varying degrees of confidence in the role that prereflective tendencies and intuitions play in guiding us toward it, both appeal to the Way as the standard for proper action. Those actions that follow or are in accord with the Way "feel" right because they manifest this deeper ethical ideal.

33. In *Confucian Moral Self Cultivation*, I argue that Confucian thinkers of various times and persuasions employed different and at times incompatible views about the character of human nature and the proper path of self-cultivation. I propose a variety of models, for example, "development," "reformation," and "discovery" models, to describe these different views and their related conceptions of self-cultivation.

34. David B. Wong and T. C. Kline III have dramatically advanced our understanding of this aspect of Xunzi's thought. See Wong's "Xunzi on Moral Motivation" and Kline's "Moral Agency and Motivation in the *Xunzi*," both in *Virtue, Nature, and Agency in the* Xunzi. Kline is the first to describe the way Xunzi thinks aspects of our basic nature can be "conscripted" into the cause of morality.

35. As Paul Kjellberg points out, in Zhuangzi's story about carving up an ox, the cook's movements are even likened to the movements of classical ritual dances. See Paul Kjellberg, *Zhuangzi and Skepticism* (Ph.D. diss., Stanford University, 1993), 34–37. See especially 35, n. 1.

36. The *Daodejing* advocates a level of social development that requires a variety of tools and village organization. We are to go only so far "back"—to the stage of an agrarian utopia—not to the stage of hunters and gatherers (who also have tools and their own form of social organization).

37. Bernard Faure, while he defines and deploys a much more ornate definition of "rhetoric," argues that Chan Buddhists deploy a related sense of rhetoric in their advocacy of doctrines such as "sudden" enlightenment. See *The Rhetoric of Immediacy: A Cultural Critique of Chan/Zen Buddhism* (Princeton, NJ: Princeton University Press, 1991).

38. See Kupperman, "Confucius and the Problem of Naturalness."

39. Ibid., 29. A. C. Graham expresses a similar idea in distinguishing early Daoists from Western Romantics. See A. C. Graham, trans., *Chuang-tzu: The Inner Chapters* (Reprint, Indianapolis, IN: Hackett, 2001), 14.

40. Kupperman, "Confucius and the Problem of Naturalness," 88.

41. Ibid., 29. A. C. Graham seems to endorse something like this idea in his comment about our need to cultivate the "selfless, mirror-like objectivity" that ensures that our spontaneous response reflects all and only the promptings of Heaven. See Graham, *Chuang-tzu*, 16.

42. Mary Midgley offers the most revealing and profound account of this interplay. See *Beast and Man: The Roots of Human Nature*, rev. ed. (London: Routledge, 1995), 203–317.

43. For a trenchant exploration of this aspect of Xunzi's views on the nature and function of ritual, see T. C. Kline III, "Sheltering under the Sacred Canopy: Peter Berger and Xunzi," *Journal of Religious Ethics* 29, no. 2 (Summer 2001): 261–282.

44. I discuss this aspect of early Daoist thought in the particular case of Zhuangzi in Carr and Ivanhoe, *The Sense of Antirationalism*, 173.

45. For a discussion of these issues, see Midgley, *Beast and Man*, 25–49.

46. For a more thorough defense of these claims, see my "Nature, Awe, and the Sublime."

47. For a revealing discussion of such differences, see A. C. Graham, *Reason and Spontaneity* (London: Curzon Press, 1985); *Unreason within Reason: Essays on the Outskirts of Rationality* (La Salle, IL: Open Court, 1989). See also my review of the latter work in *China Review International* 1, no. 1 (Spring 1994): 107–123.

48. Charles Taylor makes a similar point concerning the history of the Western notion of authenticity. See *The Ethics of Authenticity* (Cambridge, MA: Harvard University Press, 1991).

49. Charles Taylor makes a similar point in regard to the nature of practical reasoning: "To make practical reason substantive implies that practical wisdom is a matter of seeing an order which in some sense is in nature. This order determines what ought to be done. To reverse this and give primacy to the agent's own desires or his will while still wanting to give value to practical reason, you have to redefine this in procedural terms" (*Sources of the Self* [Cambridge, MA: Harvard University Press, 1989], 87).

Contributors

Eirik Lang Harris (Ph.D. University of Utah) teaches in the Department of Philosophy at Santa Clara University. His major interests are in Chinese moral and political philosophy. Currently, his research focuses on the role of morality in politics and how early Chinese philosophers such as Xunzi and Hanfeizi can contribute to contemporary debates on this issue.

Chun-chieh Huang (Ph.D. University of Washington) is distinguished professor of history, National Taiwan University. He specializes in East Asian Confucianisms and Chinese intellectual history and has written many books on these topics, including *Mencian Hermeneutics: A History of Interpretations in China* (Transaction Publishers, 2001), *New Perspectives in the History of East Asian Confucianisms* (National Taiwan University Press, in Chinese, 2004), *Taiwan in Transformation 1895-2005* (Transaction Publishers, 2006), *Tokugawa Japan's Interpretation of the Analects* (National Taiwan University Press, in Chinese, 2006), *East Asian Confucianisms: Dialects between Classics and Interpretations* (National Taiwan University Press, in Chinese, 2007; Japanese translation, 2010) and *Xu Fuguan and His Thought in East Asian Confucian Perspective* (National Taiwan University Press, in Chinese, 2009).

Philip J. Ivanhoe (Ph.D. Stanford University) specializes in the history of East Asian philosophy and religion and its potential for contemporary ethics. He has written, edited, or co-edited more than a dozen books and published more than thirty articles and numerous dictionary and encyclopedia entries on Chinese and Western religious and ethical thought. Among his publications are *Confucian Moral Self Cultivation* (Hackett, 2000), *The Daodejing of Laozi* (Hackett, 2003), *Readings from the Lu-Wang School of Neo-Confucianism* (Hackett, 2009) and *On Ethics and History: Essays and Letters of Zhang Xuecheng* (Stanford University Press, 2009).

Shirong Luo (Ph.D. University of Miami) is assistant professor of philosophy at Simmons College, Boston, Massachusetts. He teaches philosophy of religion, world religions, Greek philosophy, and Asian philosophy. He previously taught at Mount Holyoke College. His research interests include East Asian philosophy and religion, comparative philosophy, and ethics.

Heiner Roetz is professor for Chinese history and philosophy at Ruhr-University, Bochum, Germany. His major research fields and teaching subjects are classical Chinese philosophy, history of Chinese ethics, Chinese culture and human rights, comparative philosophy and cross-cultural hermeneutics. Among his English publications is *Confucian Ethics of the Axial Age* (State University of New York Press, 1993).

Julia Tao is professor in the Department of Public and Social Administration, City University of Hong Kong. She specializes in comparative applied philosophy, contemporary ethics, and public policy analysis. Her recent publications include an edited book *China: Bioethics, Trust, and the Challenge of the Market* (Springer, 2008), a co-edited volume *Governance for Harmony in Asia and Beyond* (Routledge, 2010), and an article on "Between Market and State: Dilemmas of Environmental Governance in China's Sulphur Dioxide Emission Trading" in *Journal of Environment and Planning C: Government and Policy*, Vol. 27, 2009 (with D. Mah).

Justin Tiwald (Ph.D. University of Chicago) is an assistant professor of philosophy at San Francisco State University. He has published several articles on Confucian ethics and political philosophy, and is working on a book on the ethics of Dai Zhen. He has been a visiting professor at the University of California, Berkeley.

Kam-por Yu (Ph.D. Hong Kong University) is a senior lecturer in the Faculty of Humanities of the Hong Kong Polytechnic University, and formerly an associate professor in the Department of Public and Social Administration of the City University of Hong Kong. He has been a visiting research fellow in Bonn University, the University of Edinburgh, and Harvard University. His major interests are Confucian ethics and applied ethics. His most recent publications include a series of papers on the Confucian views on harmony, war, peace, and multiple values.

Qianfan Zhang obtained his Ph.D. in Government from University of Texas at Austin (1999). He taught comparative constitutional law and administrative law at

School of Law, Nanjing University, and served as the Chief Editor of the faculty law journal, *Nanjing University Law Review* before he joined the law faculty in Peking University in 2003, where he is now the director of the Center for the People's Congress and Parliamentary Studies and the senior deputy director of the Constitutional and Administrative Law Center. He has published several books and numerous articles in public law, including a two-volume treatise *The Constitutional Systems in the West* (2nd ed., 2004/2005), *Constitutional Commentary in Daily Life: Between Ideal and Reality* (2007), *Introduction to the Study of Constitutional Law* (2nd ed., 2008), *Selection of Classical Constitutional Cases* (2008), *Comparative Administrative Law: Systems, Institutions, and Processes* (2008, first author), *From Constitution to Constitutionalism: A Comparative Study of Judicial Review* (2008, first author).

Index

acedia, 165, 179n14
act-centered moral theory, 123
action, 9, 28, 36, 165, 184, 186, 187, 191. See also *wuwei*
aesthetics, 183, 184, 196, 200
After Virtue, 205n30
agent-based, agent-focused, and agent-prior virtue ethics. See *under* virtue ethics
agent-centered moral theory, 123
agrarianism, 195, 206n36
agriculture, 40, 75, 113, 192, 205n28
akrasia, 165, 179n14
alienation, 187
Allison, Henry, 201n4
all-round excellence. See under *zhongyong*
altruism, 103, 108, 109, 112, 152
Ames, Roger, 20
Analects. See *Lunyu*
analogy, 22
Ancient Learning School, 85, 91, 93
animals, 58, 59, 62, 67–68, 110, 115, 161nn30–31, 183, 184, 201n3
Anonymous Iamblichi, The, 100
Apel, Karl-Otto, 23
Apocalypse Now, 205n31
Aquinas, Thomas, 178
Aristotle, 7, 37, 112, 123, 181n26
Arrow, Kenneth, 106
audience, 13, 19, 21. See also rulers, as audience

audit explosion, 101
authenticity, 207n48
authority, distrust of, 101, 118
autonomy, 101, 119, 183, 199, 200
awareness. See consciousness

Bai, Duke of Chu, 79
Bai Ting 白珽, 96n52
Baier, Annette, 102, 103, 106
Banfield, E., 105
bangwudao 邦無道. See *wudao*
bangyoudao 邦有道. See *youdao*
barbarians, 83
Beatniks, 195–96
behaviorism, 20–21
ben 本 (root), 138
benefit, 146. See also harm; well-being
benevolence: as translation of *ren* (see under *ren*); nature's, 197; and trust, 106
Bi Gan, 48n2
biophilia, 192, 197, 198
Blind Man (father of Shun), 73, 83, 86–89
Bok, Sissela, 105, 106
Boli Xi, 182n33
Book of History. See *Shangshu*
Book of Rites. See *Liji*
Bu She 不奢, 79
Buddhism, 32, 203n13, 206n37

cannibalism, 161n31

213

care and caring, 7, 115, 119, 124, 133, 155, 185, 193; empathic, 123; by extension (*tu ji ji ren* 推己及人), 110, 116, 118; impartial, 77
categorical imperative, 54, 112
Cheng Shude 程樹德, 180n23
Cheng Yi 程頤, 28, 41, 48n5, 49n15, 83, 161n41
cheng 誠 (sincerity), 28
Cheng-Zhu School, 93, 145
children, 81, 103, 111, 185, 192, 197, 203n11
Chinese Community Party (CCP). *See* government, of PRC
Cho Ik 趙翼, 88
choice, 100, 193, 199
Chosŏn period, 88
Christianity, 18, 105–06
Chu Ni 鉏麑, 79
circumstances, 70, 87, 107, 125, 130, 135, 137–38
civil society. *See under* society
claims of truth or validity. *See* truth claims
cliques. *See under* rulers
comfort, 189, 196–97; metaphysical, 187, 190, 191, 192, 193, 194, 198, 199, 201, 204n18, 204n24
commerce. *See* trade
common people, 13, 39, 41, 45, 55, 60, 63, 67, 68, 69, 70, 113–14
community: intellectual, 13, 15; moral, 103–04
comparative approach to Chinese thought, 2–3, 17–18. *See also* contrastive approach
compassion, 57–58, 62, 68, 71n2, 72n20, 109, 124, 167, 172, 185. See also under *ren*; rulers
compromise, 85–86
Confucius. *See* Kongzi
conscience, 59
consciousness (*jue* 覺), 159n16

consequentialist ethics, 131
constitution, 70, 72n24, 72n27, 101, 104
continence. *See* enkrasis
contingency, 8–9, 60, 163, 170, 176, 182n39
contractarianism, 200
contracts, 104, 111; social, 119–20
contrast, 38–40
contrastive approach to Chinese thought, 2–3, 17–18, 20, 21. *See also* comparative approach
Cooper, John, 111
corveé labor, 114
courage. *See yong*
critical thinking, 42, 119, 151
Csikszentmihalyi, Mihalyi, 202n9
cuanchen 篡臣 (usurping ministers), 78, 82
culture, 6, 9, 105–06, 118, 188, 195, 196, 199. *See also* socialization

Dai Zhen 戴震, 7–8, 90, 91, 93, 145, 149, 149–57
Daiqing luli 大清律例 (*Collection of Law of the Great Qing*), 90
dance, 206n35
dao 道 (way), 6, 38, 77, 78, 82–83, 109, 119, 124, 165, 167, 180n23, 186, 195, 201, 204n17, 206n32; as basis of Confucian morality, 6, 125–127; Confucian, 193; delighting in (*le* 樂), 168, 180n23; of Heaven, 56; of the kings, 95n29, 159n14; knowing (*zhi* 知), 168, 180n23; liking (*hao* 好), 168, 180n23; of the minister, 82; and *ren*, 126; and virtue, 180n22
Daodejing 道德經 or *Laozi* 老子, 77, 178n6, 195, 203n17, 206n36
Daoism, 9, 77, 178n6, 184, 186, 191–93, 195–96, 197, 198, 200, 202n10, 203nn12–14, 203nn16–17, 205n25, 205n28, 206n32, 207n44

Darwall, Stephen, 161n32, 161n38
Dasguta, P., 106
de 德 (virtue), 124, 164, 178n8. *See also* virtue(s)
death, 80; fear of, 156
deficiency, 37, 38–39
definitionalist interpretation of Confucian ethics, 127
Defoort, Carine, 203n10
delight, 189, 190, 192. See also *dao*, delighting in
democracy, 5–6, Chap. 5; and distrust of authority, 101; institutions of, 107
deontology, 80, 111–12, 131
depression, 161n32
desires (*yu* 欲), 7–8, 9, 78, 84–85, 95n29, 145, 165, 166, 168–69, 176, 179n16, 187, 190, 192, 193, 199, 200, 207n49; attribution to others, 146, 147–48, 150, 159n10, 160n23; fulfillment (*sui yu* 遂欲), 149, 155; informed, 152–53, 155; rectification of, 150–51, 157; relation to well-being, 148–50; self-harmful or self-sacrificial, 153, 161n32; and spontaneity, 184
dignity, 4, 58, 59–61, 72n20, 109, 184
disobedience, loyal, 119
disorder. *See* order and disorder
dissent. *See* protest
Du Yu 杜預, 76
Duan Yucai 段玉裁, 48n4
duan 端 (end[s]), 34–35, 42, 50n19
Dubs, Homer, 127
due process, 101
duty, 58, 76, 78, 87, 89, 103, 112, 113, 115, 117, 118; as translation of *yi*, 130

e 惡. *See* immorality
economics, 25n29, 100. *See also* equality, economic; growth and development; redistributive policies

education, 38, 68, 70–71, 107, 115, 116, 188. *See also* learning
elderly people, 111
elections. *See* democracy; government, elected
elites, 203n16
emotions, 139, 145, 157, 161n39, 167, 195
empathy, 123. See also *shu*
end(s), human beings as, 54, 59, 60–61
enkrasis, 181nn26–27
enlightenment, 206n37
environment, 193. *See also* nature
equality, 60, 201; economic, 104, 106–07, 114; of humanity, 112, 174; of love, 110; moral, 109
Erikson, Erik, 105
ethics, definitions of, 1
ethnocentrism, 16, 18
eudaimonia, 123, 160n25
excellence. See *pianzhi; zhongyong*
excess, 37, 113, 114, 174–75, 186, 187, 190, 191, 195, 197
exchange theories, 100, 112
eye-level principle (*Prinzip Augenhöhe*), 3, 15, 21, 23

facts, 22
fairness, 78
family, 6, 43–44, 75, 82, 92, 103, 105, 108, 110, 111, 114, 116, 118, 119. *See also* filiality
fan gong 反躬. *See* self, returning to
Fan Ye 范曄, 29
Fang Yizhi, 50n19
Faure, Bernard, 206n37
fear, 166, 184, 201n3; of death (*see under* death)
feelings (*qing* 情), 8, 58–59, 157, 162n46, 167, 195
filiality (*xiao* 孝), 39, 73–74, 78–81, 82–83, 84, 86–87, 109, 110, 114, 116, 126, 153, 161n30. *See also* family

five relationships, 40, 80–81, 108, 110, 116
flow, 202n9
foolishness, 131, 132, 133, 134
Foot, Philippa, 8, 163, 164, 166–67, 169, 170, 172, 176, 179n9, 179nn15–16, 179n20, 181n27, 202n6
forgiveness, 35–36
fraternality, 116
freedom, 58–59, 60, 70–71, 72n27, 102, 188, 199, 200, 201
Fremdverstehen. See understanding of otherness
Freud, Sigmund, 198, 205n25
friendship, civic, 112
Fukuyama, Francis, 105
Fung Yu-lan, 51n

Gadamer, Hans-Georg, 14–15, 16–17
games, 189
Gao Yao 皋陶, 73, 83, 86–89
Gaozi 告子, 85, 159n16
Gazette of Human Nature. See Renwu zhi
gentleman (*junzi* 君子), 36, 37, 39, 44–45, 49n11, 51n34, 55, 60, 64, 67, 78, 79, 84, 85, 95n29, 126, 131, 135, 136, 137, 138, 139, 142n32. Cf. *xiaoren*
Gibbard, Allan, 204n24
globalization, 119
Golden Rule, 51n36, 72n20, 104, 112, 128, 156–57, 158n2, 159n9, 204n21
gong 公 (public realm, public responsibility), 5, Chap. 4; abstract meanings, 76–78, 92; Chinese character, 74–75; concrete meanings, 76, 92; definitions, 74–81, 160n23; meaning "clan leader," 75; priority over *si*, 77–78, 83–84, 95n29; whether reconcilable with *si*, 81–83
Gongduzi, 174

Gongzi Zhuo 公子卓, 79
good(s) (*shan* 善), 27; common, 111, 116–17, 119, 120; multiple, Chap. 2; and practices, 205n30; psychological, 187, 203n17; supreme, 149. See also *duan* 端; value(s)
government, 4, 5–6, 35, 37, 39, 40–42, 43–44, 51n34, 54–55, 61–69, 75–77, 82, 89–90, 92, 95n47, 102, 108, 125, 159n14, 160n26, 172; accountability in, 101; checks and balances in, 101; democratic, *see* democracy; division of powers in, 101; duties of, 114; elected, 65–66, 69, 72, 101; Heaven as model for, 77; institutionalist account of, 102; as model, 95n47; monarchical, 55, 69; of PRC, 54, 64, 69, 70, 72n27; production of trust by, 104, 107, 113–16; purposes of, 113, 115, 118; royal succession, 78–79; self-, 68, 69, 102, 119; and well-being, 149; of Western countries, 61–62, 70. See also rulers
government, benevolent. See *renzheng*
Graham, A. C., 175, 206n41
Graham, Gordon, 51n35
Granet, Marcel, 19, 20
Great Commonality, 50n19
growth and development, economic, 105, 107, 108
Gu Yanwu 顧炎武, 91
Guangzhou, 4, 53

habit, 186, 188, 191
Hall, David, 20
Hampton, Jean, 182n34
Han Fei 韓非 and *Hanfeizi* [text], 22, 74, 77, 78
Han 漢 period, 90, 97n65
Hansen, Chad, 18, 19
happiness, 147, 148. See also well-being
Hardin, Russell, 100, 101–02, 106, 112, 114, 117

Hare, R. M., 33–34
harm (*huo* 禍), 146, 186, 187, 190, 191, 195, 204n18. *See also* benefit
harmony, 149, 161n41, 186, 187, 190, 193. *See also* society, harmony in
He Yan 何晏, 181n25
Heart of Darkness, 205n31
heart or heart-mind (*xin* 心), 56–61, 62, 72n20, 84–92, 109, 114, 150
Heaven, way of. See under *dao*
Heaven: as model for government, 77; nobility of, 109; as source of inclinations, 182n39; as source of propriety and righteousness, 85; as source of spontaneity, 206n41
Heavenly principle. See *Tianli*
hermeneutics, 3, Chap. 1
Hershey, John, 167
Hinduism, 106
History of the Later Han Dynasty. *See* Houhanshu
Hobbes, Thomas, 183, 199, 200, 201n3
holistic excellence. See *zhongyong*: as all-round excellence
Houhanshu 後漢書 (*History of the Later Han Dynasty*), 29
Hu Shih 胡適, 72n25
huai 懷. *See* love
Huainanzi 淮南子, 39
Huang Zongxi 黃宗羲, 91
Hui, King, of Liang, 65
humanity, 103, 110, 191; as translation of *ren* (see under *ren*)
Hume, David, 123
Hutton, Eric L., 180n23, 204n19

immorality (*e* 惡), 131
inappropriate acts, 90–91
inclinations, natural or innate, 9. 168, 175, 185, 191, 193, 195, 197, 202n10, 203n12, 204n25 (*see also* nature, human)

Ingelhart, R., 105
instinct, 185, 196. *See also* nature, human
institutions, 41, 72n25, 104, 106, 113, 116; democratic, 107
instrumentalist interpretation of Confucian ethics, 127
intellectuals, 15. *See also* community, intellectual; scholar-officials
intelligence. *See* wisdom
interest(s): conflict of, 81; encapsulated, 100, 112; others', 7–8; public, 95n47 (*see also* good, common); self-, 55, 65–69, 78, 100, 106, 110, 116, 117, 119, 120, 153–56, 158n8, 160n23, 161n36, 174–75 (see also *si* 私)
internalism, 27, 33, 48n5
international community, 92
Ireland, 106
Islam, 105
Itō Jinsai 伊藤仁齋, 91, 93
Ivanhoe, Philip J., 142n21, 180n24

Japan: Confucianism in, 74, 85; law in, 91; trust in, 106
Jaspers, Karl, 23
Ji, Viscount, 48n2
Jia 賈, 76
Jin 晉, State of, 76
Jin, Marquis of, 76
jingtian 井田. *See* well-field
jiujing 九經 (nine guiding principles), 40–41
joy, 149, 183, 188, 191, 193, 194, 196, 201
judgment, about values. *See under* values
judicial review, 101
jue 覺. *See* consciousness
Jung, C. G., 205n25
junzi 君子. *See* gentleman
justice and injustice, 56, 60, 78, 91, 107, 111, 116, 125

Kanaya Osamu, 35
Kant, Immanuel, 54, 58–59, 60, 66, 112, 132, 170-71, 184, 199, 200, 202n5, 202n7
Katō Jōken 加藤常賢, 75
Kjellberg, Paul, 206n35
Kline, T. C., III, 206n34, 206n42
knowledge, 167–68. *See also* moral knowledge; wisdom
Kong Yingda 孔穎達, 42
Kongzi 孔子 (Confucius), 6–7, 28, 32, 39–40, 42, 49n11, 54, 55, 60, 61, 81–82, 85, 95n43, 99, 108, 112, 114, 120, 124, 126, 127, 128, 129, 132, 135, 136, 137, 138, 156, 164–66, 167, 169, 179n10, 179n20, 181n25, 189, 192, 204n21
Korea, Confucianism in, 74, 88
Korsgaard, Christine, 171
Kupperman, Joel, 192, 195–96, 197, 203n11

La pensée chinoise, 19
land allocation. *See* well-field system
language, 16; descriptive, 20; function of, 19–21; as medium, 20, 21; performative, 21; perlocutionary, 19; prescriptive, 20; propositional, 19–20, 21
Laozi 老子 [person], 202n10
Laozi 老子 [text]. *See Daodejing*
Lau, D. C., 7, 124, 125, 128, 129–40
law, 51n34, 73–74, 75, 79, 82, 83, 84, 86–87, 90–91, 95n29, 95n43, 97n65, 100, 101, 107, 114, 115, 119–20, 132, 201. *See also* government; moral law
learning (*xue* 學), 130, 131, 132, 134, 168, 185, 186, 187–88, 189, 202n10, 204n19. *See also* education
Legalism, 13, 67
Legge, James, 40–41, 180n23

legitimacy, 101, 113
Levi, Margaret, 104
Li Ji 驪姬, 78
Li Ke 里克, 79
Li Si 李斯, 13
Li Zhi 李贄, 51n34
li 理 (pattern of the universe), 180n23
li 禮 (ritual; ritual propriety; good order), 56, 85, 124, 145, 150, 158n3, 170, 173, 180n23, 197; as basis of Confucian morality, 6, 127–29; dance, 206n35; internalization of, 189; and music, 204n22 as object of learning, 132; origins of, 192; purposes of, 128–29, 190, 204n24, 206n43; and *ren*, 127–29, 138–39; as social behavior, 189; and spontaneity, 189
Liang Qichao 梁啟超, 72n25
life (*sheng* 生), 159n16: cultural, 80; definitions of, 159n16; flourishing and satisfying, 187, 190, 191, 197, 199, 201, 204n24 (*see also* satisfaction); fulfillment (*sui sheng* 遂生), 8, 149, 155; as a good, 149–50; love of, 156, 161n36, 167, 182n33
life-producing processes (*sheng sheng* 生生), 149, 155
Liji 禮記 (*Book of Rites*), 39, 42–43
Ling, Duke, of Jin, 79
literature, 205n31
Liu Shao 劉劭, 30
Lloyd, G. E. R., 19
Locke, John, 114
love, 60, 109, 110, 111, 114, 115, 116, 128, 139, 154–55, 161n32, 170. *See also* self-love
loyalty, 76, 78–81, 109, 119
Lü Buwei 呂不韋, 13
Lu Gong, 76
Lunyu 論語 (*Analects*), 28, 31, 36–37, 42, 44, 54, 82, 99, 109, 110, 112, 113–14, 119, 124, 126, 127, 128,

129, 131, 132, 133, 135, 136, 137, 138, 142n32, 159n9, 164–66, 168–70, 172–75, 177, 179n10, 181n25, 192
Lüshi chunqiu 呂氏春秋 (*Master Lü's Spring and Autumn Annals*), 13, 76–77

Machiavelli, Niccolò, 113
MacIntyre, Alasdair, 205n30
Mandate of Heaven. See *Tianming*
Margalit, Avishai, 71n13
market, 119
Marsalis, Wynton, 205n30
May Fourth Movement, 95n43
Meiji period, 91
Mengzi 孟子 [author] and *Mengzi* [text], 9, 22, 31–32, 44, 49n11, 54–69, 72, 81–89, 92–93, 96n52, 109, 110, 114, 116, 119, 124, 142n32, 162n42, 164, 170–71, 174, 175, 177, 179n10, 179n20, 182n33, 192, 194–95, 203n12, 204n22, 205n28
metaphor, 22, 205n28
metaphysical comfort. See comfort, metaphysical
metaphysics, 59
Midgley, Mary, 206n42
Mill, J. S., 158n8
Minglu 明律 (*Laws of the Ming*), 90
minyi 民意 (popular will), 119
moderatism, 27
Moeller, Hans-Georg, 17, 18, 20
monarchy. See *under* government
moral caution, 51n35
moral community. See *under* community
moral knowledge, 165
moral law, 58
moral normativity, 202n5
moral reciprocity, 158n2
moral sentimentalism, 123
morality: decline of, 53; and human nature, 206n34; as translation of *yi*, 130, 137. See also immorality

motivation, 9, 57–58, 64, 100–01, 110, 111, 112, 116, 127, 130, 132, 137–39, 141n8, 154–55, 161n36, 163, 165, 166, 173–74, 176, 182n36
mourning, 129, 138, 151, 161n39, 191
Mozi 墨子 and *Mozi* [text], 31, 68, 77, 78
multiculturalism, 102
music, 129, 134, 180n23, 188, 189, 190, 193–94, 204n19, 204n22, 205n30

narcissism, 170. See also self-love
nature, 9, 49n10, 149, 159n16, 159n20, 176, 184, 187, 191, 193, 194, 196, 197, 198–99, 201, 205n31, 207n49 (*see also* environment); human, 8, 38, 42, 55, 56–64, 68, 69, 108–11, 148, 149, 166, 168, 173, 174, 175, 176, 191, 192–96, 199–201, 206nn33–34 (*see also* inclinations; instinct); second, 9, 188, 193, 194, 196, 205n31
needs, 192, 193, 197
Neo-Confucianism, 145, 156, 158n3, 203n13. See also *names of individual Neo-Confucians*
Nicomachean Ethics, 181n26
nine guiding principles. See *jiujing*
Nishida Taichirō 西田太一郎, 75
Nivison, Daivd S., 178n8
nobility, 60, 63, 109
Noddings, Nel, 7, 123
nonaction. See *wuwei*
norms, social, 88, 127–28, 184, 190–93, 197, 200, 204n24
Nu Shuqi 女叔齊, 76

obedience, 100, 126
Oberth, Mathias, 17–18
objectification: of human beings, 3, 14; of texts, 14, 20–21
objectivity, 206n41

Of Liberty and Necessity, 201n3
Offe, Claus, 104
Ogyū Sorai 荻生徂徠 (物茂卿), 85
omens, 95n47
ontology, 55
optimism, 167
order and disorder, 6, 13, 95n47, 145, 198–99, 202n6, 207n49
other(s). *See* self, and others; interests, others'; understanding of otherness
overcautious way, 31–32, 49n11, 49n13

Pang Pu 龐樸, 50n21
peace, 187, 188, 190, 191, 193, 196, 204n18
people, common. *See* common people
perfection(ism), 44, 56, 160n26
perspective-taking, 4, 7, 146, 148, 151, 157, 187. See also *shu* 恕
petty person. See *xiaoren*
philology, 14–16,
"philosophy, Chinese" [term], 13, 18, 19
philosophy, political, 4, 55, 69–70, 113
philosophy, Western, 5, 10, 18, 19, 100, 138, 163, 207n48. *See also names of individual philosophers*
pianzhi 偏至 (excelling in one aspect), 29, 30. Cf. *zhongyong*
pity, 49n11, 61, 63, 64, 71n13, 72n20
plants, 159n16, 183, 184
play, 185, 192, 193–94, 197, 203n11
pluralism, 27
poets, 183, 184
politics of recognition, 48n3
poverty, 53, 61, 71n13, 149, 158n3
Power, Michael, 101
power, political, 89–90, 92, 93, 101
practice, 9, 43, 110, 127, 128–29, 185, 187–88, 189, 195, 196, 199, 200, 202n10, 203n12, 205n30
pre/trans fallacy, 204n25
pre-Qin period, 81, 85, 184

principles, nine guiding. See *jiujing*
private (realm or responsibility). See *si*
propriety, 109, 128. See also *li*; *yi* 義
prosperity, 147. *See also* well-being
protest, 107, 119
prudence, 131, 157
psychological conditions, 169
public (realm or responsibility). See *gong*
public [noun]: as audience, 13, 21
public opinion, 89–90
Putnam, R. D., 105

qi 氣 (vital force), 91
Qin 秦 dynasty, 21, 67
Qin 秦, State of, 13
Qing 清 dynasty, 72n25
Qu Boyu, 48n2

reason and rationality, 59, 60, 100, 102, 146, 152–53, 198, 200, 208n49
reciprocity, 112, 158n2
redistributive policies, 104, 106–07, 114
reflection, 9, 174–75, 185–86, 187–88, 189, 191, 193, 197, 198, 199, 200, 202n10, 203n12
reform, 41, 72n25, 104
relationships, five. See five relationships
religion, 193, 196, 205n25
ren 仁, 4–5: acquisition of, 131-32; as basis of Confucian ethics, 6–7, Chap. 6; as "benevolence," 4, 6, 55, 62, 68, 108, 113, 118, 124, 130, 133, 137, 167, 170–71, 173, 190; as "caring," 124; the Chinese character 仁, 71n2, 129; as "compassion," 124, 134; and *dao*, 126; and emotions, 139; fondness for, as a virtue, 132; as "humanity," 4, 54, 55, 56–61, 67, 68, 69–70, 72n20, 108–09, 110, 115, 119, 124, 133, 134, 139, 149, 153, 156, 161n36, 162n42; innate, 56–61 (*see also* nature, human); as lacking its

own moral guarantee, 130–40; and *li* (ritual), 127–29; and *shu*, 162nn41-42; as superior or supreme virtue, 109, 110, 116, 134, 135–36; translations of, 54–55; and trust, 108–16; and *yi*, 136–37

Renwu zhi 人物志 (*Gazette of Human Nature*), 30

renzheng 仁政 (benevolent government), 4, 54, 61–71, 113–14

Republican period, 72n25

respect, 4, 6, 14, 15, 36, 37, 40, 41, 42, 43, 50n22, 54, 58, 60, 63, 64, 68, 70, 71, 71n13, 110, 111, 115, 118, 119, 133; self-, 181n31, 182n34

rhetoric, 22, 36–38, 50n21, 63, 206n37. *See also* analogy; metaphor

righteousness, 128. *See also yi*

rightness. *See yi*

rights, 70–71, 72n27, 101, 117, 119

Roberts, Robert C., 163, 164, 169, 170, 172, 176

Roellicke, Hermann-Josef, 17

Romanticism, 197, 199–200

root. *See ben*

Rousseau, Jean-Jacques, 119

rule-based ethics, 128

rulers: as audience, 13, 19, 55, 63, 65–69; and cliques, 78, 82; compassionate, 62, 172; duty to depose, 116, 119; as fathers, 80–81, 89; and *gong* (public responsibility), 75–76, 92; and ministers, 80–81, 82; as models, 127; and people, 68–69, 113; remonstrating with, 119; as root of order, 95n47; virtuous, 61. *See also* government

Russell, Bertrand, 110

sage(s), 30, 32–33, 60, 62, 65, 87, 115, 149, 158n3, 159n14, 160n26, 161n32, 182n33, 204n22

satisfaction, 67, 102, 127, 148–49, 153, 189, 190, 191, 193, 196, 198, 200, 205n30. *See also* life, flourishing and satisfying

Scheler, Max, 16

scholar-officials, 78, 87, 89, 96n47, 119, 126. *See also* intellectuals

Segalen, Victor, 16

self, 193, 194; dear, 170; nature of, 108; and others, 44–45, 109, 132 (*see also* care); returning to (*fan gong* 反躬), 156

self-cultivation, 7, 69, 109, 115, 124, 128, 131, 138, 170–71, 205n28, 206n33

self-determination, 201n4

self-examination, 156

self-government. *See* government, self-

self-interest. *See* interests, self-

self-love, 163, 167, 170–72, 176, 181n31, 182nn33–34. *See also* love

self-respect, 181n31, 182n34

self-restraint, 162n46

Sen, Amartya, 153

shame (*chi* 恥), 56–57, 139. *See also yi* (righteousness)

shan 善. *See* good(s)

Shangshu 尚書 (*Book of History*), 49n15, 75, 95n29

She Gong 葉公, 82

Shelley, Percy Bysshe, 200

sheng sheng 生生. *See* life-producing processes

shi 士 (scholars). *See* intellectuals; scholar-officials

Shijing 詩經 (*Book of Odes*), 75, 180n23

Shiyu, 48n2

Shu Xiang, 76

shu 恕 (empathy), 112

shu 恕 (sympathetic understanding), 7–8, Chap. 7, 185, 197; definitions of, 158n2; effects of, 151; as naive, 7,

shu 恕 (sympathetic understanding) (*continued*)
151–52; as perspective-taking, 151–53; and *ren*, 162nn41–42

Shun 舜 (legendary emperor), 32–33, 42, 57, 63, 73, 82, 86–89, 92, 115, 204n22

Shun, Kwong-loi, 127

Shuowen jiezi 說文解字 (*Explaining Single-component Graphs and Analyzing Compound Characters*), 74

si 私 (private realm, private responsibility), 5, Chap. 4; abstract meanings 76–78, 92; Chinese character 私, 74–75; concrete meanings, 76, 92; definitions, 74–81, 160n23; meaning "personal favorites," 77; whether reconcilable with *gong*, 81–83. *See also* interest, self-

Sima Guang 司馬光, 83, 96n52

sincerity. See *cheng*

sincerity. See *zhong* (sincerity)

Sinology, 2–3, 16–21

situatedness of ethical distinctions, 80

Sivin, Nathan, 19

Sizukuisi Kōkichi, 95n43

Slingerland, Edward, 180n23

Slote, Michael, 6–7, 123–24

social behavior, 189

socialization, 186, 188, 191, 193, 196, 200

society: civil, 6, 15, 99, 118; Confucian-influenced, 105; Daoist model, 206n36; effecting changes in, 19, 21–22; harmony in, 48n3, 116, 129, 204n22; modern, 81; morality of, 53, 57; welfare, 61–62, 70, 113

Song xingtong 宋刑統 (*Compendium of Song Punishments*), 90

Song 宋 period, 84, 86

Song-period Confucians, 49n13, 83, 85, 91. *See also individuals' names*

spontaneity, 9–10, Chap. 9; cultivated, 9, 187–94, 197–201; definitions of, 183–84, 199; and desire, 184; and fear, 184; and free will, 184, 201n3; and ritual, 189; untutored, 9, 185–87, 188, 190, 192, 197–201, 202n10; and voluntary actions, 201n3

Spring and Autumn period, 76, 78, 79, 82

sprouts of virtue, 9, 56, 58, 59, 109, 119, 173, 182n35, 192. *See also li* (ritual, etc.); *ren* (benevolence; humanity; etc.); *yi* (righteousness, etc.); *zhi* (wisdom, etc.)

Stange, Hans-Otto, 19

Stompka, Piotr, 101

strangers, 103, 105, 111, 117, 118

strength, 35–36

Su Che 蘇轍, 83–84

sublime, 200

sui sheng 遂生. *See* life, fulfillment

sui yu 遂欲. *See* desires, fulfillment

suicide, 78–81, 92

Sun Zhigang 孫志剛, 4, 53, 70

Suzuki, D. T., 127

sympathetic understanding. See *shu* 恕

synthesis, 35–36

taking as. *See* self-determination

Tang 唐 period, 90

Tanglu 唐律 (*Laws of the Tang*), 90

Tao Ying 桃應, 73, 81, 83, 86, 92–93

Taylor, Charles, 48n3, 207nn48–49

technology, 61, 192, 198

temperance, 166

temptation, 8–9, 132, 163, 165, 166, 181nn27–28

theology, 182n39

Tian Chang 田常, 79

Tianli 天理 (Heavenly principle), 5, 84–88, 90–93

Tianming 天命 (Mandate of Heaven), 119, 165, 189
Tianxia 天下 (All under Heaven; the world), 5, 87–92, 97n65
Tokugawa period, 85, 91
tolerance, 35–36, 49n11
trade, 107, 111
tradition, 5, 9, 193–94, 197, 199, 205n30
translation, 16, 20, 54
Trauzettel, Rolf, 17, 20, 21
trust, 5–6, Chap. 5; as civic virtue 111–12, 118–19; Confucian approaches to, 108–16; definitions of, 100; effects of, 106; as familial virtue, 6, 110–11; generalized, 5, 103–04, 106, 116–17; information necessary to, 100; moralistic (i.e., as a moral good), 5–6, 102–08, 110, 111, 112, 117–18, 120; particularized, 5, 103–04, 106, 116–17; as political virtue, 113–16, 120; as result of state actions, 104, 107, 113–16; strategic, 5, 100–02, 106, 117–18
"truth" [term], 18, 19
truth, whole vs. partial, 30, 33–34, 49n11
truth claims, 3, 10, 14, 16, 18, 19, 22–23
Tu Wei-ming, 127
typology, 25n29

understanding: definitions of, 14–17, 20–21, 181n25; of otherness (*Fremdverstehen*), 16; of ritual, 190; sympathetic (see *shu* 恕)
undisciplined way, 31–32, 49n11, 49n13
universal concepts. See *Tianli*; *Tianxia*
Uslaner, Eric, 6, 102–08, 118
utilitarianism, 80, 158n8, 171
utility, 123, 153

validity claims. See truth claims
value(s), 27; absolute, 80; deficiency of, 37, 38–39; distinguishing among, 42–46; excess of, 37; judgment about, 42, 48n3, 119; multiple, 3, Chap. 2, 77–81, 85–92; multiple-value model, 49–42; one-value model, 36–38; synthesis of, 35–36; two-value model, 38–40. See also good(s)
Van Norden, Bryan W., 175, 178n6, 182n33
vice(s), 166–67, 169, 171, 181n27
Vietnam War, 205n31
virtue ethics, 6–7, 123, 163, 164, 173, 177, 182n34; agent-based, 6–7, 123, 124, 127, 130–31; agent-focused, 123; agent-prior, 7, 123; Confucian, 164, 177n1; foundations of, 177n1; objections to, 131
virtue(s), 8, 30, 119, 125, 126, Chap. 8; civic, 111; as correctives, 8–9, 163, 166–70, 171, 173, 175–77, 181nn30–31, 182n39; cultivation of, 128; and *dao*, 180n22; definitions of, 164, 166; inclinational, 9, 164, 172–75; internalization of, 167, 179n20; and vices, 166–67, 169, 181n27; *virtus*, 178n8; and will, 166, 179n15. See also *de*
voluntary actions, 201n3
voluntary associations, 104–05

Waley, Arthur, 180n23
Wang Anshi 王安石, 83, 96n52
Wang Fuzhi 王夫之, 32, 49n13, 49n15, 88
Wang Guowei 王國維, 41–42
Wang Yangming 王陽明, 161n41
Warring States period, 74, 76, 78, 81, 82, 85
way. See *dao*
Weber, Max, 21, 25n29

Weber-Schaefer, Peter, 16, 17
welfare. *See* well-being
welfarism, 159n20
well-being, 4, 10, 145, 147, 149, 158n8, 185, 186; "full-information" theory of, 153. *See also* benefit; happiness; joy; prosperity
well-field (*jingtian* 井田) system for land allocation, 114–17
Wen and Wu, Kings, 40, 65, 66, 77
Wen, King, of Han, 97n65
Wilbur, Ken, 204n25
will, 8, 95n43, 166, 169, 176, 179n15, 199, 200, 207n49; free, and spontaneity, 184, 201n3; good, 132; popular, see *minyi*
Wilson, E. O., 192, 197
wisdom. See *zhi*
Wong, David B., 206n34
world (as transcendent principle). See *Tianxia*
World Values Surveys, 105
wudao 無道 (the condition of *dao* not prevailing in a state), 126
wuwei 無爲 (nonaction), 186, 187, 203n14

Xi Qi 奚齊, 79
Xian, Duke of Jin, 78
xiao 孝. *See* filiality
xiaoren 小人 (petty person), 126, 135, 137, 174. Cf. gentleman
Xie, minister, 115
Xu Shen 許慎, 74
Xu Zhongshu 徐中舒, 75
Xuan, King, of Qi, 62, 66
xue 學. *See* learning
Xun Xi 荀息, 79
Xunzi 荀子 and *Xunzi* [text], 21, 30, 37, 49n10, 55, 64, 77, 78, 82–83, 85, 95n29, 95n47, 124, 159n20, 174, 178n6, 179n20, 192–94, 195, 198–99, 202n10, 205n30, 206n34, 206n43

Yan Hui, 34, 168, 180n25
Yan, King, of Xu, 67
Yang Liang 楊倞, 95n29
Yang Shi 楊時, 86
Yangzi [Yang Zhu 楊朱], 31
Yanzi 晏子, 76
Yao 堯 (legendary emperor), 57, 63, 115
Yi Ik 李瀷, 89
Yi Meng, 96n52
yi 義 (rightness; righteousness; propriety; etc.), 44–45, 56, 78, 82–83, 85, 95n29, 124, 137, 170–71, 173, 190; as basis of Confucian morality, 7, 125, 128, 129–40; definitions of, 130, 134–35, 137, 142n32; as having its own moral guarantee, 137; and *ren*, 136–37; as superior or supreme virtue, 135–37
Yin Tun 尹焞, 180n23
Yin Zhou zhidu lun 殷周制度論, 41–42
yoga, 190
yong 勇 (courage), 109, 135–36, 142n32, 166
yong 庸 (use; common), 49n15
youdao 有道 (the condition of *dao* prevailing in a state), 126
Youzi, 126, 138
Yu Pian 庾駢, 76
Yu Yunwen 余允文, 84
yu 欲. *See* desires
Yu, the Great 大禹 (legendary emperor), 67
Yuan 元 period, 96n52
Yueji 樂記 (*Record of Music*), 156-57

Zai Wo, 138
zaizhong 在中 (unbiased state), 28. See also *zhongyong*
Zhang Dainian, 49n15

Zhang Shi 張栻, 85
Zhang Shizhi 張釋之, 97n65
Zhao Dun 趙盾, 76
Zhao Xuanxi 趙宣子, 79
Zhao, King of Chu, 79
zhi 智 (wisdom; intelligence; etc.), 16, 32–33, 49n14, 56, 133–34, 160n26, 173, 179n15, 199, 207n49
zhizhong 執中 (holding on to middle ground), 30–31. Cf. *zhongyong*
zhong zhi dao 中之道 (appropriateness), 28. See also *zhongyong*
zhong 中 (unbiased state; appropriateness), 27; definitions of, 28, 48nn4–5
zhong 忠 (sincerity), 112
zhongdao 中道 (synonymous with *zhongyong*, q.v.), 27, 31–32
zhongxing 中行 (synonymous with *zhongyong*, q.v.), 27, 31–32, 49n13
Zhongyong 中庸 (*Doctrine of the Mean*) [text], 28, 32–38, 40–43, 48n2
zhongyong 中庸 (harmonious mean, etc.), 3–4, 27; as all-round excellence, 29–32, 36; in Buddhism, 32; consultation as necessary to, 33–34, 42–43, 48n3; impossibility of achieving, 28; as supreme virtue, 28–29
Zhou 周 dynasty, 57, 61
Zhou 周 period, 15, 21, 55, 74, 75, 81
Zhou, Duke of, 41–42, 65, 83
Zhou, King, of the Yin dynasty, 48n2
zhouquan 周全 (holistic; all-round; synonymous with *zhongyong*, q.v.), 29, 30
Zhu Xi 朱熹, 28, 48n5, 49n15, 84–85, 86–88, 91, 150, 161n41, 180n23, 181n25
Zhuangzi 莊子 [author] and *Zhuangzi* [text], 21, 49n10, 77, 178n6, 192, 195, 202n10, 203n11, 203n17, 206n35, 207n44
Zhuzi dayu 朱子答語, 97n65
Zhuzi yulei 朱子語類 (*Classified Conversations of Master Zhu*), 86–87, 180n23
Zigong, 40, 99, 181n25
Zilu, 35–36, 135
Zimo, 31
ziran 自然 (so of itself), 186, 202n7
Zuozhuan 左傳 (*Zuo's Commentary to the Spring and Autumn Annals*), 76